Hits and Misses in the Baseball Draft

*What the Top Picks Teach Us
About Selecting Tomorrow's
Major League Stars*

ALAN MAIMON *and*
CHUCK MYRON

McFarland & Company, Inc., Publishers
Jefferson, North Carolina

LIBRARY OF CONGRESS CATALOGUING-IN-PUBLICATION DATA

Maimon, Alan.
    Hits and misses in the baseball draft : what the top picks
teach us about selecting tomorrow's major league stars / Alan
Maimon and Chuck Myron.
        p.   cm.
Includes bibliographical references and index.

ISBN 978-0-7864-7031-0 (softcover : acid free paper) ∞
ISBN 978-1-4766-0436-7 (ebook)

1. Baseball draft—United States—History.   2. Baseball players—
United States—History.   I. Myron, Chuck, 1979–   II. Title.
GV880.25.M35 2014
796.357'64—dc23   2013047164

BRITISH LIBRARY CATALOGUING DATA ARE AVAILABLE

Front cover: Pitcher Kris Benson of the Baltimore Orioles in 2006
(Keith Allison)

Manufactured in the United States of America

*McFarland & Company, Inc., Publishers
  Box 611, Jefferson, North Carolina 28640
  www.mcfarlandpub.com*

For Cindy, who was there every step of the way, and for Franklin, who will enjoy this book more than anyone I know — Chuck Myron

For all those who almost made it — Alan Maimon

Table of Contents

Table of Contents

Acknowledgments

A few years ago, as we were chatting away on the phone as we often do, Alan Maimon floated the idea of a book about professional sports drafts, and why this year's top selection isn't necessarily next year's All-Star. We realized this is especially the case in baseball, where a draftee's major league career can end before it begins. I was intrigued by the idea, and couldn't wait to help my friend polish his book, as he had graciously allowed me to do with his previous works.

Little did I know that I would be doing a lot more than polishing this one. I can't thank Alan enough for the opportunity to co-author this book. It means a lot coming from him, since I think that if there were a draft for up-and-coming sports book authors, he'd be the top pick (and he'd deliver on all that promise, too). Our friendship, which has endured more than ten years with each of us living in three different states, means even more.

Once I got to work, I encountered some of the best and most forthcoming people both in and out of baseball who provided source material. I'd need another book to properly thank each one individually, but I hope they all understand how much I appreciate their time and willingness to help me examine the draft as thoroughly as possible. In telling their stories and giving their insight, they've contributed to the greater understanding of baseball, and for that they've served the betterment of the game we all cherish.

There were many others whose names don't appear in the book, but whose help was crucial to its completion. Scott Dressel connected me to the Florida Athletic Coaches Association showcase that proved to be one of the cornerstones of our research. If journalism has lost you for good, Scott, we're all the worse for it. Barbara Price provided invaluable

Acknowledgments

Chicago-style guidance to a pair of AP Style devotees, and her constant willingness to do for others in the writing and editing community, even if it's simply to provide moral support, makes her a Hall-of-Famer in her field.

I wouldn't have written a word without the teachers who showed me what I could do, just as they've helped countless others realize their dreams. These are the real heroes in our society, and I was lucky to have so many open new doors for me. Stan Eggleston's recognition of, and faith in, my writing ability set me on the path I walk now. Dave Ashby encouraged me to see the world a different way, and I try to use that vision every step of the way. They are two out of dozens.

Then there are the many friends and family members I haven't seen or spoken to nearly as often as I would have liked as I've dedicated my time to this book. Thanks for your understanding. Now that this project is over, let's get together — before I start the next one.

— Chuck Myron

I couldn't have asked for a better collaborator than Chuck Myron. His keen eye for detail and tremendous baseball acumen greatly elevated the quality of my first three books. I looked forward to the day when he and I could co-write a book.

During the writing of this book, I relocated my family from Nevada to New Jersey. In addition to having to acclimate to new environs, my wife and daughters also had to put up with me disappearing for hours at a time to write and research. I appreciate their patience — and owe them a trip to Six Flags.

I can't adequately express my appreciation for my parents, Mort and Elaine, whose love of language, books, and the written and spoken word set my sister and me on the course we're on.

More than anything, this book is about falling short of realizing dreams. Nobody better conveyed the joy, pain, regret, and acceptance of this condition than David Yocum. He spent a great deal of time sharing his story, and in the end, became almost invested in the subject matter of the book as Chuck and me.

Special thanks to Kevin Towers and John Mozeliak, who candidly discussed many aspects of the draft process with us. Their insights gave us a better understanding of how baseball general managers prepare for and conduct the annual event.

Through hours of conversation with Dallas Green, whose memoir I co-wrote, I learned an amazing amount about scouting and player development. Those master classes gave me a deeper appreciation for a lot of the issues discussed in this book.

—Alan Maimon

Preface

Some top baseball draft picks adjust to the level of competition, put mind over matter, and fulfill their promise. And some do not. Since professional teams first began assembling their rosters in the 1800s, and since the modern draft began in 1965, figuring out who has what it takes to become a major leaguer has proven a thoroughly confounding exercise. Baseball executives use advanced statistical metrics, detailed scouting, in-home visits, and just about every resource available to evaluate potential draft picks. They then apply the metrics and scouting, plus careful physical and mental health care, to nurture those players through the minors.

Yet, according to most recent data, only two-thirds of the players taken in the first round of the June draft even make it to the major leagues, and far fewer become stars.

Why is that?

This is the question this book attempts to answer.

The question begets other questions: Why do some stars emerge from obscurity to shock the baseball cognoscenti? Why do teams, with all the advances in statistics and technology available to them, continue to swing and miss at draft time? How did the explosion of major leaguers from Latin America in the 1990s affect the career trajectories of top draft picks? Attempting to answer those questions, more than simply identifying successes and failures, is the mission of this book. If the answers were simple, teams would have figured them out long ago, and in so doing, would have solved the sport's equivalent of the nature-versus-nurture debate. By shedding light on these mysteries, we stand to learn more about the game we love, and possibly about performance issues in other walks of life as well.

The players we have chosen to study are those who were drafted from 1990 through 2006, specifically those taken in round one. For context, we also examine rounds five and ten. The careers of the players from this time frame are recent, and in some cases still going on. For the most part, though, their fates have already been defined. These prospects have all had a chance to prove worthy of their draft position, and while a fair number of these draftees were still awaiting their major league debuts as they toiled away on the farm in 2013, it is safe to assume the teams that drafted them have long since written most of them off as losses.

There are other compelling reasons to study this era. This was a time when the economics of baseball took center stage. Clubs that raked in high revenues, like the New York Yankees and Atlanta Braves, began to spend more freely and pile up pennants. The Pittsburgh Pirates and Kansas City Royals typified the small-market teams that changed from competitive, successful organizations in the '70s, '80s and early '90s, into the dregs of their respective leagues. The bitter strike that wiped out the World Series in 1994 reinforced the notion that the game itself was secondary to the business of baseball. Scott Boras and other "superagents" began to demand top dollar not only for their major league clients, but for freshly minted draftees as well, at times preventing teams from so much as signing their picks to their first pro contracts and reaping a day's worth of value out of their selections. It was a decade and a half of revolution in baseball, from expansion to wild cards to interleague play, and a period in the history of the sport that would make a compelling study as a whole.

To quantify teams' success in turning top draft picks into major leaguers, we analyzed draft data from Baseball-Reference.com, and to a lesser extent, from TheBaseballCube.com.

While other books, including Michael Lewis' *Moneyball* and Jonah Keri's *The Extra 2%: How Wall Street Strategies Took a Major League Baseball Team from Worst to First*, examine how individual teams, the Oakland A's and Tampa Bay Rays, respectively, built teams through free agency, trades, and the draft, no book has ever specifically investigated the draft and how it affects all of baseball. The writer, to date, who has provided the most thorough holistic examination of various draft-related issues is Rany Jazayerli, co-founder of *Baseball Prospectus.* His work and that of several other baseball writers, including Rod Beaton of *USA Today,* Jim Callis of *MLB.com,* and Jerry Crasnick of *ESPN.com,* helped us frame many key issues. For scholarly analysis of the issues at hand, we consulted journals including *NINE: A Journal of Baseball History and Culture.*

To augment our research, we traveled to a major league showcase, spring training complexes, and minor league parks to gain firsthand knowledge from players, scouts, and other baseball figures who personify the draft.

Introduction

The big leaguers are long gone, having headed north to begin their 162-game season. But the Florida ball fields they occupy in the spring are not empty. Those parks are occupied by young men recently pegged as the best high school and college players in the country. For some of these prospects, this is the beginning of their professional baseball careers. But for most, this is the beginning of the end. In the High Class A Florida State League, players will either glimmer against the backdrop of the shimmering tropical sun or get blown away like palm fronds in an afternoon thunderstorm.

From 2010 through 2012, Jake Mauer managed the Fort Myers Miracle, an affiliate of the Minnesota Twins. He is intimately familiar with the story of prospects who make it to the top as well as the vast majority of others who never do. He spent parts of three minor league seasons playing alongside his now-famous little brother, Joe, watching him develop into a star while his own hopes faded. Their last season together was with the Miracle in 2003, when Joe's numbers validated his status as the first overall draft pick in June 2001. Jake, whom the Twins selected in the twenty-third round of the draft that same year, enjoyed far less success.

Based on what he's seen as a player, a manager and a brother, Jake Mauer knows this is the level where players begin to distinguish themselves.

"Obviously they're still developing their tools, but this is where you really start to try to apply them to the game," Mauer said. "You try to develop them not only physically, but also mentally. A lot of guys that get out of here and do well in Double-A have a pretty good shot of making the big leagues."[1]

Introduction

There are no stars in A-ball, only stars in the making, but some players command more attention than others, if for no other reason that they were former first-round draft picks. The Miracle opened 2011 with three such players on the roster. Though all still young, each came into the season at a different point in his career, and each wound up enduring struggles that may have caused fans, not to mention the organization's brass, to wonder why they were drafted so highly.

Center fielder Aaron Hicks began the season widely regarded as the top position-player prospect in the Minnesota Twins organization. Though he had never played above Class A, the fourteenth overall pick in the 2008 draft had displayed an enticing combination of speed, plate discipline and defensive prowess in three seasons of professional baseball. Assigned to Fort Myers to begin 2011, he spent spring training under the tutelage of Hall-of-Fame former Twins outfielder Rod Carew, a sign of the respect the Twins had for Hicks' abilities. Hicks called the experience a "blessing," as Carew, one of the greatest contact hitters of all time, shared pointers on his approach at the plate.[2] Little appeared out of reach for the player *Baseball America* once ranked as the 19th-best prospect in the game.

In Fort Myers, where ninety-degree days are not uncommon in April, Hicks nonetheless took a while to heat up, just as he did the year before while in Wisconsin at Class A Beloit. But Hicks, who rebounded to make the Midwest League All-Star Game in 2010, was unfazed by another slow start in 2011. He broke out in May, improving his average to .250 by the end of the month, with an on-base percentage (.349) nearly one hundred points better. The pattern follows a story Mauer tells his players about his brother.

"Down here early in his Florida State League career, I was his roommate and teammate, obviously, and he was struggling the first week," Jake Mauer said. "It might have been two or three weeks. I think he was hitting .190, .180 or something like that, but he didn't change his approach. He didn't change anything, and then before you know it, at the All-Star break, I think he was hitting .340 or whatever it was, and getting moved up [to Double-A]. And that's a 20-year-old kid, the first time he ever had any failure. He didn't panic or anything, just stayed the course. It all kind of shakes out in the end."

Jim Rantz, who served as the Twins' director of minor leagues from 1986 through 2012, saw Joe Mauer and plenty of other players persevere during his front-office career, which began right after his playing days ended in 1965.

"When someone has as much talent as Hicks, and other guys who've got talent, they figure it out," Rantz said. "Some take a little bit longer than others, but they usually figure it out and move up the line."[3]

Usually.

The Twins' other first-round pick from 2008, right-handed pitcher Shooter Hunt, began 2011 with much less fanfare. He was no longer considered a top prospect, having failed to post an earned-run average of less than 5.00 at any of his past three stops in the organization. His minor league career began auspiciously in 2008 at rookie-level Elizabethton, Tennessee, where he posted a 0.47 ERA in four starts. He was quickly promoted to Beloit, and there his struggles began. He went just 1–4 in seven starts there, posting a 5.46 ERA. That was nothing compared to what happened in 2009. He opened up with the Gulf Coast League Twins, the lowest rung on Minnesota's ladder. He did little to persuade the organization to move him up, going 0–4 with a 9.60 ERA in seven appearances, but he was nonetheless recalled to Beloit, where his ERA was 10.70 in seven more games. He spent the rest of the season on the disabled list with a groin injury. According to the (*Newark, N.J.*) *Star-Ledger*, a newspaper near his hometown of Westwood, he then began collaborating with fitness professional Jay Lally, working on, among other exercises, "Ginastica Natural," a Brazilian training method designed to improve flexibility, strength, balance, breathing and endurance.[4]

The exotic workout did not pay immediate dividends. Having started all but four games in his professional career, Hunt was shifted to the bullpen in 2010, and continued to struggle with his control, walking 84 batters in 67⅓ innings at Fort Myers. He returned to Fort Myers in 2011 and walked 28 while putting up a 5.84 ERA in 24⅔ innings during the first two months of the season.

Still, Rantz remained upbeat about the former first-round pick in the summer of 2011.

"Shooter Hunt has come a long ways from last year to where he is this year," Rantz said in 2011. "He's still not, I don't think, where he wants to be, but I think he's moving in a positive direction."

In December 2011, the St. Louis Cardinals selected Hunt in the minor league portion of the Rule 5 draft. He didn't pitch a single inning in 2012 or 2013.

Whatever ailed Hunt appears to be contagious. Alex Wimmers, the Twins' first-round pick in 2010, taken twenty-first overall, followed up an impressive post-draft debut with a disturbing start to 2011. The right-hander was held back in spring training because of a pulled quadriceps muscle, and then bombed in his first regular-season start at Fort Myers. He faced just six batters, and walked them all. He threw four wild pitches, three of which went all the way to the backstop. The Twins placed him on the disabled list with "flu-like symptoms,"[5] and two months into the season, Wimmers had yet to appear in another game. He came back to win two games for Fort Myers by the end of 2011.

So, what happened to the two-time Big Ten pitcher of the year who followed up his final college season with a 0.57 ERA in four starts at Fort Myers in 2010?

"We're kind of wanting to figure that out ourselves," Rantz said. "I wish I had an answer for it."

If it wasn't something physical, Wimmers would be far from the first player to encounter hurdles inside his own mind.

"Psychology is playing such a big part of what goes on in the game," Rantz said. "There are more mental casualties than there are physical casualties."

With regards to Wimmers, who received a $1.3 million signing bonus in August 2010, Mauer sees a young man for the first time coping with failure, or at least not immediate success.

"I think it may have been the first time he ever had some adversity, really," Mauer said. "That's part of development, too, that things aren't always going to go your way. You may have been a big fish in a small pond in high school and college, and now it's the opposite. You're in the ocean now. There's going to be teams that you're going to match up with and there's going to be situations where it's not going to go your way."

For Wimmers, the battles have been both psychological and physical. In 2012, he made one start each in the Gulf Coast League and at

Double-A New Britain before undergoing surgery to repair a ligament in his pitching elbow.[6] In 2013, he came back to make six starts in the Gulf Coast League, registering a 7.20 ERA in 15 innings.

For this book, we will look at the players drafted between 1990 and 2006 and what they can tell us about why some are household names and others have already been forgotten. There were 685 players drafted and signed in the first round, including supplemental picks, during this time frame. Alex Rodriguez, Roy Halladay and Chipper Jones established themselves as stars, while Brien Taylor, Matt Brunson, and Mark Farris are busts who never wore a major league uniform. In all, 36 percent of the first-rounders from the 1990s did not even make it to the major leagues for a single game. A whopping 64 percent failed to have major-league careers of five years or more while maintaining a positive wins-above-replacement value, the minimum requirements for what we will define as a "serviceable" career. (Wins above replacement indicates the number of extra wins a team can expect to have in a season with a particular player in the lineup instead of the average Triple-A call-up who might replace him.) So that means that close to two-thirds of the players taken in the first round in the '90s could not so much as muster passable major league production over a five-year stretch. This book provides evidence that teams made significant strides in turning top picks into major leaguers during the first decade of the 2000s.

Of course, some organizations have proven more successful than others at converting draft picks into valuable, or at least employable, major leaguers. For instance, according to data through the 2012 season, the Twins, Seattle Mariners and Los Angeles Angels, each of whom have enjoyed multiple playoff appearances in the last 15 years, are the only organizations to have drafted first-rounders in the 1990s whose careers averaged more than seven years in length. The Philadelphia Phillies and Tampa Bay Rays, who met in the 2008 World Series, parlayed successful drafts in the early 2000s into positive results on the field. Conversely, first-rounders taken in the '90s by the Brewers, who only in recent years have become competitive again, averaged only 2.79 years in the majors. The next lowest number of this list belongs to—who else?—the long-suffering Pirates, whose draftees averaged 3.07 years in the bigs during the '90s.

Some of the other findings of our study:

- Seventy-two percent of first-round draftees in the 1980s played in the major leagues. Organizations took a step back in the '90s, when only 64 percent of first-rounders made the majors. The percentage was 70 percent from 2000 to 2006.
- Not surprisingly, players drafted in the first round have a markedly better chance of making the majors than players picked in the fifth (31 percent) and tenth rounds (20 percent).
- Seventy-four percent of players drafted out of college, compared to fifty-nine percent of players taken out of high school, made the bigs.
- Through 2013, fifteen percent of first-round picks from 1990 to 2006 went on to make at least one major league All-Star team.
- Of all the positions, right-handed pitchers are most likely to be picked in the first round of the draft. But players drafted as third basemen are most likely to ascend to the major leagues.
- First-round picks who do not make the majors are as likely to top out at the Triple-A level as at lower levels of the minor leagues.
- Between 1990 and 2006, 44 percent of first-round picks came from high schools or colleges in California, Florida, and Texas.
- The higher a player is drafted in the first round, the more likely it is that he will make the major leagues. Seventy-five percent of players in the '90s selected with between the first and seventeenth overall picks saw time in the big leagues. That percentage drops to 45 percent for players taken in the last third of the first round.

To what extent can baseball be compared to other sports when it comes to the draft? The preparations are similar. So are the "war rooms" on draft day, where executives huddle over last-minute decisions. But while the National Football League and National Basketball Association drafts are made-for-TV events, the Major League Baseball draft is primarily a behind-the-scenes affair that only recently has been broadcast to a national audience. And while the NFL draft has seven rounds and the NBA only two, the MLB draft can last up to forty rounds.

Whereas top draft picks in the NBA and NFL are often household names before even starting their professional careers, the best amateur baseball players in the country, with rare exceptions, are unknowns.

This makes the baseball draft process inherently different from its counterparts.

When highly drafted NBA or NFL players don't pan out, the backlash is enormous. For evidence of that, consider the numerous quarterbacks over the years whose impressive college performances didn't carry over to the NFL, or the basketball big men tabbed as the future of an NBA franchise but as busts a few years later.

It would be unreasonable to expect as high a percentage of amateur baseball draftees to attain the level of success of their counterparts on the gridiron and basketball court. One reason is that the collegiate athletic systems in football and basketball have long served as a farm system for professional leagues. In contrast, baseball has an actual farm system, with every organization fielding teams in leagues ranging from rookie ball to Class AAA. It is in these leagues that players are mercilessly weeded out, with only a small fraction going on to make the majors. It would be unheard of in the football or basketball drafts for fourteen first-round picks in a year never to play a minute in the NFL or NBA. Yet in baseball, that is the average annual number of first-round selections between 1990 and 2006 who never reached the major leagues.

To understand why so many of these draftees had such short, unproductive careers, it is helpful to understand who some of these players are.

When Chad Mottola, the fifth overall pick by the Cincinnati Reds in 1992, hung up his spikes after a sixteen-year professional career, he finished with 1,884 hits, an impressive total for an outfielder who was pegged as a sure thing coming out of the University of Central Florida.

The bitter twist for Mottola was that all but twenty-five of those hits came in the minor leagues, where his consistently strong performance, which included a year at Triple-A, where he stole more than thirty bases and clubbed more than thirty home runs, never translated into a prolonged stint with a big league club.

Mottola's story is a cautionary tale of how even the most highly touted major league prospects, even those who put up gaudy numbers down on the farm, are far from guaranteed a shot at baseball's top level. Adding to the intrigue of Mottola's near-miss career is that he was selected with the pick right before the Yankees took Derek Jeter.

"I don't get my feelings hurt when the Jeter question gets asked," said Mottola, who took a job coaching in the Blue Jays organization after retiring from professional baseball in 2007. "If I took someone with the fifth overall pick, I'd want them to be in the big leagues for fifteen years. People can call me a bust, but it's a lot more complicated than that."[7]

It is not hard to see what major league organizations found appealing about Mottola, a Florida native who initially was drafted out of high school in the tenth round by the Baltimore Orioles in 1989 but chose to go to college instead of signing with the team. He had all the tools that jumped out at scouts: size, speed, and an impressive throwing arm.

His stock only rose while at UCF, and a performance during his junior year in an exhibition game against the Royals cemented his status as a first-round pick. In that contest, he went 3-for-4, stole a base, and recorded a pair of outfield assists nailing runners at third.

The Reds gave Mottola, who was not represented by an agent, a $450,000 signing bonus. By contrast, the Yankees gave $800,000 to Jeter, who had the assistance of agent Casey Close.

The Reds nonetheless seemed to regard Mottola as a budding star.

"We like his arm, we like his speed and we like his bat," Reds scout Clay Daniel told the *Sun Sentinel* on the day of Mottola's signing. "He's got all three plusses, and that's what you need to make it to the major league level. The sky's the limit for him."[8]

Mottola spent three and a half seasons in the Reds' system before being promoted to Triple-A Indianapolis, where he put up solid, if not spectacular numbers. *Baseball America* rated him the forty-eighth best prospect in the game going into the 1994 season.[9] In 1996, Mottola's fifth year of pro ball, Reds general manager Jim Bowden told the *Sun Sentinel* that the organization still expected great things from Mottola: "We've all been waiting for his bat to come, and it has. He already could do everything else. He can be a superstar."[10]

At the end of the 1996 season, the Reds rewarded Mottola with a promotion to Cincinnati when major league rosters expanded to forty players in September. He did not know it at the time, but that month turned out to be his one chance to show the Reds he could compete at baseball's highest level. He had seventy-nine at-bats with Cincinnati and hit only .215. He stayed in professional baseball another eleven years, but more than half his major league at-bats came that season with the Reds.

A taste of the majors was more than the man drafted two spots higher than Mottola ever got. B.J. Wallace, a left-handed pitcher out of Mississippi State University and the third overall selection by the Expos in the 1992 draft, never played a game above the Double-A level. It is much easier to explain why Wallace failed to fulfill expectations: he underwent major shoulder surgery during his second year of pro ball and never fully recovered. Wallace was one of fifteen first-round picks in the 1992 draft not to play in the majors.

Mottola never suffered any career-changing injuries, which makes his story much more worthy of examination.

After the 1996 season, which from a statistical standpoint did not differ greatly from his previous seasons, the Reds' brass stopped uttering superlatives about Mottola and dealt him to the Texas Rangers. In 1999, he signed as a free agent with the Chicago White Sox and put up impressive numbers at Triple-A Charlotte that included twenty home runs, ninety-four RBIs, and a .321 batting average.

But Mottola would soon be on the move again, this time going as a free agent to the Blue Jays.

Still only twenty-eight years old, his best production was yet to come.

In 2000, at Triple-A Syracuse, Mottola won the International League MVP award, bashing thirty-two home runs, knocking in 103 runs, stealing thirty bases, and hitting .309.

He hoped that season would put to rest any concerns about his ability: "Some people were labeling me as a long swing guy who can't really hit. Everybody had their scouting report already, and I think they were looking to move on to a young kid they thought had more potential than me. If that season didn't change their minds, I didn't know what would."

A monster year in the International League used to be a path to major league stardom. In the '70s, recipients of the IL MVP award included Jim Rice, Dwight Evans, and Bobby Grich. But all Mottola's breakout season got him was nine September at-bats with the Blue Jays and a trade to the Marlins at season's end.

Mottola kept plugging away in the minors, seeing time in the Boston, Tampa Bay, Baltimore, and Toronto organizations. But he never got more than sixteen at-bats in a season at the major league level, and he never made more than $15,000 a month during his career.

When he retired at the end of the 2007 season, Mottola had the third most hits of any International League player in the 2000s.

Mottola's first coaching job with the Blue Jays came as a hitting instructor in the rookie-ball Gulf Coast League.

"I didn't want to know what round my players were drafted in, because to me they were all equal and I wanted to evaluate them," Mottola said. "But there's a business side of the game that you can't ignore. You better make sure those top picks make it or the guys above you are in trouble. I always try to see a level playing field, but nowadays if a guy got $3 million to sign, there will be certain expectations. You're not allowed to fail."

Mottola went on to become a roving instructor in the Blue Jays organization and a hitting coach for their Triple-A affiliate.

Mottola chooses not to view his career as a failure, but among other things as a learning experience he can share with the young players he coaches: "It's easy for me to relate to players, whether they're first-round picks or guys just hanging on, because I've been in both places. I think there are guys who go up to the majors and fail, but they are given a second chance. Other guys aren't given a second chance."

Mottola reflects back on his playing career almost every day: How might things have been different if he had taken steroids like a lot of other guys were doing? Should he have been more assertive and cocky? What ultimately went wrong?

He is not alone. More than 250 first-round picks from his era either did not make the majors or failed to have average careers there.

Here is the story of why that happened.

1

A History of the Draft

Hundreds of baseball players in small towns all across the country waited each year to find out if they would be among the lucky few chosen to go to the big time. Other players took different routes to the major leagues, bypassing the draft altogether, but ballclubs still saw the draft as an important mechanism of constructing their teams, and the game's leadership found it a key to controlling player movement. All of the draft-eligible players had spent years honing their craft on baseball's proving grounds, hoping one day to be a part of the games that they'd spent a lifetime imagining themselves playing. This was their chance.

This was true in the 1890s, just as it was in the 1990s.

Major League Baseball was the last of the four major North American professional sports to institute an amateur draft, but baseball came up with the idea of a draft long before any of the other leagues existed. Big league clubs began selecting players from the minor leagues using a draft system instituted in 1892. While this draft was fundamentally different from today's amateur draft, which introduces high school and college players to the minor leagues, it represents the genesis of structured player allocation. Its vestiges are seen in today's Rule 5 draft, wherein veteran minor leaguers left off the big league team's 40-man roster are eligible to be selected by other major league clubs. This primordial draft was a part of the framework that resulted in the first stratification of the minor leagues and played a significant role in shaping the player development system we know today.[1]

The original draft was part of the National Agreement of 1892, a general accord that governed player movement between the National League, the sole "major league" at the time, and all of the other "minor" leagues. The NL had emerged from a bitter labor dispute as a 12-team monolith atop baseball, and with power consolidated within its clutches, it sought to bring some order to player movement. The adoption of the draft was also a mechanism to depress salaries by removing competition among National League clubs for a player's services.[2] Major league and minor league teams were free to come to their own agreements involving player transfers apart from the draft, and this was long the primary method by which top-flight minor league talent made it to the bigs. Still, the draft allowed the majors to fill their rosters without having to negotiate with minor league teams for each player. The basic structure of the draft stipulated in the agreement held that players could be drafted at any time during the offseason, by any club. If a player was drafted by multiple teams, the name of the team that got to keep the player was drawn out of a hat.[3] This was later amended to a first-come, first-serve policy, whereby the first team to stake a claim to a player was awarded his services.[4] It wouldn't be until decades later that the notion of a draft order that allowed teams with poorer records to pick first was considered.[5]

Far from brokering a lasting peace between the National League and the minors, the draft set forth in the 1892 agreement represented the beginning of a contentious coexistence. The draft helped lead to the creation of the American League when the 1896 Western League champion Minneapolis Millers were picked clean of their talent. The team struggled to avoid last place the following season, threatening the viability of the franchise.[6] Western League president Ban Johnson, never a fan of the National League, responded by withdrawing his league from the agreement and reforming it so that by 1901, it was rechristened the American League and had begun competing with the NL for major league talent.[7] The NL and AL were soon able to peacefully coexist, but the stormy relationship between the majors and minors did not change. The National Agreement of 1903 brought an end to an unsettled period of player movement brought on by the creation of the AL, but quibbles over matters such as how many players could be selected from any one team and, most often, the amount of money a major league club had to pay a minor league team for selecting one of its players, were *de rigueur* for years. The fee incurred for each draft pick began at $500 in 1892 and rose to $2,500 for players at the highest level of the minor leagues in 1912.[8] By 1921, it was $5,000.[9] The $5,000 figure was negotiated following a two-year hiatus during which there was no agreement, and therefore no draft, between the majors and minors. It coincided with the appointment of iron-fisted Kenesaw Mountain Landis as the game's first commissioner, and Landis, characteristically, was at the center of more turmoil over the draft system throughout the 1920s. Major league owners grew to resent the 1921 agreement, which held that only one player could be selected from each of the clubs at the two highest levels of the minors.[10] This led to a significant decline in the use of the draft, as major league teams resorted to the more expensive practice of negotiating the purchase of player contracts from minor league clubs rather than drafting the players outright.[11] Still, the establishment of "options," which allowed major league teams to send players to the minors without losing the rights to their services, was one of the building blocks of a new relationship between the majors and the minors.

There was one other significant development in 1921 that made it a landmark year for player development. For the first time, major league teams and minor league teams could be under the same ownership umbrella.[12] That meant individual major league franchises could wield much greater control over talent, as they could buy up minor league clubs and stock them with talent not quite ready for the bigs. In other words, the concept of a farm system was born. Branch Rickey, perhaps the most widely known baseball executive of the first half of the twentieth century, is widely credited with inventing and popularizing the idea. Yet with the ability to own both major and minor league clubs in place, it's easy to suppose that if Rickey hadn't done it, someone else soon would have. Before the practice was legal, Rickey, and others preceding him, had long engaged in secret player-development arrangements with minor league clubs.[13]

The formal development of farm systems helped further establish the majors as the one and only venue for top-flight baseball. No longer could a talent like Lefty Grove be left in the minors long enough to compile 108 wins over five seasons for Baltimore of the International League.[14] As farm systems became widespread in the 1930s, major league teams would promote players from their affiliates when they were deemed ready, without having to negotiate a deal or wrangle with the vagaries of the draft system.

The draft in the 1930s began to function much more like the Rule 5 draft of today. In 1931, a new agreement allowed major league teams to draft any player in the minors with four years of minor-league playing experience.[15] Thus, pitcher Bobo Newsom, who bounced around the minors for a few years before winning thirty games in 1933 for the Los Angeles Angels, a top-level affiliate of the Cubs, was drafted by the St. Louis Browns and inserted into their starting rotation in 1934. Major league teams weren't so much poaching the minors as they were poaching each other. This presaged the next phase of controversy in player development, one that led directly to the establishment of the amateur draft.

In 1941, the Tigers shocked baseball by signing University of Michigan star Dick Wakefield to a contract that included a then-record $52,000 signing bonus. He took $1,400 of it to buy a Lincoln Zephyr, a curious purchase considering he did not know how to drive.[16] He spent most of the next two years in the minors but was the Tigers' everyday left fielder in 1943, batting .316, earning selection to the All-Star Game, and finishing sixth in MVP voting. A combination of war service, injury, and pressure to live up to his bonus derailed his career, however, and he never played a full season again, finishing his career with only 625 hits. Still, his impact was felt for years to come.

In an effort to curb such extravagances, baseball instituted a bonus rule soon after the end of World War II. From 1946 to 1950, if a team signed a player for more than the limit, which varied from year to year but was usually around $5,000, the player had to be carried on the major league roster.[17] The rule failed to have the intended effect of curbing hefty payments to unproven amateur talent; instead, bonuses continued to escalate. In 1950, Branch Rickey, then in charge of the Pirates' front office, paid baseball's first $100,000 bonus to left-handed pitcher Paul Pettit, who won just one career major league game.[18] Teams took advantage of loopholes in the system, and rumors abounded of teams creating a few loopholes of their own with under-the-table payments and other gifts. Baseball temporarily abandoned the bonus restrictions, but with more and more money being paid to the top amateur talent, stricter regulations were put in place in 1953. Amateurs who signed deals that gave them more than $4,000 or lasted longer than one year had to be immediately promoted to the big leagues and remain on the major league roster for at least two years.[19]

The result was more of the same, with a slew of players who did little more than take up space on rosters. Hall-of-Famer Sandy Koufax never pitched an inning in the minor leagues, but spent the entire 1955 season riding the bench for the Brooklyn Dodgers, appearing in only a dozen games. Yet for every Koufax or Harmon Killebrew, there were many more players like Paul Giel, Mel Roach or Frank Zupo, who never delivered for the clubs that had committed valuable roster space to them. Teams that kept highly regarded prospects in the minor leagues, however, risked losing out on a star. The Dodgers went to great lengths to obfuscate the skills of nineteen-year-old Roberto Clemente in 1954. Max Macon, Clemente's manager at Triple-A Montreal, would take him out of games when his bat appeared to be heating up and leave him in whenever he was slumping, depressing his batting average to .257.[20] Renowned scout Clyde Sukeforth was not fooled, however, and he convinced the Pirates' front office to draft Clemente at the end of the season.[21] The Pirates made him their everyday right fielder in 1955 and stuck with him as he struggled to establish himself. Clemente made his first All-Star Game during Pittsburgh's championship season of 1960 and went on to collect 3,000 hits, all of them with the Pirates.

On the heels of the Braves' signing Bob "Hawk" Taylor to a $112,000 bonus that established a new record, the bonus rule was once more abandoned in 1957.[22]

Over the next six years, teams would combine to spend more than $50 million in bonuses.[23] In 1959, a modified attempt at a bonus rule was made in the form of the Rule 5 draft. Minor leaguers who had spent more than a year as professionals were subject to the draft if they were left off a major league team's 40-man roster. A team that drafted a player, however, had to keep him on the major league roster for the entirety of the next season.[24] This did little to stem the bonus tide. The wave crested in 1964 when the Los Angeles Angels signed Rick Reichardt from the University of Wisconsin for $205,000. Four other amateurs signed for six figures that year.

It was time for baseball, which seventy-two years earlier had pioneered the notion of stocking its clubs by drafting professional players, to follow the lead of professional football, basketball and hockey, all of which drafted amateurs. The proponents of an amateur draft hoped it would not only curb escalating bonus payments, but also restore competitive balance to the game.[25] Of the thirty-eight pennants won between 1946, the year of the first bonus rule, and 1964, twenty-three of them were taken by either the Yankees or the Dodgers. Not surprisingly, neither the Yankees nor Dodgers were in favor of the plan. Johnny Johnson, director of the Yankees' farm system, labeled the idea of a draft "communistic."[26] Others were concerned that the draft would endanger baseball's longstanding antitrust exemption.[27] Still, the draft's opponents in major league front offices were outnumbered. A notable convert was Buzzie Bavasi, the Dodgers' general manager, who once called the draft "a form of socialism" that "penalizes the industrious."[28] On the eve of the draft's approval, he instead encouraged cooperation amongst all the clubs. "There may be some kinks that need to be ironed out," Bavasi told the Associated Press, "but we can always make some slight changes or amendments, if necessary."[29] The last hurdle would involve approval from the minor leagues. According to the same Associated Press story, the minors fell in line when they were informed by three U.S. Supreme Court justices that a challenge to the draft based on restraint of trade would meet with the court's opposition. The day after the minors approved the draft in December 1964, the majors followed suit.

For all the hand-wringing leading up to the event, little fanfare accompanied the proceedings of the first amateur draft in 1965.[30] The Kansas City A's, who were awarded the top pick based on their last-place finish in 1964, made Rick Monday the first-ever selection. Monday, who went on to make two All-Star Games over the course of a steady nineteen-year career with the A's, Cubs and Dodgers, received a $104,000 signing bonus in 1965, more than $100,000 less than Reichardt had received the year before.[31] No draftee received a bonus better than Monday's until 1975, and no one exceeded Reichardt's 1964 bonus record until well after Reichardt played his final major league game in 1974. Just who exceeded Reichardt's take is unclear. *Baseball America* lists a $208,000 payout from the Yankees to Todd Demeter in 1979 as the record-breaker,[32] while Rany Jazayerli, writing for *Baseball Prospectus*, cites the $235,000 the Padres gave Andy Benes in 1988 as the bonus that finally surpassed the mark.[33] Doug Pappas, in a 1998 Society for American Baseball Research newsletter, called Darryl Strawberry's $210,000 bonus from the Mets the record-breaker.[34] What is clear is that for many years, the draft effectively held down bonuses, just as teams had hoped.

The early focus of the draft was on high schoolers. A rule implemented in 1967 held that college players could not be drafted until they were juniors or had turned twenty-one.[35] These collegians were also shunted off to a secondary phase of the draft.[36] Before 1972, players who were drafted out of high school but chose to go to college instead of signing weren't eligible for the regular phase of the draft when they left college.[37] In 1975, all college juniors were finally made eligible for the draft, regardless of their age.[38] The result of all the restrictions on college talent helped lead most clubs to draft high schoolers instead.[39] Only twenty-nine of 184 first round picks from 1967 to 1974 were college players. This was not an era of great success for draftees, either, as nearly 25 percent of the players drafted through 1980 failed to so much as advance past Class AA.[40]

One player development experiment from this era represented an attempt to get a step ahead of the draft and presaged the way many clubs mine talent in Latin America today. In 1970, owner Ewing Kauffman of the Kansas City Royals, an expansion team that hit the field the year before, opened the Kansas City Royals Baseball Academy in Sarasota, Florida. Kauffman was convinced that expert baseball skills could be taught to those with little more than rudimentary knowledge of the game.[41] The Royals' scouts concentrated on finding talented athletes who hadn't concentrated on baseball growing up, and the team brought in a research psychologist who had previously worked with NASA to determine the ideal physical, psychological and mental traits of a top-flight baseball player.[42] The approach was highly unconventional, but it appeared the Royals were onto something in 1971, when they debuted a team made up entirely of academy players in the short-season Gulf Coast League, the lowest rung of the minors. That team sprinted to a record of 40-13, lapping the field behind players such as Frank White, a future five-time major league All-Star; Ron Washington, who reached the majors and later found greater fame as manager of the Texas Rangers; and Orestes Minoso, stepson of White Sox legend Minnie Minoso. They had a deep corps of pitching, as they threw eleven shutouts and a dozen different pitchers earned wins, but the team's greatest asset was speed. They swiped 103 bases, including nine in one game,[43] and finished with forty-eight more steals than any other team in the league. They legged out thirty-one triples, while no other Gulf Coast League team had more than eighteen. The academy had brought in Wes Santee, a former member of the U.S. Olympic track team, and University of Kansas track coach Bill Easton to work with the students on baserunning.[44] This paid lasting dividends. The academy team led the Gulf Coast League in steals in every year of the school's existence, and many of the experimental techniques, such as using a stopwatch on the field, became widely accepted practice throughout the majors during the stolen-base boom of the '70s and '80s.[45]

White, who enjoyed a lengthy tenure as the Royals' everyday second baseman from 1976 until 1989, was the academy's greatest success story. He never played high school baseball, and yet he was a linchpin on all seven Royals teams to have advanced to the postseason in club history. His frequent double-play partner, shortstop U.L. Washington, was another academy graduate, as was Rodney Scott, the starting second baseman on the only playoff team in Montreal Expos history. In all, fourteen academy players made it to the majors.[46] Even though White was in Kansas City by 1973, the academy's dividends were not immediately clear. It met resistance from traditionalist executives within the Royals' front office, and the declining performance of the Gulf Coast League team after 1971 spelled trouble.[47] Kauffman, who had spent $1.5 million to open the academy and $700,000 a year in operating expenses, closed the camp in 1974.[48] No other such venture has been undertaken by any other major league team in America, yet countless camps and academies dot the Latin American landscape, teaching fundamentals in lands where formal baseball instruction, if not passion for the sport, is otherwise nonexistent. These are the primary entry points to organized baseball for countless future major leaguers. The major difference is that the foreign camps work in territories where the draft, which by rule draws from only the U.S., Canada, and Puerto Rico, is not a factor. Yet both Latin American camps and the Royals Academy represent baseball's eagerness to look outside the confines of the draft for talent, and they illustrate the draft's inherent blind spots and fallibilities.

Perhaps no one player personifies the shortcomings of the early years of the draft more than Danny Goodwin, an elite catching prospect in the early 1970s.[49] Drafted first overall by the White Sox in 1971, he elected not to sign and instead attended Southern University. His draft prospects, by default, seemed to have nowhere to go but down. Yet he upheld his reputation in college and was again made the first overall selection in 1975, taken this time by the Angels. He signed with the club and received a $125,000 bonus, breaking Monday's record set ten years prior.[50] Goodwin appeared briefly in the majors that very same year, but never once appeared as a catcher during seven seasons as a fringe major leaguer. Used mostly as a designated hitter, he never totaled more than 172 plate appearances in a single season and finished with 150 hits and thirteen homers for his career. It was embarrassingly meager production for a man twice deemed the nation's top amateur player.

One step taken to help teams better judge draft-eligible talent was the creation of the scouting bureau in 1974. One of the initial concerns upon the implementation of the draft was that it would make scouting more difficult.[51] The bureau consolidated operations, allowing owners to contribute to the pool of scouts who travel the country and set up camps to look at draft prospects. Teams still have their own talent scouts, but the bureau's reports provide a basic sketch of the available talent to serve as a basis for additional observation. Originally set up by the owners as an independent group, the bureau became part of the commissioner's office in 1985.[52] Today, the bureau employs close to three dozen full-time scouts and another dozen part-timers.[53]

Over the first twenty-five years of the draft's existence, teams gradually became more sophisticated about the talent they chose, and changes in the makeup of the draft class began to take place. In particular, teams began to select significantly more college players in the 1980s. Though the rules regarding collegians had been loosened in the early '70s, the strategic shift didn't occur for several years. Prior to 1981, college players represented only about a quarter of the first-round selections.[54] The 1981 draft was the first to feature fewer than ten high schoolers picked in the first round, and from that point forward, the rate of high schoolers to college players has stayed the same: roughly 50-50.[55] The rate at which first-rounders made the majors jumped from about six in ten in the '60s and '70s to 71 percent from 1981 through 1989.[56] This coincided with an increasing number of pitchers being taken in the first round. The number of pitchers taken in the '80s rose 10 percent over earlier totals, and jumped another five percent or so in the 1990s.[57] Teams seemed to be detecting patterns and exploiting them. Yet at the same time, players were beginning to become more sophisticated in their approach to the draft as well.

The name Billy Cannon is most closely associated with the Tigers — the LSU Tigers football team, that is. The 1959 Heisman Trophy winner and his son, Billy Cannon Jr., made it clear their baseball loyalties were to the Yankees. In 1980, the elder Cannon sent a telegram to the other twenty-five teams notifying them that his son, a highly touted shortstop prospect, would only sign if given a record signing bonus.[58] The Yankees took Cannon in the third round, but, upon complaints from the other teams, the draft pick was voided and the Yankees were barred from signing him. This attempt at legerdemain from a player would pale in comparison to what would be introduced the very next year.

In 1981, the Mariners selected pitcher Mike Moore out of Oral Roberts University. Moore went on to be a solid presence in Seattle's rotation for seven years, winning seventeen games in 1985 before moving on to Oakland in 1989, when he won a career-high nineteen games for the World Series champion A's. The pitcher the Mariners really wanted, however, was Yale's Ron Darling, who was a key figure on the Mets team that won the 1986 World Series.[59] But Darling wanted a $110,000 signing bonus, while Moore was commanding only $80,000.[60] Darling was still available when Texas took him with the ninth pick, and he became the first draftee to negotiate his first contract through an agent.[61] Quickly thereafter, players represented by an agent became the rule instead of the exception.

An entirely different set of high-dollar deals began to affect the

24

draft in 1979. For the first time, teams that signed top-tier free agents had to give up their first-round pick. In 1982, the clubs that lost their free agents also began to receive additional picks tacked on to the end of the first round, known as "sandwich picks." The free-spending Yankees, before they began to place a somewhat higher value on in-house talent in the 1990s and 2000s, were without a first-round pick from 1986 through 1989.

Another player fired a salvo at the draft system in 1985, when Pete Incaviglia, having just set an NCAA record of 100 career home runs at Oklahoma State, including forty-eight in his final season,[62] sought to set another mark. The Expos drafted him eighth overall, but Incaviglia refused to sign with the team unless he was given a signing bonus larger than any other in baseball history. He was willing to sign for less to go elsewhere, however, so the Expos agreed to a sign-and-trade with the Rangers five months after the draft, getting Jim Anderson, a utility infielder who never played another major league game, and pitcher Bob Sebra, who lost fifteen games for the Expos in his only full season in the bigs. Incaviglia immediately assumed the role of starting right fielder for the Rangers and hit thirty home runs in his rookie season. He had left the Expos with little to show for their pick by making an end run around the draft to play for a team more to his liking. Major League Baseball subsequently closed this loophole for players by essentially outlawing such sign-and-trades, prohibiting teams from trading drafted players until a year after they signed.[63]

Baseball made another couple of key adjustments to prevent teams and players from circumventing the system. While draft eligibility was once open only to players born in the fifty states, this was expanded to include anyone who attended high school domestically after the Brewers signed Connecticut high schooler Juan Nieves, a native of Puerto Rico, to a free-agent contract that included a $110,000 signing bonus in 1983.[64] Before the 1991 draft, eligibility expanded to include players from Canada, Puerto Rico and all other U.S. territories.[65] The ultimate extrapolation of such incremental changes, a universal system that would allow teams to select the best players from around the globe and put baseball's draft in line with other sports, has remained the subject of proposals, discussions and rumors, but nothing more. As Latin America continues to consistently produce top-flight major league talent, the draft is still just one of many gateways to professional baseball.

For draft-eligible players, it has become an increasingly lucrative gateway over the past two decades. From 1988 to 2000, a new signing bonus record was achieved almost every year.[66] The average signing bonus given to first-round picks in 1989 was $176,000.[67] That figure increased nearly three times from 1989 to 1992, and shot up more than ten times by 1999, when the average bonus was $1.81 million.[68]

An infusion of TV money helped fuel the spending spree. In 1988, baseball agreed to jump from a joint arrangement with NBC and ABC to CBS for a four-year deal worth more than a billion dollars.[69] At the same time, the Yankees signed a twelve-year, $500 million deal for local TV rights,[70] and in 1989, a national cable package involving all twenty-six major league clubs was struck for the first time. ESPN paid $400 million for the rights to multiple games every week.[71] Teams were flush with cash, and agents helped funnel that to their clients.

Agent Scott Boras, as he has done consistently ever since, jumped on the opportunity. In 1990, he negotiated a three-year, $1.2 million major league contract for 14th overall selection Todd Van Poppel,[72] who appeared mostly as a reliever during 11 seasons in the bigs and finished with a career ERA of 5.58. The next year, Boras got a record-shattering $1.55 million signing bonus for top pick Brien Taylor, more than doubling the previous mark.[73] A shoulder injury kept Taylor from ever appearing in a major league game. Jeff Moorad, later an executive and part owner of the Diamondbacks, got third baseman and fifth overall pick Josh Booty a record $1.6 million signing bonus in 1994.[74] Booty saw action in a grand total of thirteen major league games.

Baseball's mistakes didn't end with inflated payouts to the wrong personnel. In 1996, the Twins, Expos, Giants and White Sox failed to tender contracts to four of the top twelve picks within the required 15-day time frame following the draft. As a result, the players (Travis Lee, John Patterson, Matt White and Bobby Seay) were declared free agents, able to sign with the highest bidder.[75] The massive contracts they got as a result, ranging from $3 million for Seay to $10.2 million for White, a player who never made the majors, helped further inflate the market for first-round talent.[76]

The next year, many teams were cautious about who they drafted, passing up the most talented player available in favor of a player more willing to sign.[77] Phillies draftee J.D. Drew, the second pick in 1997, sought to take advantage of the events of 1996 when he held out for an $11 million contract, $1 million higher than the payout the Phillies had made to Lee, the No. 2 pick the year before.[78] The bitter negotiations between the team, which offered a little more than $2 million,[79] and Drew, a Boras client, dragged on for months. Drew signed to play with the independent Northern League, and while Boras contended his client would become a free agent a week before the 1998 draft, Major League Baseball declared Drew's rights would remain with the Phillies in perpetuity until he signed.[80] The players' union filed a grievance, and eventually Drew was simply placed back into the draft pool for 1998.[81] The Phillies had the top pick in the draft that year, but passed on him. The Cardinals took Drew fifth and gave him a contract that guaranteed him $7 million.[82] The Phillies used their pick on Pat Burrell and gave him a contract that guaranteed him $8 million, a total greater than the 1997 World Series champion Marlins, who had gutted their roster, were spending on their entire major league team in 1998.[83]

High-profile contract squabbles that resulted in major money on the table, combined with the posting of draft picks on MLB.com for the first time in 1998,[84] led to a slight uptick in notoriety for the draft. Originally, results from the second round onward weren't made public for weeks.[85] The draft was also somewhat easier to follow thanks to the imposition of a fifty-round limit in 1998.[86] Still, the draft didn't become a televised event until ESPN2 broadcast the first round in 2007.[87] By contrast, both the NFL and NBA drafts have been on TV since the early 1980s, and both are now highly anticipated prime-time events.

Bonuses continued to spiral out of control until 2000, when the commissioner's office began making recommendations on the size of the bonuses clubs should pay to each draftee according to the order in which they were taken. The White Sox nonetheless gave twelfth overall pick Joe Borchard a record $5.3 million signing bonus that year.[88] Still, bonuses increased by only 3.5 percent across the board in 2000, after jumping by about 30 percent each year during the 1990s.[89] In 2003, first-round bonuses dropped 16.2 percent,[90] but they soon returned to record-setting levels. Two different marks fell in 2011. The Royals helped convince Bubba Starling to eschew a chance to play quarterback at the University of Nebraska by giving him a $7.5 million signing bonus, the largest ever to go to a player drafted out of high school.[91] Top overall pick Gerrit Cole received $8 million from the Pirates, setting the overall bonus mark.[92] Part of the reason bonuses continued to rise is that multisport athletes, like Starling, wield the hammer of having another field to pursue.[93] Other teams simply waited until most of the other picks had been signed so that they weren't called to task by the commissioner's office for affecting the payouts to the rest of the draft class.[94] This practice was curbed somewhat in 2007 when baseball set an annual deadline of August 15 for teams to sign their June draftees, moving it up from the beginning of classes, if a player were to return to school, or a week before the next year's draft.[95] The new rule also held that if a team were unable to sign a player taken in the first three rounds, the team would receive a comparable selection in the next year's draft.[96] While teams that violated the recommendations drew the ire of the commissioner's office,[97] they weren't barred from doing so. In 2008, the average first-round bonus was a record-setting $2,458,714.[98] This figure declined in 2009 and 2010, but spiked again to a new high of $2,653,375 in 2011.[99] The idea of "hard slotting," or making the recommendations binding, is an issue that baseball has tried to push, only to meet with resistance from the players' union. Small-market clubs have demonstrated their willingness to pay a premium for top-flight talent from the draft rather than spend comparable amounts on middling veterans,[100] so an overwhelming appetite for strict limits did not exist on either side. According to Jim Callis of MLB.com, then writing for *Baseball America*, the potential that hard slotting might have been instituted for 2012 led teams to increase their budgets for 2011 draftees, fearing a strict cap on bonuses would make it more difficult to sign players, especially high schoolers.[101]

Hard slotting was not a part of the changes made in the collective bargaining agreement for 2012, but the deal does lay out specific and significant penalties for teams that exceed spending limits. Each year, teams are assigned an aggregate spending limit for their picks in the first ten rounds.[102] The limit is specific to each team based on its position in the draft order.[103] Teams exceeding the cap by less than 5 percent pay a

75 percent tax on the overage, and teams that go beyond the limit by 5 to 10 percent lose a first-round pick on top of having to pay the tax.[104] Outspend the limit by 10 to 15 percent, and a team gets hit with a 100 percent tax and the loss of a first-round and a second-round selection.[105] That second-rounder becomes an additional first-rounder for any team that spends more than 15 percent above the cap.[106] While many executives initially believed this would significantly change the draft, the limits, negotiated by Major League Baseball and the players union, are quite liberal compared to the earlier slot recommendations, which were unilaterally handed down from the commissioner's office.[107] The high ceilings counter the opinion that the agreement was unfair to small-market clubs that had been baseball's most profligate draft spenders,[108] and they were no doubt crucial in convincing those teams to go along with the deal. The small markets also benefit from the institution of a draft lottery that distributes a dozen supplemental first- and second-round picks to low-revenue teams each year.[109] The agreement additionally bars clubs from immediately signing draftees to major league contracts and moves up the August 15 signing deadline by a month to coincide with the All-Star Game.[110]

Perhaps more significant in the long term are the limits the agreement places on international spending. Much like the draft, teams are now given a cap on what they can spend on international signees each year, with taxation penalties for teams that exceed the cap.[111] The agreement stipulates the penalties will get more harsh if a worldwide draft isn't in place by 2014.[112] Thus, there is incentive for baseball to soon make what would be the most significant change to the amateur draft in its nearly fifty-year existence.

Whatever changes are in store for the draft system in the coming years, there's little historical evidence to suggest that major league teams will be able to rein in the marketability of top amateur baseball talent. Clubs have shown a continued willingness to find loopholes to get the players they want, and players and agents have long been determined to push for the best possible deal. The draft is, and will likely continue to be, a high-stakes gamble. Yet compared to the disorganized machinations that preceded the draft, and the contentiousness between the majors and minors that existed prior to the evolution of the farm systems, the existing draft and player development system is clearly an improvement for the teams. There's no doubt that the power of agents and the torrent of cash available for highly drafted players help make a few years of minor league bus rides more palatable, so it seems unlikely players will lobby too hard for substantial change, either. Baseball has spent 120 years figuring out the best way to funnel talent to the game's highest level. Now, it appears the greater task is to figure out how to continue to make more efficient use of that system and get greater return on escalating investments.

2

Analysis of Draft Data

On June 7, 2005, the Arizona Diamondbacks made 17-year-old Justin Upton, a high school shortstop from the Hampton Roads area of Virginia, the first overall pick of the June draft. The team paid Upton a record-setting $6.1 million signing bonus and soon got a worthy return on its investment. Two years after being drafted, Upton was already in the majors, and by the age of twenty-three, he had already represented the National League twice in the All-Star Game. In January 2013, the Diamondbacks traded Upton to the Braves for a package of five players that included a former All-Star and four prospects.

Upton wasn't the only one of the forty-seven first-round picks in 2005 to quickly get to the big leagues and achieve success there. Including Upton, eight of the first twelve picks that year were All-Stars before the age of thirty. The others, in order of selection, were Alex Gordon (Royals), Ryan Zimmerman (Nationals), Ryan Braun (Brewers), Ricky Romero (Blue Jays), Troy Tulowitzki (Rockies), Andrew McCutchen (Pirates), and Jay Bruce (Reds). All of these players made their first All-Star appearances with the team that drafted them.

Despite not landing any of these players, arguably the biggest winners of the 2005 draft were the Boston Red Sox, who became the first team in baseball history to have their first four picks of a draft class reach the majors within three years.[1] They were Jacoby Ellsbury, Craig Hansen, Clay Buchholz, and Jed Lowrie. Boston's fifth and final first-round pick in 2005, Michael Bowden, was called up to the majors just a few months after the three-year anniversary of his selection. The success of the Red Sox in the 2000s, which includes three World Series titles, can be attributed only in part to the team's ability and willingness to spend money on big-time free agents. As the second decade of the century got under way, it became even more apparent that Boston had also been successful at improving its team through the draft.

So had several other teams—and the 2005 draft was a main reason why.

By the end of 2013, the opening round of the 2005 draft had produced two MVPs, ten All-Stars, four top-three finishers for Rookie of the Year, and thirty-six major league players. Each of these numbers is likely to rise as already established major leaguers add to their résumés and still more draftees from that class make the breakthrough from the minors to the majors.

The bountiful first round in 2005 prompted Tom Verducci of *Sports Illustrated* to call that year's complete draft the best in history.[2]

Compared to the drafts that immediately preceded it, 2005 wasn't an aberration.

The first rounds of the prior two drafts also yielded overwhelmingly positive results for many teams. Between 2003 and 2005, 77 percent of first-rounders (96 of 124 players) reached baseball's highest level. Some of the twenty-eight players who didn't get to the majors were already out of baseball by 2013, while many others remained active minor leaguers still with a shot at making the bigs.

It's no fluke that five of the eleven first-round picks between 1990 and 2006 who won a Rookie of the Year award were drafted between 2003 and 2006.

The results of these drafts are in stark contrast to a three-year period from 1997 to 1999 when just fifty-seven percent of first-round picks got to the majors.

Why the disparity?

When considering that the number of non-drafted Latino players in the majors spiked dramatically between the mid–1990s and mid–2000s, the answer likely lies with the way teams are identifying and cultivating talent, and to a lesser extent with the ever-changing economics of baseball.

Since 1965, major league organizations have tried with varying degrees of success to acquire stars of the future through the draft. Logically, the higher a player is drafted, the higher the expectations are that he will flourish.

Still, the baseball draft process is inherently different from its counterparts in other sports.

Barring injury very early in their careers, it is a given that the most highly touted amateur football and basketball players will at least play for a time in the NFL or NBA. That's not the case with baseball. The first round of the MLB draft is rife with players who for a variety of reasons never ascend to the game's highest level.

The single point that best demonstrates how baseball differs from its counterparts: Only twenty-one baseball players since 1965 have gone directly from high school or college to the major leagues.[3] Just three of those players went from the prep level to the majors.

The conclusion here is that baseball's real testing grounds are the minor leagues.

That fact makes the draft an annual exercise in uncertainty.

It's worth briefly exploring the reasons behind why more baseball players, especially those who have excelled at the best college programs, don't make a direct jump to the majors.

A popular explanation for why position players spend at least some time in the minors involves the equipment differences between the amateur and professional ranks. Keith Law of ESPN contends that amateur baseball's use of aluminum bats makes the sport a different breed from the professional game. In an article in which he calls on colleges to switch to wood bats, Law writes, "Talk to enough scouts and you'll hear references to 'aluminum-bat swings.' If it's possible for a hitter to have a swing that works in college baseball but that doesn't work at all in the pros, are we really playing the same game?"[4]

In his column, Law points to the experience of the Red Sox' Lowrie, who hit nearly .400 with a .734 slugging percentage at Stanford but came nowhere close to matching those numbers early in his minor league career. But, as noted earlier, Lowrie quickly adjusted to the minors and was promoted to the Red Sox within three years of being drafted.

This prompts a question: Is equipment the primary reason why players aren't major league–ready out of high school or college, or is the explanation more complex?

Law's column doesn't address why amateur pitchers rarely forgo the minors. But using his thesis, couldn't it be argued that some of the most talented college hurlers, those who have already established themselves in the metal-bat version of the game, would be ready to immediately try their luck against major league hitters and their wood bats?

While Law is silent on this topic, his ESPN colleague, Jerry Crasnick, weighs in with some thoughts. He notes that Mike Leake, who played at Arizona State in 2009 and then with the Cincinnati Reds the next year without a stop in between, was the first major league pitcher since 1994, and the first starting pitcher since 1988, not to play a day in the minors. Crasnick explains this bit of history through a quote from Detroit Tigers scout Eddie Bane, who, like Leake, jumped from ASU to the majors in 1973: "The hardest thing for these kids is that you go from pitching every Friday night to pitching every five days. I think that's the biggest hurdle they have to overcome, more than the talent or anything else."[5]

Bane knows from experience the rigors of adjusting to the major leagues. He went 0–5 with the Minnesota Twins in his rookie year and went on to win just seven career games.

The reasons can be debated, but the reality is that high schools and colleges aren't producing ready-made major league talent. And that's what makes the baseball draft interesting. More so than other sports, baseball allows fans across America to look at the potential of tomorrow in the minors as they keep an eye on the results of today in the majors.

This book provides a year-by-year analysis of the first round of every major league draft between 1990 and 2006, a period in which teams cast their lot and entered into contracts with 685 amateur players from the United States, Canada, Puerto Rico, and in one case, Cuba. While other rounds of the draft are examined for comparative purposes and to note individual teams' success rate of turning draft picks into major leaguers, this book does not provide a holistic assessment of the drafts during this time frame. Rather, it uses the opening round as a window into larger issues about how major league teams identify, select, and cultivate young talent.

2. Analysis of Draft Data

For purposes of analysis, the book divides first-round selections into three primary categories: those who made the major leagues, those who did not make the major leagues, and those who had "serviceable" careers in the major leagues. A serviceable career is defined as one in which a player was or has been active in the majors for at least five years and had or has had a positive wins-above-replacement value as determined by Baseball-Reference.com.

Insufficient data existed on roughly twenty players, or more than 7 percent of those drafted between 2000 and 2006. Any active player who had reached the major leagues but had fewer than five years' service at the end of the 2013 season fell into this category.

This chapter provides an in-depth analysis of the draft data and poses several questions that will be studied in later chapters. Among them: Do the successful first rounds of the mid–2000s show that teams have become more effective at scouting, drafting, and developing players? In what areas do major league teams still need to improve? What role have skyrocketing signing bonuses played in the drafting and player development process? How has the influx of non-drafted players from Latin America affected these processes?

The patterns and trends revealed by the data help provide context to these issues.

A higher percentage of first-round picks have reached the majors in the first seven years of the 2000s than in the 1990s. Major league teams still have work to do, however, if they hope to achieve the 72-percent success rate they saw in the 1980s.

Table 1.

First-round draft picks (1990–1999)

reached MLB	256 of 398	64%
serviceable MLB career	145 of 398	36%

First-round draft picks (2000–2006)

reached MLB	200 of 287	70%
serviceable MLB career	109 of 263	41%

With a sizeable number of players drafted between 2000 and 2006 yet to achieve the peak of their careers, the percentage of these players to make the majors is almost certain to rise. It serves to reason that this increase will also result in at least a slight increase in the number of players drafted in this time frame who will go on to have serviceable careers.

Additional analysis shows that players drafted in the fifth and tenth rounds make the majors at a rate of about 30 and 20 percent, respectively. These percentages were about the same in the 1990s and 2000s. Later chapters of this book will examine lower-round picks who exceeded expectations to become major league stars.

The analysis also shows that the higher a player is drafted in the first round, the more likely it is he will make the big leagues. That provides a partial explanation for why the first round of the drafts of the 1980s produced a higher rate of major leaguers. No round in the 1980s included more than thirty-two picks, whereas the 1990s and 2000s each averaged more than forty picks per first round. The rise in the number of picks per round was due to major league expansion and more liberal distribution of compensatory picks for teams that lost free agents or were unable to sign their draft picks from the year before.

Table 2. Dividing up the first round in sections

Reached MLB (by pick)	1990s		2000-06	
Picks 1-17	126 of 167	75%	92 of 117	79%
Picks 18-35	104 of 168	62%	80 of 121	66%
Picks 36-52	26 of 63	41%	28 of 49	57%

First-round picks of the 1990s who did not make the majors were more likely than not to plateau before even reaching Triple-A. It is difficult to provide a similar analysis for 2000–2006 because many draftees from this period are still active minor leaguers.

Alphabetically, the players under consideration range from David Aardsma, the twenty-second overall pick by the San Francisco Giants in the 2003 draft, to A.J. Zapp, the twenty-seventh pick by the Atlanta Braves in the 1996 draft. In terms of their accomplishments, they range from Chris Stowe, the only first-round pick between 1990 and 2006 not to make it past rookie ball, to Chipper Jones, Derek Jeter, and Roy Halladay, all likely future Hall of Famers.

The amount of money they've earned out of high school or college has increased significantly over the years. In 1995, the average signing bonus of a first-round pick was $875,000.[6] Ten years later, it had jumped to $2 million.[7]

Eleven of the 685 first-round picks between 1990 and 2006 won Rookie of the Year honors—Jeter, Braun, Evan Longoria, Nomar Garciaparra, Ben Grieve, Kerry Wood, Jason Jennings, Bobby Crosby, Justin Verlander, Huston Street, and Chris Coghlan. In 1994, 2004, and 2006, the Rookies of the Year in both the American and National leagues were former first-round selections.

One of only two first overall picks to retire without having made the majors was Brien Taylor, a left-handed pitcher whom the New York Yankees selected in 1991. The other was 1966 No. 1 overall pick Steven Chilcott. They could soon have company, however. Matt Bush, the top pick in 2004 by the San Diego Padres, hadn't reached the majors by the end of the 2013 season. He wasn't even playing baseball. He was serving a three-and-a-half-year prison sentence for a DUI hit-and-run.

Taylor was the only left-handed pitcher during the time frame of the study to go first overall in the draft. The most accomplished player chosen in the 1991 draft was a Dominican-born high school player from New York City named Manny Ramirez, who went to the Indians with the thirteenth pick. With the second pick of the 2004 draft, the Tigers selected Verlander.

Money wasn't an obstacle for the Yankees when they drafted Taylor. The same wasn't true for the Padres. Four other first-round picks signed for more money than Bush, suggesting that potential alone isn't the sole criterion for drafting a player.

Bush, who was drafted as a shortstop, later became a pitcher. This is not rare. Several first-round picks have been converted to other positions at some point in their minor league careers.

Every year's draft has its share of hits and misses, a point that can be shown in many ways. For example, it may surprise some baseball observers to know that 1990 was the last time the first three picks of the draft went on to become All-Stars. They were Chipper Jones, Tony Clark, and Mike Lieberthal. The fourth player taken that year, pitcher Alex Fernandez, was not an All-Star, but won at least 16 games in three different seasons.

A strong baseball pedigree doesn't guarantee major league success.

Dave Parrish, a first-round pick by the Yankees in 2000 and the son of eight-time All-Star Lance Parrish, left baseball after the 2008 season without ever having made the majors. Preston Mattingly, a top pick of the Los Angeles Dodgers in 2006 and the son of former MVP Don Mattingly, topped out at High-A ball in 2011. The Mariners' first-round pick in 2001, Michael Garciaparra, whose brother Nomar won the Rookie of the Year award and made six All-Star teams, also didn't make it out of the minors.

On the flip side, Prince Fielder, the son of former slugger Cecil, has made a strong impact in the majors after being taken by the Milwaukee Brewers in the first round of the 2002 draft.

The career paths of pitchers taken in the 1999 draft may best exemplify the hard-to-predict nature of spotting and nurturing baseball talent.

That draft produced Josh Beckett, Barry Zito, and Ben Sheets, all of whom enjoyed successful big league careers. But of the twenty-seven players from that year's first round who didn't make the majors, twenty were pitchers. Shockingly, seven of those hurlers, five righties and two lefties, never made it above Class A.

So what are major league organizations looking for in a first-round pick?

Though shortstops have long enjoyed a reputation as the best all-around athletes, at least on high school baseball teams, they comprised only 11 percent of first-round picks from 1990 to 2006. That list included Jones, Jeter, and Rodriguez, all of whom were drafted out of high school.

Interestingly, four overall top picks — Jones, Rodriguez, Bush, and Upton — were drafted as shortstops, making that position second only in this regard to right-handed pitchers, of whom five were top overall selections.

The drafts of the 2000s were notable for the number of star players who were drafted as third basemen. Some of these players, including Longoria and David Wright, remained at that position. Others, including Braun and Mark Teixeira, were shifted elsewhere in the minor leagues or early in their major league careers.

By contrast, only one player, Todd Walker in 1994, was drafted as a second baseman. Walker went on to enjoy a twelve-year major league career, during which he played more than a thousand games at second base.

Table 3.

First-round picks by position	1990s		2000-06	
RHP	97 of 149	65%	71 of 111	64%
LHP	35 of 58	60%	35 of 47	74%
C	14 of 22	64%	11 of 15	73%
1B	14 of 22	64%	7 of 8	88%
2B	1 of 1	100%	6 of 9	67%
3B	17 of 19	89%	13 of 20	65%
SS	28 of 42	67%	24 of 34	71%
OF	50 of 85	59%	32 of 43	74%

The increased percentage of first-round draft picks making the majors in the 2000s can be attributed to teams' improved success rate in turning left-handed pitchers and outfielders into big leaguers.

Only thirty-five of fifty-eight left-handed pitchers drafted during the 1990s made the majors. A few of those players, most notably Zito, CC Sabathia, Billy Wagner, and Mark Mulder, went on to have solid careers. But for every Sabathia, who had won 205 games through the 2013 season, there were several lefty pitchers like C.J. Nitkowski, who went 18–32 during a ten-year career with eight different teams. As of opening day 2013, Sabathia, Zito, and Mulder, who retired due to injury in 2010, were a combined 154 games over .500. The 31 other left-handers taken in the 1990s were a combined 65 games under .500. Matt Thornton was the only pitcher of that group who was active in 2013. Those figures do not take into account the accomplishments of pitchers like Wagner, who became stellar relievers. But the point remains the same: For all the emphasis teams put on left-handed pitching, they were largely unsuccessful in drafting players from this position in the first rounds of the 1990s.

From 2000 to 2006, teams fared better with southpaw pitchers. Of the forty-seven players picked, thirty-six had reached the majors by the end of the 2013 season, including nine of eleven picked in the first round of the 2004 draft. The drafts of the 2000s produced 2011 and 2013 Cy

Young winner Clayton Kershaw and 2008 World Series MVP Cole Hamels, both lefties.

What can be gleaned from these data?

In explaining the reason major league teams actively seek left-handed pitchers, Paul Nyman of *The Hardball Times* wrote, "As hitters grow up, they do not face many left-handed pitchers, especially quality ones. At the younger/lower levels of amateur baseball, 90 percent of the pitches they see come from a pitcher throwing from the right-hand side of the mound."[8]

There appears to be a greater risk in gambling on a left-handed pitcher in the draft.

A 2010 study by the Center for Sports & Motion Analysis at Texas Metroplex Institute for Sports Medicine and Orthopedics found the physical mechanics of pitchers at this position made them more susceptible to arm injuries.[9] Whether major league teams acknowledged this fact in the 2000s and changed the way they nurtured lefty hurlers is a topic that will be discussed later in this book.

Many baseball observers have speculated that left-handed pitchers tend to find spots on major league rosters because of their relative scarcity. The data support this. Despite the overall lack of success of highly drafted lefty pitchers in the 1990s, the average length of the careers of those who made the majors was six years, the same as their right-handed counterparts. And a higher percentage of lefties than righties drafted in the '90s had serviceable careers.

Generally speaking, outfielders are far less of an enigma than left-handed pitchers. But the drafts of the 2000s suggest teams have developed a better system for drafting both. Fifty of eighty-five outfielders drafted in the 1990s made the majors, a 59 percent success rate, compared to thirty-two of forty-three drafted between 2000 and 2006, a 74 percent rate. This improvement is due in large part to the eventual fate of high school draftees. In the 1990s, just twenty-two of forty-eight high schoolers drafted as outfielders made the majors. In the 2000s, 15 of 23 such players have so far gotten there.

During the 1990s, major league organizations picked high school players with their top selections more often than college players. This was despite a clear trend showing college players make the major leagues at a far higher rate than their high school counterparts.

Perhaps in belated acknowledgment of this fact, teams reversed course and selected more college players in the 2000s.

Table 4. College vs. High School
Percentage of players to reach MLB (by school type)

HS vs. Coll vs JC	1990		2000-06	
HS	110 of 195	56%	81 of 129	63%
Coll	141 of 194	73%	116 of 152	76%
JC	4 of 8	50%	3 of 7	43%

The 346 college players picked in the first round between 1990 and 2006 came from 121 different schools. Stanford led the pack with 16, all of whom made the major leagues. The University of Texas produced 12 picks, the second most of any college or university, but only seven of those players got to the big leagues.

Though every first-rounder from Stanford got to the majors, only seven of fifteen have had serviceable careers. Insufficient data exist to determine the career arc of one other player. By far the most accomplished player in that group is Mike Mussina, who was selected twentieth overall by the Baltimore Orioles in 1990. Through the 2013 season, Mussina and outfielders Jeffrey Hammonds and Carlos Quentin were the only three of the sixteen Stanford products to make an All-Star team. Mark Appel, a right-handed pitcher who played at Stanford, was the first overall pick of the 2013 draft.

Table 5. Colleges and universities

Colleges with most 1st round picks (1990-2006)		reached MLB
Stanford Univ.	16	16
Univ. of Texas	12	7
Arizona State Univ	11	7
Florida State Univ	11	7
Rice Univ	10	7
UCLA	10	5

Sarasota (Florida) High School produced three first-round picks who signed professional contracts. Bobby Seay, a left-handed middle reliever, was the only of the three to have a serviceable career. Doug

Million, a 1994 pick of the Marlins out of Sarasota High, was named High School Player of the Year by *Baseball America* but died of a severe asthma attack during an instructional league game in 1997. Matt Drews, a right-handed hurler who was selected by the Yankees in the 1993 draft, rounds out that group. Drews' career plateaued at Triple-A.

Though a player who played high school ball in one state might attend college in another, it's still instructive to examine what states are producing the most first-round picks. From the standpoint of where a player was discovered by scouts, actual hometown matters little. The exceptions to this are the handful of players who were drafted out of high school but attended college, making them liable to be taken again in future drafts.

Certain states dominate the baseball draft landscape.

Between 1990 and 2006, 44 percent of first-round picks came from California, Florida, and Texas. During the 1990s, 72 percent of players from those states reached the majors, compared to 59 percent of players from all other places.

In the 2000s, that gap was closed. Thirty-three percent of first-rounders came from the Big Three states between 2000 and 2006, and those players made the bigs at about the same rate as players from every other state.

Virginia in particular became a hotbed for talent in the 2000s. All-Stars Upton, Wright, Verlander, Zimmerman, and Joe Saunders, all drafted in the 2000s, came from high schools or colleges in Virginia. Wagner and Michael Cuddyer were the only players drafted from the state in the 1990s who became All-Stars. Other states, including Tennessee and Alabama, have also become places teams increasingly are looking for talent, and notably, all three are Southern states.

Still, major league teams enjoy a strong track record of turning to familiar places for top players. Nearly 80 percent of first-round picks from California colleges went on to make the majors, including a staggering twenty-nine of thirty-two (91 percent) from 2000 to 2006. Nearly half of these players have had serviceable careers, and twelve have played in at least one All-Star Game.

Table 6.
1990s

State	Draftees	Got to MLB	Pct
CA	78	56	72%
FL	47	34	72%
TX	36	26	72%
LA	17	12	71%
GA	16	11	69%
AZ	15	10	67%
SC	15	8	53%
VA	14	8	57%
2000–2006			
CA	62	46	74%
TX	40	25	63%
FL	37	25	68%
GA	14	11	79%
VA	13	11	85%
LA	13	8	62%
TN	12	7	58%
AL	8	6	75%

Later chapters will examine how technology has improved teams' ability to identify and scout players in a wider variety of places.

What teams have been most successful at turning first-round picks into successful major leaguers?

The sample size for each franchise ranges from the Tampa Bay Rays, who had just 10 first-round picks from 1990 to 2006, to the Athletics, who made thirty-seven first-round picks in that period. Because this book doesn't offer a comprehensive assessment of the draft, a few basic criteria were used to measure how well teams have done in picking amateur players: percentage of first-round selections who made the majors; their average length of service in the majors; and a subjective analysis of the impact of all drafted players.

While several teams have a strong track record of turning top picks into major leaguers, later chapters in this book will focus on the San Diego Padres, St. Louis Cardinals, and Minnesota Twins, three teams that used the draft in remarkably distinct ways.

In this chapter, we'll briefly take a look at the Rays and Philadelphia

Phillies as examples of teams that drafted successfully, parlaying their wise choices into a meeting in the 2008 World Series. Of the thirty major league teams, the Phillies and Rays rank near the top in the average career length of first-rounders selected between 2000 and 2006. All six of the Phillies' first-round picks in this time frame had reached the majors by 2012, and all but one of the Rays' top selections had done the same.

During the '08 season, the Phillies had the 13th largest payroll in the majors at over $98 million.[10] The Rays, meanwhile, were the second thriftiest team in baseball, behind the Marlins, with a payroll of just $43.8 million. In the years that followed, the Phillies would vault up the list of highest payroll while the Rays would remain near the bottom.[11]

Several key components of Philadelphia's championship in '08 were players the team picked in the first round of the draft between 1998 and 2002. They included World Series MVP Hamels, starting pitcher Brett Myers, left fielder Pat Burrell, and second baseman Chase Utley. The most powerful bat in the Phillies' lineup, first baseman Ryan Howard, was the team's fifth-round pick in 2001. And another starting pitcher, Joe Blanton, was a first-round pick of the Athletics in 2002.

In contrast, none of the organization's first-round picks from 1991 to 1996 went on to have serviceable major league careers. This poor track record is reflected in the team's struggles during the years when these players might have blossomed as major league standouts. It can be argued the Phillies went from an also-ran in the late 1990s and early 2000s to a perennial contender by the late 2000s based as much on the draft as on the trades and free-agent acquisitions of players including Roy Halladay and Cliff Lee, neither of whom were a part of the 2008 championship.

The Rays' roster in 2008 was a veritable who's-who of first-round draft picks through the years. Some of those players were selected by the Rays and came up through their organization, while others were obtained by Tampa Bay through trades and free agency.

Rays home-growns includes Longoria, B.J. Upton, David Price, and Rocco Baldelli. The imports include Matt Garza, Scott Kazmir, Carlos Pena, Cliff Floyd, J.P. Howell, Trever Miller, and Gabe Gross.

That means nearly half of Tampa Bay's World Series roster was composed of former first-round draft picks, a list that doesn't include the team's top pick in 2004, Jeff Niemann, a right-handed pitcher who put together three consecutive winning seasons between 2009 and 2011. Nor does it include 2010 American League MVP Josh Hamilton, who was the first round pick of the then–Devil Rays in 1999. The organization severed ties with him, however, after it appeared he might not win a long battle against drug addiction.

Though Hamilton's circumstances were somewhat unique, he represents an important category of player: those who leave the organization that drafted them and subsequently become stars. The reasons for this are several: contending teams often trade promising prospects for already established players and small-market teams sometimes can't afford to re-sign burgeoning stars when they become free agents.

What teams have struggled to turn top picks into stars?

Start with the Pittsburgh Pirates. After making three consecutive National League Championship Series in the early 1990s, the Pirates floundered in the second part of the decade, finishing a total of seventy-seven games under .500 from 1995 to 1999.

It's not a coincidence that only six of Pittsburgh's fourteen first-round picks in the '90s made the majors, and only two had serviceable careers.

Pittsburgh's struggles to make the most of its draft picks lasted into the 2000s.

In his junior year at Kent State University, John Van Benschoten led the NCAA in home runs with thirty-one and had a slugging percentage of .982. He also dabbled in pitching, and after the Pittsburgh Pirates took him with the eighth overall pick of the 2001 draft, the organization decided that he could help them most on the mound.[12]

Van Benschoten struggled with injuries, but more than that, he just struggled. Through the 2013 season, he had a major league record of 2–13. The right-hander signed a minor league contract with the San Diego Padres in the summer of 2011, and posted a 7.52 ERA in 26⅓ innings for Triple-A Tucson. He hasn't appeared in organized baseball since.

Some teams, like the Yankees, don't need to build through the draft.

Only eleven of the Bronx Bombers' twenty-one first-round draft picks between 1990 and 2006 made the majors. Just six of those eleven had serviceable careers, three of them with teams other than the Yankees. But one of the six who became a star for the Yankees was Jeter.

Of all the Yankees draft picks who failed to make the big leagues, none has symbolized failure more than Brien Taylor. Every year, it seems, Taylor's name is invoked to illustrate the capriciousness of the draft.

There was a lot to like about Taylor when the Yankees took the tall left-handed pitcher with the top pick of the 1991 draft. Pushed into a corner by agent Scott Boras, the Yankees gave him a $1.5 million signing bonus, a record at the time.

Taylor went straight to High Class-A ball in Fort Lauderdale, where he acclimated well to the minor leagues, posting a 2.57 ERA in twenty-seven starts. That performance earned him a promotion to Double-A Albany the following season. There, he went 13–7 with a 3.48 ERA.

As expected, Taylor was blazing a path to the major leagues. Nothing suggested he would enter the annals of baseball history for never playing a day in The Show.

It wasn't lack of ability that ended Taylor's chances of big league stardom. It was a fistfight in his North Carolina hometown that left his prized left arm in tatters.[13] After returning from his arm injury, Taylor went 3–15 the rest of his minor league career.

It's easy to understand why Taylor is considered the ultimate draft bust. He was an overall number -one pick, by the mighty Yankees, no less. He was the first amateur player to leverage his use of an agent into such a huge signing bonus. And the fight, in which he stuck up for his brother, is an episode right out of a piece of tragic American literature. The fact that Taylor got into trouble with the law after his playing days ended in 2000 made the story all the more melancholy.[14]

But what about the two players selected immediately after Taylor in the 1991 draft? Mike Kelly, an outfielder taken by the Atlanta Braves out of Arizona State University, spent six seasons in the majors with four different teams, accumulating career totals of 684 at-bats, twenty-two home runs, 86 RBIs, and a .241 average. The third pick, Dave McCarty, a first baseman out of Stanford, lasted eleven years in the majors with seven different teams. Like Kelly, he finished his career with mediocre numbers.

While Taylor is the poster boy for a draft bust, he had a lot of company in 1991. Only two of the first ten players drafted that year finished their careers with positive WAR values. A weak draft class that year was headed by Ramirez and Floyd.

Many other highly drafted players between 1990 and 2006 also have compelling stories that provide insight into why the draft is an inexact science. This book is about more than data. It goes behind the numbers to tell the stories of players who failed to fulfill potential.

3

Faces of the Draft

There are almost as many reasons why draft picks fail to pan out as there are failed draft picks. Injuries, poor decisions, psychological hurdles, and a simple lack of resilience or ability are common factors, but it becomes easier to understand the greater phenomenon of under-performing prospects when you look at individual examples one-by-one. In this chapter, we'll look at all twenty-eight first-round selections from the 1995 and 2000 drafts who failed to reach the major leagues. That list includes three players, two of them pitchers, drafted in front of Roy Halladay. Six were taken in a span of seven picks in 1995. Half of the top fourteen picks in 2000 are here, all of whom went off the board before the Phillies took Chase Utley at No. 15. The six draft picks taken immediately prior to the selection of All-Star pitcher Adam Wainwright all failed to reach the majors, and all of them are profiled below. Here's how more than two dozen of the best amateur prospects in baseball lost their way.

1995

JAIME JONES

The Marlins followed up a record $1.6 million[1] signing bonus for 1994 No. 5 overall pick Josh Booty with $1,337,000 for high school out-fielder Jaime Jones, the No. 6 pick in 1995.[2] It was the largest bonus for any player drafted that year aside from No. 1 overall selection Darin Erstad,[3] and a clear indication that the third-year franchise made build-ing through the draft a priority (a strategy it would abandon the very next year with a spending spree on major league free agents that led to a World Series title). Alas, Jones, like Booty, would fail to live up to his promise. He entered the 1996 season as *Baseball America*'s thirty-first-rated prospect,[4] but hit just .249 with eight homers in 237 at-bats in Class A that year. Wracked by injuries, he played fewer than 100 games in five of his first seven professional seasons, and quit baseball after 2001. He came back with the Diamondbacks organization in 2003 and put up perhaps his finest season, batting .291 with a career-high 12 homers in 107 games, spent mostly in High Class A. He never approached those numbers again, and despite a 2005 stint with the Royals' Triple-A affiliate, he was out of pro baseball after 2006.

MIKE DRUMRIGHT

A twenty-one-year-old taken eleventh overall by the Tigers out of a successful college program at Wichita State, pitcher Mike Drumright seemed not far off from the majors. His steady, if unspectacular, progress at High-A and Double-A in his first two pro seasons brought him even closer, as he was *Baseball America*'s No. 35 prospect going into 1997.[5] He earned a promotion to Triple-A that year, but plateaued. He never missed significant time due to injury, but could never climb the final rung of the ladder, compiling a 5.76 ERA in seven seasons at Triple-A for four different organizations. While he couldn't build on the potential he displayed in Wichita, he's found success building homes there,[6] starting a business that oversees the construction of forty to sixty homes a year.[7]

ANDREW YOUNT

Pitcher Andrew Yount got off to a slow start after the Red Sox took him with the fifteenth pick, compiling a 5.15 ERA in just thirteen appearances in Rookie and Low-A ball over his first two seasons. His career nearly ended in 1996, when he severed tendons in his pitching hand while crushing a glass because he was distraught over the death of his best friend.[8] He underwent multiple surgeries and missed the next two seasons, returning in 1999 with the Tigers organization. He struggled for two more seasons in Class A, walking 100 batters and striking out ninety, before the Tigers tried converting him to an outfielder. Yount posted an encouraging .816 OPS at Low-A Oneonta in 2001, but batted .147 the next season. Despite a brief comeback attempt as a pitcher at the Rookie level with the Reds in 2006, he finished his pro career having never made it above Class A.

RYAN JARONCYK

Right after the Blue Jays took Roy Halladay, a player who became known for his dedication to the game almost as much as his dominance on the mound, the Mets took shortstop Ryan Jaroncyk at No. 18. Two years later, Jaroncyk rejoiced in taking a box of mementos from his baseball career and throwing them in a dumpster.[9] Tired of pursuing his father's dream of a life in baseball rather than his own desires, the deeply religious Jaroncyk quit baseball a month into his third professional season.[10] He decried "immorality" in the game,[11] even though he spent more time in the rookie-level Appalachian League, a circuit of Bible Belt towns, than at any other stop. He was one of several high-profile Christian athletes bilked through an investment scheme by convicted felon John W. Gillette, to whom Jaroncyk lost $100,000,[12] a fraction of his $850,000 signing bonus.[13] The Dodgers took a flier on him in the Rule 5 draft in 1999, and convinced him to briefly come out of retirement. He played a total of twenty games for the organization in 1999 and 2000, and gave up the game for good, never having played above High-A ball.

JUAN LEBRON

Almost a decade before one man named Lebron fulfilled unprecedented promise in another sport, another embarked on a much less successful journey. The Royals took Puerto Rican outfielder Juan Lebron with the nineteenth pick, and watched him make slow but steady progress for four seasons. He combined an .810 OPS with a career-high eighteen stolen bases at Class A in 1998 before the Royals shipped him to the Mets for major league third baseman Joe Randa. Though Randa was never an All-Star, he was Kansas City's starting third baseman for six years, and it soon became clear the deal was a victory for the Royals. Lebron missed all of 1999 after injuring his shoulder in spring training and was never the same again.[14] He spent the better part of three seasons at Double-A for three organizations, compiling a .718 OPS and stealing ten bases over 274 total games. He spent 2003 through 2007 bouncing around independent leagues and the Mexican League, receiving a lifetime ban from the Golden Baseball League for throwing his bat and helmet at an umpire during a game in 2006.[15]

DAVID YOCUM

Perhaps it is fate, when you share the same last name as renowned orthopedist Dr. Lewis Yocum, that your arm will not withstand the rigors of pitching a baseball for a living. That was the case for Florida State lefty David Yocum. Dodgers scouting director Terry Reynolds told the *Los Angeles Times* at the time of the draft that he was surprised Yocum slipped to the team at No. 20.[16] He got off to a fast start, putting up a 2.96 ERA in eight appearances at High-A after signing in 1995, but that ERA ballooned to 6.14 at the same level the next season, his last before arm trouble forced him out of the game. Yocum's college teammate, right-hander Jonathan Johnson, was also taken in the first round that year, at seventh overall by the Rangers, but he didn't pan out either, compiling a 6.63 ERA in forty-two appearances over six major league seasons. Yocum's full story will be profiled later in this book.

ALVIE SHEPHERD

If you just looked at his draft position and the number of wins (ten) he put up over twenty-two appearances at Double-A in 1997, you'd think right-handed pitcher Alvie Shepherd was on a fast track to the majors. His won-loss record that season belied a 5.33 ERA, and it was the farthest the twenty-first overall pick by the Orioles would go. He pitched in only nine games the next year, and put up a combined 8.13 ERA for four minor teams in two different organizations in 1999, the last of his four seasons in professional baseball. His development might have been sidetracked by lengthy contract negotiations with the Orioles,[17] who decided against having him pitch in 1995 after finally signing him in late August.

DAVID MILLER

Despite his first-round pedigree, David Miller faced a tough road to the majors when Cleveland took him with the twenty-third pick. The Indians were well-stocked with talented position players in the late 1990s, with Albert Belle, Manny Ramirez, Kenny Lofton, David Justice and Jim Thome, among others, at Miller's positions in the outfield and first base. He had plenty of competition at the minor league level, too, sharing a Triple-A outfield with future big leaguers Richie Sexson and Brian Giles.[18] Miller didn't do much to force his way up the ladder with his debut season in 1996, hitting just .254 with seven homers in 488 at-bats in High-A, but he nonetheless opened 1997 at Double-A Akron. He enjoyed his finest season there, batting .301 while stealing twenty-two bases in 509 at-bats. His numbers were down at Triple-A the next year, though, and the Phillies made him a Rule 5 draftee. He failed to make Philadelphia's big-league club out of spring training, which brought tears to the eyes of the Philly native, who had hoped to make the team in honor of his late grandmother. "She was the biggest Phillies fan on the planet," he told the *Philadelphia Inquirer*. "It was always a dream of mine to play for the Phillies. This breaks my heart."[19] He returned to Cleveland's Triple-A affiliate for 1999, scuffling again while putting up an OPS of .651. Miller never played 100 games in a season again and his professional playing career ended after 2003.

COREY JENKINS

Corey Jenkins made it to the highest level of his sport. Unfortunately for the Red Sox, who drafted him 24th overall, that sport was football, not baseball. He earned promotions after his first two seasons in the Boston organization despite lackluster numbers, and slugged eighteen homers in 426 at-bats despite a .239 batting average at Class A in 1997. His third promotion, to High-A, didn't go as smoothly, and after thirty-nine games with the White Sox organization in 1998 and 1999, his baseball career was over at age twenty-two. He had been an All-State quarterback in high school, and found he still had it after enrolling at Garden City Community College in Kansas, where he became a two-time Junior College All-America selection.[20] He transferred to the University of South Carolina and became the starting quarterback there, but switched to defense for his final two games to impress NFL scouts.[21] The move worked well enough for the Miami Dolphins to take him in the sixth round of the 2003 NFL Draft. He played two NFL seasons with the Dolphins and the Chicago Bears.

SHEA MORENZ

He was referred to as "the steal of the draft" in the same *New York Daily News* article that wondered whether he might be the next Mickey Mantle,[22] but Shea Morenz, the twenty-seventh overall pick by the Yankees, is more notorious for his two other careers. He was the starting quarterback for nearly two seasons while majoring in finance at the University of Texas, showing pro potential with his ability to throw the deep ball. His baseball skills were more highly regarded, however, and he signed with the Yankees for a $650,000 bonus in 1995.[23] He was hardly impressive in his first three stops, but showed a power bat at Double-A in 1998, hitting fifteen homers in 409 at-bats. Still, the Yankees shipped him that August to the Padres for two pitchers who could help the big league bullpen,[24] and Morenz was out of baseball after a disappointing 1999. He later became involved with one more iconic institution, rising through the ranks of Wall Street to become a managing director at Goldman Sachs.[25] He was in the news again in 2012 for his involvement in a controversial hedge fund that was detailed in documents released by WikiLeaks.[26]

CHRIS HAAS

Cardinals draftee Chris Haas had advantages along the way to becoming the twenty-ninth overall pick, but it's not as though he didn't work hard to get there. Haas is the son of a pharmaceutical company CEO who sold the $300 million operation to a major corporation and retired at age 45, but he grew up on a cattle farm in Kentucky, baling hay, building fences, bush-hogging fields, taking care of animals and doing other backbreaking physical labor.[27] The elder Haas had played minor league ball for four seasons in the system of the Milwaukee Braves, but lacked the dedication to make it to the bigs, a lesson he imparted to his son, whom he coached in high school.[28] Chris Haas took it to heart and focused on improving his defense after a forty-two-error season as a Class A third baseman in 1996. He never had more than twenty-five errors in a season again. His next assignment was to cut down on his strikeouts, which crested at 182 in 1997, when he hit twenty-one home runs while splitting time between Class A and High-A ball. He made progress the next season, striking out 129 times while hitting twenty homers and batting .274 at Double-A. The K's were back up again, to 155, at Triple-A in 1999, and he spent most of the next season back at Double-A. The Cardinals waived him, and after he struck out 151 times at the Cubs Double-A affiliate in 2001, it appeared this was one hurdle his work ethic could not help him overcome. He spent the next two seasons mostly at Double-A for three different organizations, and after 2003, his career ended without time in the major leagues, just like his father's.

2000

MIKE STODOLKA

Considering there have been others drafted higher than Mike Stodolka who failed to make the majors, it was probably a bit harsh when ESPN.com editor David Schoenfield ranked the left-handed pitcher taken out of high school as the nineteenth worst draft pick ever, in any sport.[29] The fourth overall selection by the Royals compiled a 5.04 ERA over his first two full seasons, which he played exclusively at Class A. He spent most of 2003 and part of 2004 recovering from Tommy John surgery, and despite regaining most of his velocity, struck out just sixty-six batters in 124⅔ innings while posting a 5.92 ERA at Double-A in 2005.[30] The Royals decided to try to convert him to a hitter, and he experienced more success as a first baseman and corner outfielder than he did on the mound. He followed up an .845 OPS at High-A in 2006 with an .871 OPS the next season at Double-A, but hit a wall at Triple-A in 2008 as lagging power and walk numbers brought his OPS down to .771 in just seventy-five games, the last he would play in professional baseball.

MATT HARRINGTON

It's easy to think of, and question, the decisions that teams make involving the draft. After all, they're the ones who seem to have all the choice in the matter, while players are simply told where to go. The story of Matt Harrington reveals just how many decisions a player can make when he goes into professional baseball, and what happens when nearly every one of those decisions goes wrong. The right-handed pitcher was taken seventh overall by the Rockies. Under the guidance of agent Tommy Tanzer, Harrington rejected an eight-year, $4.9 million offer from the Rockies because, instead of awarding the money as a bonus, it would have spread the money over the life of the contract and wiped out arbitration rights as well.[31] The Rockies never upped their offer,[32] and Harrington went back into the draft the next year and was taken in the second round, fifty-eighth overall by the Padres. The San Diego organization had concerns about his health,[33] and after months went by with still no deal, Harrington and his family fired Tanzer and filed a lawsuit,[34] which was later settled out of court, alleging the agent mishandled negotiations. The man Harrington hired to replace Tanzer was Scott Boras,[35] the superagent known for driving a hard bargain with teams. Boras said the Padres never made an offer in writing, but the Harringtons and then Padres GM Kevin Towers insist $1.2 million was on the table.[36] That same year, Harrington went to pitch for the independent league St. Paul Saints, but put up a 9.47 ERA in six appearances. He pitched for two more independent league teams in 2002, posting another inflated ERA of 6.75, and after watching one of his performances, the Padres told him to re-enter the draft.[37] Tampa Bay took him in the thirteenth round in June 2002 and then offered him less than $100,000,[38] another deal Harrington left on the table while he toiled in independent ball. He was drafted again in 2003, by the Reds in the 24th round, and in 2004, by the Yankees in the 36th round. He didn't sign with them, either, and with his stock sinking with each passing year, Harrington's story sounded increasingly like that of a casino gambler who had hit the jackpot and foolishly kept trying to double down. He wound up working jobs at Target[39] and Costco.[40] Yet according to Amy K. Nelson of ESPN.com, Harrington still became a millionaire, thanks to the Tanzer settlement and an insurance policy his parents had taken out on his arm with Lloyd's of London in 2000.[41] Harrington had been bothered by nagging injuries leading up to a minor shoulder surgery that scuttled any chance he had of signing with the Yankees in 2004.[42] He once threw ninety-seven-mile-per-hour fastballs in high school,[43] but by 2004 his speed was a below-average eighty-seven,[44] allowing him to collect on the insurance policy.[45] By 2006, still plugging away for the independent Fort Worth Cats, he got in shape and brought his fastball back above ninety miles per hour, and finally signed a contract with an affiliated organization. His minor league deal with the Cubs included no signing bonus, and Harrington would have to impress the team to earn a spot on a farm team's roster out of spring training.[46] He didn't, and returned to the independent leagues, re-injuring his shoulder after four games that brought an end to a confoundingly obscure professional baseball career.[47]

MATT WHEATLAND

Matt Wheatland's right shoulder failed to allow his right arm to do what it did best. He was the fourth right-handed pitcher to be taken in the top eight picks, and like the other three, he failed to deliver on his promise. He pitched in just sixteen games for the Tigers organization before three shoulder surgeries caused him to miss the entire 2002 and 2003 seasons.[48] He returned, with his velocity cut from ninety-five miles per hour to ninety,[49] to post a respectable 3.12 ERA in eighteen appearances for Houston's Class-A affiliate, but it was not enough to revive his pitching career. He spent parts of the next two seasons trying to make a go of it as a position player in Independent League baseball, but left the professional game without ever having played above Class A.

MARK PHILLIPS

Mark Phillips was *Baseball America*'s fifty-fourth best prospect coming off his second professional season in 2001,[50] having compiled a 2.91 ERA at three stops in the Padres system that year. The signs were less encouraging after 2002, when he posted a 4.19 ERA and a strikeouts-to-walks ratio that was just 156-to-94, but *Baseball America* still ranked him eighty-fourth, and the Yankees considered him the top prospect in the Padres system when they traded for him during March of 2003. "The key component in this deal, for us, is Mark Phillips," General Manager Brian Cashman told the *New York Times* when the deal was struck. "That's not to put any extra pressure on him, but adding an extra power arm to our system was important."[51] The Yankees soured on him quickly after one season at High-A, during which he had a career-high 5.76 ERA and walked fifty-one while striking out fifty in 70⅓ innings. The Yankees kept him in extended spring training in 2004, but he continued to struggle with his command. As a Yankees official told the *San Diego Union-Tribune* that year, "Some things you can't explain."[52] He never pitched in a game for an affiliated team again, despite a brief independent league comeback in 2007.

JOE TORRES

Joe Torres was the third left-handed pitcher picked in the 2000 draft when the Padres took him with the tenth pick. All three were taken out of high school, and remarkably, all three failed to make the majors. Torres came the closest, posting a career-best 2.24 ERA mostly at Double-A in 2011. It was a long road filled with injury and "a mental block" just to get to that point.[53] He showed no signs of the struggle to come when he arrived in Low-A ball after the draft, recording a 2.54 ERA in eleven appearances, ten of which were starts. He couldn't duplicate that success the next three seasons, peaking at Class A in 2002, a season when he had a respectable 3.52 ERA but walked nearly as many batters (sixty-six) as he struck out (eighty-seven). He began the 2003 season in High-A, but after eight appearances and a 5.88 ERA, he was headed for Tommy John surgery that kept him out the entire 2004 season. The two seasons after he returned, he was even worse than he was before, with an atrocious 10.29 ERA in 73 appearances at Class A and High-A. "The first year I had a lot of issues with the elbow. The second year it was a big mental block, a big mental struggle," Torres told Minor League Baseball's website.[54] The Angels finally let him go after that, but he latched on with the White Sox in 2007 and began to show improvement. He brought his ERA down to 3.76, and lowered it again the next two seasons. He posted a career-best 2.24 ERA in 2011, mostly for Colorado's Double-A affiliate, but his ERA ballooned to 7.11 at Triple-A in 2012, and he spent 2013 with independent league teams.

SHAUN BOYD

The Cardinals had gone nine years without taking a high school position player before selecting Shaun Boyd with the thirteenth pick in the 2000 draft, and his performance surely made them wish they'd stuck with their policy. It didn't look that way in 2002, when he batted .313, hit twelve homers and stole thirty-two bases at Class A. The next year, split between High-A and Double-A, his power and contact numbers dipped, but he still wound up with thirty steals. His speed became less of a factor the next season, when his at-bats were cut nearly in half, and even in 562 at-bats in Double-A in 2005, he stole just fourteen bases. The Cardinals, unwilling to give up on his potential, forced him up to Triple-A in 2006.[55] The results were disastrous, as he batted just .188 with a homer and four steals in 112 at-bats. The Phillies gave him a shot the next season, but after just eighty-one at-bats with their organization, he was out of affiliated baseball for good.

BEAU HALE

It's not often a player is able to fully recover from missing two full seasons because of injury, as happened to right-handed pitcher Beau Hale, who was taken by the Orioles with the fourteenth pick. Hale didn't take the mound in 2003 or 2004 because of shoulder surgery, but he posted a nearly identical ERA in the seasons before his injury and the years that came afterward. Hale had a 4.32 ERA his first two pro seasons, and pitched to a 4.29 ERA in the three seasons that followed his recovery. Both numbers nonetheless represented disappointments for a first-round pick. He pitched exclusively at the Orioles' High-A and Double-A affiliates, and retired in 2007 after another shoulder injury that caused so much pain it woke him up during sleep.[56]

MIGUEL NEGRON

In 2011, as former Blue Jays minor league shortstop Sergio Santos saved thirty games as the White Sox closer, the Sox took a shot at converting another former Toronto prospect from batter to pitcher. The experiment didn't turn out nearly as well this time, as Miguel Negron compiled a 6.23 ERA in seven Class A appearances, bringing to a close Negron's lengthy minor league career. Picked at No. 18 by the Blue Jays, Negron played twelve years, but only recorded one season of more than 400 at-bats with an OPS of .700, in 2008. By that time, he was on his fourth organization. His best asset appeared to be speed, as he stole at least twenty bases four times, but he was caught on more than thirty-six percent of his attempts on the basepaths. He spent all of 2009 at Triple-A, batting .279 with 14 steals in 27 attempts, but never returned to that level after he was suspended for the first fifty games of 2010 after twice testing positive for "a drug of abuse."[57]

DAVID ESPINOSA

David Espinosa had a long-term major league contract and a spot on a major league roster, but never played a single game in the bigs. Such an anomaly is the product of a contract drawn up by agent Scott Boras and Jim Bowden, then general manager of the cash-strapped Reds.[58] When Cincinnati took Espinosa with the twenty-third pick, the organization couldn't afford bonuses for him and the two other selections they had in the first forty-six picks.[59] They put off bringing thirty-fourth pick Dustin Moseley on board for a year,[60] and Boras, the agent for Espinosa and No. 46 pick Dane Sardinha, convinced Bowden to give his clients major league contracts.[61] That way, they spread out a guaranteed $2.95 million to Espinosa instead of paying out a smaller bonus all at once.[62] Since it was a major league contract, though, that meant Espinosa had to occupy a spot on the 40-man roster for the length of the deal.[63] Espinosa batted .262 with seven homers at Class A in 2001, but struggled defensively at shortstop and was converted to second base the next year. The Reds soured on him at that point,[64] and freed up a forty-man roster spot when they traded him to the Tigers in July 2002. Shifted to the outfield, he batted .264 with nineteen home runs and twenty stolen bases at Double-A in 2004, and spent parts of the next three seasons trying in vain to match that performance at Triple-A. Apart from sixty games at Double-A with the Mariners in 2009, he's been out of affiliated baseball since 2007. He remains active in independent leagues.

BLAKE WILLIAMS

Simply put, Blake Williams was never the same after Tommy John surgery. The twenty-fourth overall pick by the Cardinals followed up six outings with a 1.59 ERA in an abbreviated first year at Low-A ball by posting a 2.43 ERA in 17 starts at High-A in 2001. In July of that year, thirteen months after he was drafted, Williams underwent the surgery, returning ahead of schedule to pitch in 2002.[65] Two successful starts later, however, he was shelved for the remainder of the season with tendonitis.[66] The Reds claimed him as a Rule 5 draft pick after the season, but did not have a place for him at the major league level, sending him back to the Cardinals.[67] Back at High-A in 2003, he struggled to a 4.36 ERA, and compared to his 2001 season at the same level, his walks per nine innings more than doubled while his strikeouts per nine innings were down more than 50 percent. The Cardinals released him in 2004,[68] and no other major league organization took a shot on him. He played his final four seasons in independent leagues, where he posted a combined 4.04 ERA.

SCOTT HEARD

Catchers, with rare exception, aren't asked to carry their teams offensively. The Rangers probably weren't looking to replace Ivan Rodriguez's bat when they selected catcher Scott Heard with the twenty-fifth pick, ignoring doubts about his hitting and durability and focusing on his ballyhooed defense.[69] Matt Wheatland, one of Heard's battery mates at Rancho Bernardo High School in San Diego, was taken at No. 8 by the Tigers, so Heard was not unused to handling a stellar pitcher. He looked like he might turn out to be a hitter after all when he batted .351 and had a 1.016 OPS against rookie league pitching in a thirty-one-game pro debut in 2000, but he never batted above .250 at any other level. That was tough to stomach, considering his defense was a disappointment,[70] and he was out of baseball after 2003, never having played a game above High-A.

COREY SMITH

Corey Smith, who drew comparisons to Gary Sheffield,[71] was taken twenty-sixth by the Indians. Like Sheffield, Smith was a high school shortstop who was converted to third base in the pros. Unlike Sheffield, his conversion did not go smoothly, and in four of his first five seasons at that position he posted a fielding percentage below .900. His fourth pro season, at Double-A, was the first full year he had without a hundred strikeouts, but his home run bat had disappeared with the strikeouts. He rediscovered that stroke with nineteen homers in another season at Double-A in 2004, but it was his final year with the Indians organization.

He put up similar power numbers but saw his strikeouts increase and walks decrease with the Padres' Double-A affiliate in 2005, and again he was on the move, this time to the White Sox, who gave him another shot at Double-A in 2006. A career-low .238 batting average forced him to independent ball in 2007, but he latched on with the Angels the next year, belting twenty-six homers at the familiar Double-A level. He followed with twenty-one homers for the Royals' Double-A team in 2009. Perhaps the greatest similarity Smith has to Sheffield, a veteran of twenty-four professional seasons, has been staying power, as Smith continued to play affiliated baseball through 2012.

ROBERT STIEHL

Robert Stiehl, drafted by the Astros at No. 27, was another pitcher who was never quite the same after injury. He had a 1.98 ERA in fourteen appearances, twelve of them starts, at Class A in 2001 before a pair of shoulder surgeries robbed him of 2002 and most of 2003.[72] His initial return to the mound in 2003 was shaky at best, as he gave up seven hits and recorded eight outs over four appearances at Low-A. He wasn't much better in 2004, compiling a 4.09 ERA on the same team he excelled for in 2001, and it only got worse from there. He tore tendons in his ankle and shattered his fibula covering first base on a play as a reliever at High-A in 2006, and that unfortunate blow all but ended his career. He made it back and found himself at Double-A for the first time in 2007, but after ten appearances with an ERA of 7.47 and a WHIP of 1.92, he was done with pro baseball for good.

DAVE PARRISH

Dave Parrish was seen as something of an opposite of fellow catcher Scott Heard, who was taken three picks before the Yankees made Parrish the twenty-eighth overall selection. The Yankees hoped his bat would make up for his shortcomings behind the plate, though most teams saw him as a second-round pick at best.[73] His father, Lance, had displayed rare power for a catcher during his nineteen-year major league career, but the younger Parrish never hit more than eight homers in a season. He never hit .300, either, and the only reason he seemed to last was his durability and willingness to put on the catcher's gear. He made at least

200 plate appearances in seven of his first eight seasons (in 2003, the lone exception, he made 199), and caught in every one of his 595 games as a pro. The Yankees called him up to the big club in 2004, but he never appeared in a major league game.

TRIPPER JOHNSON

Tripper Johnson was the second of two players the Orioles selected in the 2000 first round, and the second who failed to reach the majors. Unlike No. 14 pick Beau Hale, Johnson, taken 32nd, had his moments at lower levels. The third baseman batted .306 in a forty-eight-game stint at rookie ball in 2000, but he never hit for an average so high again. His finest season was probably the year he showed a power stroke, knocking twenty-one homers with a .269 batting average at High-A in 2004. That earned him a promotion to Double-A the next season, but his home runs were cut nearly in half as his OPS dipped to .695. He looked even worse in thirty-six games at Double-A the next year, batting .198 with an OPS of .525, and that spelled the end for him with the Orioles. The Pirates gave him a shot the next season, but playing in the same league where he hit twenty-one homers just three seasons before, Johnson sent just ten balls out of the park despite having twenty-six more plate appearances. He enrolled at the University of Washington the next year and made a go at it in football,[74] spending two seasons as a safety and special teams player.[75]

CHAD HAWKINS

Right-hander Chad Hawkins patiently waited for the right time to become a professional, turning down the draw of playing for a living when he was drafted in the fourteenth round out of high school in 1996 and again when he was a thirteenth-round pick out of junior college the next year. After further impressing scouts while at Baylor University, he finally signed with the Rangers in 2000 when they made him the thirty-ninth pick of the first round. Hawkins became a pro after holding off for four years, but he wound up playing only three seasons once he signed. Multiple shoulder injuries derailed his career,[76] which covered only twenty-two games and ended after nine appearances with a 7.48 ERA at High-A in 2002.

Aaron Herr

A dozen picks after the Yankees took Dave Parrish, another son of a former major leaguer, the Braves made a similar appeal to genetics. They turned high school shortstop Aaron Herr into a second baseman, hoping the fortieth overall selection could man the position for more than a decade at the major league level just like his father, Tommy. Instead, they never got a game above Double-A out of him. It seemed like Herr was finally on his way in 2005 when he got to the Cardinals, the same organization for which his father had been an All-Star, and at Double-A, Aaron posted career highs in multiple categories, including batting average (.298) and home runs (twenty-one). His lack of plate discipline, with fifteen walks against 108 strikeouts, was the dark spot on his record that year, and he was off to the Reds for 2006. He was promoted to Triple-A in 2007, and had a year similar to 2005, with nineteen homers, a .274 batting average, thirteen walks and 144 strikeouts. Still, at age twenty-six, it was not enough to earn a callup. He regressed during an injury-plagued 2008,[77] and was out of affiliated baseball from then on. He wound up playing for the independent league team his father managed in their hometown of Lancaster, Pennsylvania.[78]

4

The Showcase

The heavy footsteps of a pair of top high school prospects finishing the sixty-yard dash in center field drown out the chatter from scouts. It's the Friday before Memorial Day, ten days before the 2012 draft, and close to ninety players have gathered to be seen by nearly the same number of scouts from major league teams at the Florida Athletic Coaches Association All-Star Baseball Classic in Sebring, Florida. Hours from any Interstate and nowhere near a Spring Training park, Sebring is off the map for most who visit the Sunshine State, but every year it's a prime destination for scouts from all thirty major league teams. The event, in its thirty-fourth year, has produced a list of major league alumni so long that only an abridged version appears in the program that's sold at the games. It includes Chipper Jones and Alex Rodriguez, former No. 1 overall picks, and other former top-ten picks who went on to stardom, like Dwight Gooden, Gary Sheffield, Alex Fernandez, Prince Fielder and Zack Greinke.

As this year's Florida high school all-stars run their sprints, scouts are impressed with the speed of Addison Russell and Lewis Brinson, who would soon become the first two players drafted from the 2012 FACA event, with Russell going eleventh overall to the A's and Brinson at No. 29 to the Rangers. Yet there are no "oohs" and "ahhs" from this hardened audience, whose primary concern at the moment is that the runs are accurately timed.

"Coach, get 'em behind the line!" yells one scout. "Right foot on the line, coach!"

"Whoa! Hey, turn around so we can see your numbers! Please! Thank you!" says another.

The players selected for the event are split into four teams based on the geographic locations of their high schools, with North and South squaring off in one game and East and West in another on the first day of action. The winners and losers meet each other the following afternoon. With a day of practice preceding the games, it's a tantalizing display of high school prospects in arguably the most talent-rich state in the country.

Buck Rapp, head baseball coach at Sebring High, the host school for the event, estimates that the players who've taken part in the event over the years have combined to make close to a billion dollars in baseball.[1] Considering Rodriguez alone has signed contracts totaling more than $500 million, a billion is probably an underestimate. For an event with so much at stake, the atmosphere is surprisingly laid-back, a mood befitting the languid country music piped over the loudspeakers throughout a long afternoon of practice preceding two days of games.

"It's so close to the draft. There's really not a whole lot you can do," Royals scout Alex Mesa said while waiting for play to resume after a short burst of rain.[2] "Just make sure guys leave healthy, do well and perform, make sure that they're the same guys that you thought they were."

The general tenor from scouts is that since they already have a book on these players from the past year, there isn't much anyone can do to radically alter their draft stock.

"You're not coming to watch these guys for the first time," Brewers scout Tim McIlvaine said.[3] "Some of the guys from out of the area maybe are, so it's their first look at some of those guys, but the guys who have been in the area watching them, they have a pretty good idea of who they are."

One of the primary draws for the scouts, then, is the chance to compare prospects to each other and see them square off. Thirty-one of the eighty-nine players listed on the rosters for the 2012 event were drafted the next month, including a half dozen who went in the first round. The level of competition is high.

"Comparison is such a big thing in our business," Mesa said. "When you're able to see guys from the north part of Florida, from the south part of Florida, and everywhere in between, you kind of see how they line up, and that may help you make the right decision."

No scout ever turns down another chance to evaluate talent.

"The more times you see a player, the better line you get on him, no matter where you see him," said veteran Dodgers national cross-checker Gib Bodet, in town for the event.[4]

With influential eyes upon them, the players seem eager to prove their worth, and unfazed by the proximity of the day they've long had circled on their calendars.

"The draft is probably the last thing on my mind right now," said Addison Russell, a shortstop from Pace High School near Pensacola.[5] "I just want to go out there and play some ball."

If anyone seemed to impress the scouts in the weeks leading up to the draft, it was Russell. The six-foot-one, eighteen-year-old shortstop was ranked the twenty-eighth best prospect by *Baseball America* just before the draft,[6] but the A's broke a longstanding tradition of favoring college players to make him their first selection.

Russell helped his stock by remaking his body during the spring of 2012. He said he dropped twenty-five or thirty pounds in four months through a combination of yoga, pilates and cardio workouts along with a changed diet. That prompted increased attention from scouts, he said, adding to an already intense senior year.

"It's crazy, but fun at the same time," Russell said. "My parents and grandpa and my grandma help out with all the papers that come in so I don't have to deal with all that trouble, so they've been a big help for this whole process."

Parents and family members play a key role for many at the event, and several are in attendance, watching just as intently as any scout. Some are able to offer extra insight, like Pat Borders, the 1992 World Series MVP for the Blue Jays, who spent seventeen seasons in the big leagues. Borders had recently agreed to take over the head coaching job at Winter Haven High School, where as an assistant he worked with his son, Levi, a member of the FACA west team. The elder Borders hung out down the third base line behind the dugout, displaying a calm demeanor and humble, easygoing personality that belied not only his position in baseball lore, but his role as father and mentor to a player at a critical juncture in his baseball career. Perhaps that's because Pat Borders has walked down this very path before, having played in the 1982 FACA event.

"When I got drafted, I didn't know there were any scouts in the stands," Borders said.[7] "The day I got drafted, I think I went to the beach. Somebody told me, 'You got drafted.' I said, 'Oh, good.'"

That's not the case for Levi, who plays in an era when scouts are much more visible.

"They're watching," Pat Borders said. "They know everything about you. They give you forms to fill out. They call you. They come by the house and see you.

"The pressure's a lot bigger now than when I played."

Borders coached his son, who was taken in the eleventh round by the Braves, and Tyler Pike, a third-round draftee of the Mariners. With both, he took an approach that acknowledged the stress they were under and tried to channel any anxiety into positive performance.

"When I go out there, I tell them, you have earned the right to get this attention, to have this pressure. Embrace the pressure, and have fun," he said. "Instead of just saying, 'Be happy and have fun,' it's, 'You've earned this; this is fun.'"

Craig Faulkner, the head baseball coach at Venice High School, believes distraction as well as anxiety can affect the performance of a player in line to be drafted.

"Their head leaves high school a little bit, and goes into college and the pros, and sometimes they don't play in the moment," he said.[8] "Our job as high school coaches is to try to get them to play in the moment, not looking down the road."

Playing well is only half the equation for high school prospects. Once they're drafted, they have to decide whether to sign with the team that took them or go to college in hopes of a better draft position, and better bonus money, down the line. It's a decision that must come more quickly under new rules in place for 2012, with a July 15 signing deadline designed to preclude negotiations that used to stretch out all summer. Levi Borders opted to attend the University of South Florida rather than sign with the Braves, becoming the highest drafted player from the 2012 FACA event not to turn pro out of high school. It was a decision his father strived not to influence.

"He might look back on that time and say, 'Well, I should have gone. I missed my opportunity. Dad told me this,'" Pat Borders said. "I want it to be his choice so he doesn't look back and say, 'Well, I never got that choice, because I should have gone when I had the chance.' I'm going to give him side instructions, a little bit of instruction first for his thinking, but I want him to make the decision."

The signing deadline was just one of many rule changes affecting the draft that were implemented in 2012, and their ultimate effect drew a shrug and a wait-and-see attitude from most at the FACA event. It's not the first time draft rules have been adjusted, and many are unsure if they'll make any profound change to a system that's empowered agents and led to the creation of terms like "sign-ability" to describe a player's willingness to accept a team's offer.

"It is different, and it's hard to have an idea of how it affects you, really, until after it's over," McIlvaine said. "It's how people react to it. Major League Baseball's always trying to go in the right direction, move forward and get better, and you hope this is a step in that way."

Avery Romero, a sought-after shortstop from St. Augustine, echoed most of the other FACA All-Stars who weren't terribly concerned about the effects the new rules might have.

"I guess whatever happens, happens," he said.[9] "We can't really control it, anyway."

It all worked out for Romero, who was drafted with the ninth pick in the third round by the Marlins, and signed for $700,000, well above the $458,400 slotted amount for his draft position.[10]

The system also played out in favor of Hayden Hurst, a right-handed pitcher from just a few miles up the coast in Jacksonville. He was taken in the seventeenth round by the Pirates and wound up signing for $400,000, the second highest amount any player taken after the tenth round had received, according to a tweet on July 13 from then–*Baseball America* editor Jim Callis.[11] Any amount higher than $100,000 for a player picked after the tenth round goes against the team's cap for spending on higher draftees.

Hurst wasn't willing to settle for less, and said he was prepared to go to Santa Fe Community College, turning down a scholarship from Florida State, so he could re-enter the draft in 2013.[12] Hurst was resigned to the idea that he and the Pirates wouldn't come to terms when he got a call from Pirates scout Darren Mazeroski, son of former Pirates Hall-of-Fame second baseman Bill Mazeroski, to confirm that his phone number was still the same.

"Then the phone rang ten minutes later and it was Darren again and he said, 'We got your 400,000, you ready to be a Pirate?'" Hurst said.[13] "I was ecstatic."

Mazeroski told Hurst they'd be flying him up to Pittsburgh the very next day, and Scouting Coordinator Jim Asher followed up with another call a few minutes later to say the team would email Hurst his flight information. Up to Pittsburgh he went with his mother and father, and at 7:00 a.m. the day of the signing deadline, he was at Allegheny General Hospital to begin three and a half hours of medical tests. He had lunch with Asher and Joe DelliCarri, the team's director of amateur scouting, and got word that the medical tests had all checked out fine. With the 5:00 p.m. cutoff drawing close, Hurst arrived at PNC Park at 3:30, heading up to the fifth-floor board room, where he finally put pen to paper. By 11:00 p.m., Hurst and his family were home, with Hayden off to begin his pro career five days later at the Pirates' Gulf Coast League affiliate in Bradenton, Florida.

Romero cut it even closer before joining his former FACA teammate in the Gulf Coast League, signing with the Marlins a mere five seconds before the deadline, his father said.[14] Romero had been practicing at the University of Florida for two weeks, seemingly ready to accept his scholarship there and forgo his draft eligibility for the next three years.[15] While it would have been no surprise if a player drafted at Hurst's position had gone to college, it would have been unusual for Romero. There were just nine players drafted in the first ten rounds of 2012 who failed to sign with their teams before the deadline. That's in line with the thinking of scouts who, while biased, believe the most effective way to get to the big leagues is by turning pro as soon as possible.

"If you want to see how good you really are, get into professional baseball, and you're going to find out," Mesa said. "In the college game, the only big step that you have is that first year, from a high school senior to a college freshman. There's no Division I-Super A or Super-Duper A."

If a player can turn pro when he's still a teenager, Mesa said, he's more apt to learn proper habits than if he goes to a college program, where winning, and not player development, takes precedence. In the minors, a player might be given a chance to break out of a slump that he wouldn't get in college, McIlvaine asserts.

"You go to some of the college programs sometimes, and you strike out, and you're out of the lineup for three weeks," McIlvaine said. "In pro ball, you're going to play. You're going to be in there the next day."

Yet it remains a difficult choice for players. No one wants to turn down a full athletic scholarship and the chance to earn a degree only to look back in regret after flaming out at Double-A. Russell, the eldest of three siblings, said he had his family in mind as he gave strong consideration to attending Auburn University rather than signing with a pro team. That was before the A's took him eleventh overall, however, and gave him a $2,625,000, bonus far above the cost of tuition should he go back to get his degree.

High schoolers aren't the only ones with a decision to make about college. Under the draft rules, unless a player turns twenty-one years old within forty-five days of the draft, he must wait until after his junior year in college to re-enter the draft if he chooses not to turn pro immediately after high school. That only applies to players attending a traditional four-year college, however — those attending two-year community colleges can be drafted after each year. The drawback to going the community college route is the lack of exposure those players get compared to stars at Florida, Florida State, South Carolina, or other top-ranked four-year programs that are fixtures in the nationally televised College World Series. Phenom Bryce Harper had little trouble attracting scouts to the obscure two-year College of Southern Nevada, but players of more modest reputations can be overlooked.

Right-handed pitcher Matt Kimbrel came to the FACA event hoping to avoid just that. Kimbrel knew the event would be well-attended by scouts, so he arranged for a chance to come in and be seen among the top high school talent despite already having finished his third year of college. Granted, Kimbrel isn't quite as anonymous as most from Southern Polytechnic State University in Macon, Georgia. His older brother Craig is a three-time major league All-Star and 2011 National League Rookie of the Year who quickly established himself as the closer for the Braves. The Kimbrels had similar experiences the first time they were drafted. Craig was taken in the thirty-third round by the Braves after his first season at Wallace State Community College, and Matt was Atlanta's thirty-second round selection after his second year at Shelton State Community College. Both returned to school rather than sign — Craig for another year at Wallace State, and Matt for a year at Southern Polytechnic State. The move paid off handsomely for Craig, whom the Braves snagged again, this time in the third round. Matt came to Sebring with hopes of following suit, knowing that visibility can improve the chance that he, and others, will get to prove they belong in pro baseball.

"This is a great opportunity for high school players to come here and get looked at," he said.[16] "Where I came from, in high school, we didn't have anything like this, so these guys are very fortunate to come out here and be playing in this thing."

Just like his brother, Matt Kimbrel wound up getting drafted a second time by the Braves, but Matt was taken in the thirty-first round in 2012, only one round higher than the Braves took him in 2011. It was nothing resembling the leap Craig took from his first draft to his second, but it falls in line with the lesson the younger Kimbrel said he's learned from his brother over the years. Dedication, Matt believes, is what took Craig from the bottom of the draft to the All-Star Game in a span of only four years.

"If you want it, you've got to work for it," Matt Kimbrel said. "Nothing gets handed to you in this game. It's all about how much you put into it. The more you put in, the more you'll get out of it."

Brian Kraft, an area scout for the Marlins, said he tries to get a feel for a player's drive when there's a chance to speak away from the field.

"This is a tough game; just like any job, the athlete has to get up and perform every day," he said.[17] "With that in mind, it takes someone who really wants to do it. Some kids don't. They play because they are good at it, because it is fun, but when doing it 162 games a year it becomes a grind, and those who don't have passion for the game will struggle."

There's a lot a scout can learn from speaking with a player, but it's not always possible to do so.

"It kind of varies, how much interaction you're given to the kid," McIlvaine said. "The high school ones are much easier, ease-of-access-wise, to get with. With a lot of the college guys, the coach will set up times when you can talk to them, and this and that, but they'd rather you not bother them during the year, which I can understand."

Diamondbacks general manager Kevin Towers, who did not attend the showcase in Sebring, echoed that sentiment.

"Agents and college coaches always try to be mother hens over their players," Towers said.[18] "A lot of times you don't get an opportunity to get to know a player that well."

Still, the high school players assembled in Sebring require much more seasoning than comparable college talent. Even for the most successful prospects, the time between draft day and major league debut is two or three times as long coming from high school as it is from college.

"This level is just the high school level. Then you've got rookie ball, Class A, so it's very hard, more for a high school kid, to see how good they're going to be," White Sox scout Jose Ortega said.[19] "It's very hard. It's easy for college guys because they're 21, 22, so they're ready to go. These kids, 17 years old, and they're starting now. It's tough. It's very tough."

For Ortega and other scouts, that's just one more reason to try to assess a player's makeup.

"The first thing I look at a kid from high school is how big a heart he has," Ortega said. "And here, most of the good athletes are good because they have a big heart. They want to show the scouts they can do the job."

That means a player isn't judged solely on his performance on the field, as watchful eyes peer deeply into the day-to-day lives of high school students.

"You're definitely under a microscope, so you've got to act right all the time," Russell said.

Borders believes the increased attention from scouts in the thirty years since he was drafted presents an added challenge for prospects of his son's generation.

"The kids are more aware of it," Borders said. "And the pressure's far greater than what it was, because they are aware of it. Scouts want to talk to the kid. They don't want to talk to the parents. So, seventeen, eighteen years old, talking to a scout, it's a little intimidating. You don't want to say the wrong thing."

Some scouts say they try to interact with the parents, even if it's secondary to getting to know the players themselves.

"You do talk to the parents a lot," McIlvaine said. "You try not to talk too much with them at the games, because you want to let them watch their kid play, too. It's all a part of it, to talk to them."

Kraft said a lot of scouts differ on the subject, but he feels getting to know a player's parents is important.

"Just like when meeting your wife, husband or significant other it's important to know where they are coming from," he said. "You can find out the kid's story, what kind of financial background the family comes from, are the kids spoon-fed or are they blue collar. Big leaguers come from wealthy families, less fortunate families—but I think that getting to know the actual kid is the important part. I feel you can learn a lot about the player and their families from meeting in a place where they feel comfortable to be themselves."

A team can benefit if a prospect and his family feel comfortable with the organization, Kraft said.

"While I am not trying to become great friends with the family, meeting face-to-face may help you with the flow of information through the next year in terms of when and where games and batting practices will take place, if games are canceled, if their son is sick, et cetera," he said. "It also helps at the end of the year when calling on sign-ability, and makes for a more comfortable situation when talking about financial issues."

The average player at the FACA event didn't resemble the stereotypical teenager distancing himself from his parents. Several prospects were open about the critical roles their families play in dealing with the peripheral challenges that come with having a sought-after talent.

Many of the FACA players have family ties to baseball that certainly don't hurt when it comes to getting noticed. Like Borders and Kimbrel, Jose Mesa Jr. comes from a major league household as the son of longtime major league closer Jose Mesa Sr. Grant Maris, an outfielder from St. Francis High School in Gainesville, is the grandson of legendary home run champion Roger Maris. Connections abound, and even those who don't have major league bloodlines often grow up in baseball families.

"We practice after school every day," Romero said of his family.

"My dad is one of the coaches [at the school] and therefore we are always the last ones to leave the field. My mom throws batting practice and my dad works with me on the defensive end. I guess you can say it's a family affair. I wouldn't want it any other way."

Having a large family to help spread the tasks around can be an advantage, but even a single parent can make a difference, as Brinson, the first-round choice of the Rangers, can attest.

"It's just me and my mom," he said.[20] "She's done everything, all those phone calls and stuff. She's handled all that, all the getting me places where I need to go, finding me a ride to places, getting me money to go to all these showcases. She's been there. She hasn't been able to come to all of them, but she's finding a way to get me all prepared, handling all the calls and handling all these guys coming after me. So, she's been real big."

A responsibility that often falls on parents is dealing with the player's adviser. NCAA regulations don't allow players to maintain college eligibility if they use an agent to negotiate directly with a team. Players can, however, be advised by agents as they decide whether to sign or attend school.

"I have an adviser. My dad kind of works with him and they focus on talking about all the draft stuff, talking with scouts, and they just let me pitch," Hurst said.[21]

The rule survived a court challenge from Andy Oliver, a left-handed pitcher suspended after allowing his adviser to negotiate directly with the Twins when they drafted him out of high school in 2006.[22] Oliver sued the NCAA and received a $750,000 settlement in 2009.[23] The settlement also vacated an order that barred the NCAA from enforcing the rule.[24] NCAA vice president Dennis Poppe indicated that the organization was considering changes to the rule in 2011,[25] and said discussions were taking place, but a year later the NCAA had yet to act on the issue.[26] So while high-schoolers and college underclassmen wield the leverage of returning to school, they continue to do so without the benefit of an agent at the table. Still, as advisers, agents are still an integral part of the draft experience, and serve as one more reminder that a robust, discerning support structure can make a difference for a prospect.

For some, that support is more structured than others. Two of the

FACA draftees attended academies that merge education with baseball, where students spend part of the day on academics and the rest getting baseball training. Catcher Bryan De La Rosa, a third-round pick of the Braves, went to the Bucky Dent Baseball School in Delray Beach, while Max Foody, a left-handed pitcher who was a twelfth-round pick of the Cardinals, came from the IMG Academy in Bradenton. The IMG Academy website details a typical day for a student-athlete, which begins with classes that take place at an on-campus private school and run from 7:45 a.m. to noon. After lunch, practice goes from 1:30 p.m. to 4:00 p.m., followed by weight and agility work four days a week, and "mental conditioning work" on the fifth day.[27] Students at the Bucky Dent Baseball School, founded by the light-hitting shortstop remembered for his home run for the Yankees in their one-game playoff against the Red Sox in 1978, attend one of two high schools in nearby Boca Raton for their academics before returning to the academy for daily baseball activities.[28]

The concept isn't new, and these academies are similar in many ways to the ones throughout Central America, with the cost representing a major difference. Up-front tuition for a high school boarding student at the IMG Academy was $64,205 for one year, as of 2012.[29] McIlvaine, the Brewers scout, believes that while those schools may provide the tools to set young players up for success, they come with no guarantees.

"It's a nice environment to play in," he said. "You go to school for half the day, and play baseball the rest of the day. You hope that the kid's getting better in that environment. You don't give him any kind of extra credit or anything. I don't. Maybe other people do. You evaluate him like any other kid, really."

Bodet says it all depends on the player's level of engagement.

"Overall, I think it's a good thing if the kid gets something out of it," he said of the academies. "That's part and parcel to the way it's done now. You can't bring back the way it was done sixty years ago. But saying that, for a kid to develop, he's got to have fun doing it. It shouldn't be like, 'Oh God, I've got to go do it today, because my Dad wants me to get lessons today.' I don't think lessons make a player. I don't think so. I can understand why people have their kids get them, to help them become better players, but it's what you learn as a player when you don't have adults around that helps you be a better player."

The academies worked well enough for De La Rosa and Foody, two of the thirty-one FACA all-stars taken in the 2012 draft. Only six of those thirty-one draftees opted not to sign.[30] The twenty-five signees combined for bonuses of $15,447,300, according to the Perfect Game website, not including four players taken in the late rounds whose bonuses weren't reported.[31] That figure makes it easy to understand why so many scouts decided to spend a three-day weekend in an out-of-the-way town of roughly 10,500 people.[32]

The late-setting sun left a dying light on the field as the practice day came to a close. Buses took the teams back to their hotel, the historic Kenilworth Lodge. Scouts filed out of the grandstand, taking the opportunity to say hello to a parent or chatting on a cell phone to a higher-up about what he'd just seen. A few scouts were getting ready to go to an Outback Steakhouse to meet and talk shop, taking advantage of a rare night without lengthy travel. The casual atmosphere of the weekend belied the tension of the impending draft and condensed signing period to follow. It's a pivotal time for prospects and teams alike. Careers, millions of dollars, and reputations hang in the balance of a place where the unforgiving business of baseball merges with the game's pastoral schoolboy innocence.

Scouting has played a key role in the ability of teams to maximize the draft through the years, and disagreements about the techniques and relative importance of scouts shape the way organizations approach the draft and player development. With each passing year and every additional dollar spent on unproven talent, constructing an effective scouting system and striking the right balance between trained eyes and raw data becomes increasingly vital.

5

The Scouts

Ten years ago, after Michael Lewis published his book *Moneyball*, the general perception was that scouts were going the way of the dodo bird. The story of the A's front office under general manager Billy Beane, further immortalized in 2011 when Brad Pitt took a turn as Beane in the Hollywood adaptation of the book, was to have proven that everything in the game is quantifiable, rendering a scout's power of observation moot.

Indeed, 103 scouts lost their jobs in the winter following the publication of *Moneyball*, longtime baseball executive Roland Hemond told Bill Shaikin of the *Los Angeles Times* in 2012.[1] Hemond teamed up with Dennis Gilbert, a special assistant to White Sox owner Jerry Reinsdorf, as well as scouts Dave Yoakum and Harry Minor, to form the Professional Scouts Foundation, which staged a fundraiser for out-of-work scouts in 2004. The gala, called "In the Spirit of the Game," has become an annual event, attended by Hall of Famers, commissioner Bud Selig, and Hollywood types like Harrison Ford.[2] It has helped the organization gather millions of dollars to help former scouts in need.[3]

Yet for all the elegies pronounced at the foot of the scouting profession's deathbed, it remains a vibrant and vital part of the game, and isn't soon to vanish. The A's, who made surprising playoff runs in 2012 and 2013, continue to employ a skeleton scouting crew,[4] but not every cutting-edge front office takes that approach. Blue Jays general manager Alex Anthopolous falls into the broad category of "new school" baseball executives,[5] but his stance on scouting is the opposite of Beane's. Anthopolous inherited the Jays front office in late 2009 from J.P. Ricciardi, Beane's former player personnel director. He quickly hired more scouts in anticipation of the 2010 draft, when Toronto had seven of the top eighty selections.[6] The team kept the scouts aboard, and as of 2012, the Jays had twenty-four area scouts on the payroll, the most in baseball.[7] That's given scouts less territory to cover, allowing them more time to get to know amateur prospects on and off the field.

"That's the most beneficial way," Noah Syndergaard, the thirty-eighth pick of the first round in 2010, told Jon Paul Morosi of Fox Sports in 2012. "Nothing against Billy Beane, I guess, but I don't think you can generate players with a computer."[8]

Scouts in other organizations sense the tide is turning, too. The statistical revolution made enhancements to baseball, but the key is to strike the right balance between numbers and subjective observation, Brewers area scout Tim McIlvaine contended as he spoke about the sport's infatuation with advanced metrics.

"It allowed more people to become a part of it, which is nice because it heightens the awareness of the game, but I think you're starting to see a lot of the people who were so ingrained, one hundred percent in that, are starting to swing back toward scouting," he said. "You can't make every decision based on that. You need to still have the evaluation of scouts, and with that, you make a combined decision more so than just one hundred percent scouting or one hundred percent statistics. You're trying to find the right marriage, instead of just being one way or the other."

White Sox area scout Jose Ortega, who's been working at his craft for more than three decades, said the edge a team gains when it understands a prospect as a person as well as a baseball player represents the value of scouting.

"That's what we're getting paid for, to study these kids, to tell what kind of guy they are," he said.[9] "Do they like to party too much? Do they like to drink? You have to know these kids in and out. You have to go to games. You go early to the games, make sure they're there on time, see how they react."

Ortega isn't as willing as others to give Sabermetrics their due.

"I don't believe in stats," he said. "I'm an old-timer. You have to produce in the field."

Ortega explained that statistics can be misleading, even amid the context of multiple games.

"First game, on Friday, you face a great pitcher, you go 0 for 4," he said, painting the hypothetical scenario of a three-game weekend series. "The second day, against a so-so pitcher, you go 1 for 4. Then on Sunday, you've got a bad pitcher and you go 4 for 4. So your stats say you're going to be above .400. Who'd you hit against to go .400?"

While many of today's advanced metrics are designed to correct for an opponent's relative strength, that's easier to do with established pros than with amateurs, particularly high schoolers. There's little track record to suggest whether a fifteen-year-old high school sophomore, in his first season on the varsity squad, might be a poor, average, or outstanding pitcher. The numerical results of any hitter's performance against that pitcher are influenced by the unknown. The high school landscape, crowded with thousands of teams of widely varying quality, is even further muddied by the lack of shared statistics. In an information age when anyone can pull up detailed statistical reports and player biographies from pro and college league websites, such data can be hard to come by for high schoolers. Whether to compile and distribute stats is usually up to a coach, and the information is not always reliable even when it's available. Stat-keeping is much better at amateur showcase events, which bring top talent together, but the scope of a full season is nonetheless obscured.

The best record of a player's accomplishments might be in the notebook of an area scout. They're the foot soldiers of the scouting profession, combing thousands of square miles to see prospects and could-be prospects. The same is true for associate scouts, who are essentially part-time or adjunct area scouts, filling the gaps left by area scouts, of which there are rarely as many as two dozen employed in a single organization.

Work is never in short supply for these observers, for whom diligence is a priority.

"If I can get to two, three games a day, that's great,"[10] Marlins area scout Brian Kraft said.

So much of getting to those games, and maximizing his time while he's there, has to do with technology.

"The advances in technology in relation to the cell phone and computer help us in our day-to-day work unbelievably," Kraft said. "A lot of regions in the country have group emails where coaches, parents and players can put out emails to a large group letting us know specifics of their games, starts, et cetera. I would imagine everyone would agree that being able to text or call a coach from your car or receiving an email from a player to find out the status of a game today makes our job easier."

Kraft, who's only been scouting for a few years, can't imagine having to get in his car and "roll the dice" to see if the pitcher he wanted to scout would be on the mound, or if the game would be played at all.

"Probably the biggest obstacle that scouts face is the weather," Kraft said, explaining how technology can help him avoid a dreaded rainout.

Technology also helps scouts cover territory virtually. Kraft uses Twitter and team websites, when available, to stay on top of the prospects he's targeting in between visits.

"The game hasn't changed," he said. "Scouts haven't changed. The types of players haven't changed, but the technology that we have, literally at our fingertips at any time we want to do our job, has probably changed 5,000 percent for the better. I will hear stories from guys that have been scouting for a while about pulling off the highway to get to a pay phone to check their voicemail to see when their directors are coming into town, et cetera. I just couldn't imagine trying to do this job without constant access to a phone or email. It seems impossible. We are very spoiled."

Gib Bodet is one of those guys who had to scout in the days long before Twitter, cell phones and even voicemail. He began his career as a part-timer for the Red Sox in 1969, and has been with the Dodgers since 1979. He was promoted to national crosschecker in 1998, making him one of the longest tenured top-tier scouts in baseball. Bodet echoes the sentiments of the much younger Kraft, believing the game and the nature of scouting remain fundamentally unchanged in spite of modern efficiencies.

"There have been a lot of changes, I guess," he said.[11] "We've got computers now, we've got film now, we've got videotape now, we have all kinds of tests that they give. We have psychologists, psychiatrists. It's still the same process. Does he have instincts to play the game and does he have physical ability? And does he play hard? And is it natural for him to play hard, or is it natural for him to pout when he doesn't do well?"

The thick tome of sports clichés is full of references to heart, hustle and determination, but the scrapheap of baseball is littered with talented prospects who simply didn't want to play the game as much as the next guy.

"I feel you can really learn the interest level in the game when you get a chance to sit and talk face-to-face with players," Kraft said.

Drive, more than any other characteristic, might be the primary attribute a scout looks for aside from physical ability.

"Makeup is a term that is used a lot that can mean many different things," Kraft said. "Good makeup for me doesn't mean that the player is someone that you would want your daughter to marry. That is just a bonus; not every player in the big leagues is a saint. Obviously I do not like criminals, but what I am looking for is passion for the game. If a passion for the game drives a talented kid and they enjoy playing, then it will never be 'work.'"

Of course, anyone who's ever been the parent of a teenager can attest that, even at that tender age, someone can put on airs just to impress the right person at the right time. Repeated contact becomes the key, but a scout can only spend so much time on one prospect, particularly since another team may draft him before the scout's club ever gets a chance to make its own decision.

"You never know them well enough, and it's harder now than it was years ago, because you have so many more guys to see," Bodet said. "It's just harder for you to get to know the kids as well as you'd want to, simply because you've got so much work."

Teams scour the country for talent like never before, with more major league organizations competing and much more money on the line than there was decades ago when Bodet started.

"You don't have the time, if you're an area guy," he said. "Some of these guys drive forty, fifty thousand miles a year. They don't just pop in and see a player. It's hard to get to know them as well as you'd want."

The heavy workload is what most people outside the game don't understand about scouting, Kraft believes.

"I feel that scouting is a very underrated area of baseball outside of the baseball world," he said. "I think the biggest misconception is that all scouts do is go to games, and all we do is watch baseball. Yes, we do get to go to games, which is great, but that may make up 10 percent of our day."

As much as technology allows Kraft and other area scouts to gather useful information, it also gives all of them tools they must fully utilize on a daily basis to keep up with each other. Every day presents a new logistical puzzle. Kraft begins by checking the weather, and if there's no rain, he gathers and analyzes team schedules to figure out if he has an opportunity to see multiple games. Kraft looks at maps to determine how quickly he can get between games and when he'll have to leave to beat traffic. He tries to contact coaches to confirm the lineups and pitching matchups, and make sure none of the prospects he wants to see are injured. He also asks them what time players will take batting practice.

"The day leading up to a game or games can be exhausting," Kraft said. "It's always a sense of relief when you finally arrive at the game."

The first sight of bleachers abutting a grassy field and a diamond of combed dirt puts scouts at ease, but when Bodet started, the game he attended didn't always involve a stick and a ball.

"In the old days, you would go see guys play in the offseason, and see guys play a sport that they weren't good at, maybe football or basketball," he said. "See how he competes when he's not the dominant player. They don't have an opportunity to do that as much anymore. You never see them enough."

A high school athlete's specialization in one sport or another makes sense in a logical vacuum. If practice makes perfect, more baseball would mean better baseball. It's not that simple.

"Now they have all these travel teams, and all that," Bodet said. "I don't think that necessarily makes the player who you're dealing with in this time frame better than everybody who preceded him."

With travel teams come money, and parental involvement. The prospect of a year-round commitment with little or no time off can begin to erode the passion for the game that scouts covet. A constant schedule of baseball games can negatively affect a player in other ways, as Bodet described while recalling his childhood introduction to the sport.

"We played a lot on our own," he said. "We didn't have to have eighteen guys to have a game. We played two against two, or three against three, or whatever. You hit the ball on the left side of the diamond and you're out, or whatever. Whatever the circumstances dictated. Now, most of the time, the only time they play is when they have an adult involved who says, 'OK, we're going to practice today.' Frankly, I don't see that as a great advantage. It's a great advantage if you've got a great coach, but there again, I don't think it helps develop instincts. That's just one guy's opinion; I've only been doing this forty years."

Often, it's the thought of major league millions that prompts teenagers and even younger children into specialization and an unrelenting approach to baseball. The desire for a return on that investment, as well as a thriving sports agent industry eager to deliver the largest bonus check possible, can become the determining factor in whether a prospect ever plays a game for the team that drafts him. Those factors can also play into whether a team drafts him at all or passes him up for an inferior talent who's more willing to sign. Scouts file reams of reports designed to help assess what a player is worth, but they're also expected to gauge what that player believes he's worth.

"It's arguably the most important part of the process," Kraft said. "In my brief scouting career there have been a lot of guys that I wanted to be Marlins. But it comes down to how much you value their abilities. Your evaluation of the player has to match up with the sign-ability of the player. A lot of times that is a difficult idea for eighteen-year-olds and parents to understand. Owners of clubs are not ATM machines that just spit money out at everyone that plays."

Scouts often wind up as the liaison between two starkly different perceptions of reality: the one accepted in the baseball world and the one held in the prospect's world.

"When I meet with players and their families I try and keep things extremely simple when explaining the process," Kraft said. "The analogy I use is the draft is in a way like placing a bet.

"For example, last year [in 2011] the Marlins selected Jose Fernandez with our first pick. When we signed him, essentially the club is betting two million dollars that Jose will be a starter in the big leagues. We also took players down in the draft that maybe we gave ten to twenty thousand dollars to. So in that case we are betting ten to twenty thousand dollars that they will play in the big leagues. The difference in money spent shows that clubs feel more confidence in the high-money guys making it. That is not to say that guys [taken] lower in the draft won't, because we are still betting on them. But their toolsets and abilities don't demand the same money." Fernandex won Rookie of the Year in 2013.

While baseball has sought to erode players' ability to negotiate with progressively stricter rules that assign a predetermined value to each draft slot, prospects who haven't exhausted their college eligibility wield a powerful hammer. Alex Mesa, an area scout for the Royals, acknowledges that power, and said he doesn't spend too much time worrying about how a player is going to use his leverage.

"Sign-ability and ability are two different things," he said.[12] "If they don't want to play now, it's OK. College is a great thing for a lot of kids. It really helps. Are you disappointed? Probably, but it's the nature of the beast. If you weren't disappointed, you probably didn't care. So, sign-ability is a personal decision on the player's part. You can't determine that."

Whether a draft pick signs or not is just one of many variables that go into scouting, and it's one of the few unknowns that's resolved at draft time. Most of the time, a scout must wait for years to see the fruit — whether rotten or ripe — of his work.

"I think the biggest obstacle we face is that at the end of the day you just don't know," Kraft said. "We go watch baseball games every day, see kids three, four, five times during their draft year after watching them for the past three years, scouting the 'famous' guys and the lesser known. We can think certain guys are slam dunks while others do not have a chance. Then [you go] down the road a few years and the kid that didn't have a chance is in the big leagues and the sure thing is in Low-A."

No team has come up with an infallible approach to evaluating draft-eligible talent, whether basing its system primarily on statistical evidence or keen-eyed observation. Making an educated guess about which amateurs will be All-Stars and which will be out of baseball within five years is no easy task. Kraft's approach is to maintain independent thought, and, as much as possible, resist the urge to recommend prospects based on groupthink, even if it means he might err when no one else would have.

"In terms of overall scouting my biggest fear is not getting a player wrong, but not being aggressive with those players that you do believe in," he said. "I would rather put a guy in High-And have him seen by those above me, draft him and have him not work out and find out if he is a big leaguer while wearing our uniform than be passive, not have him seen and another club signs him and he ends up playing on TV."

No matter how they do it, scouts who have proven the ability to find the right talent more often than others are craftsmen of the highest order.

"The amount of human factor that goes into the success and or failure of a player is unbelievable," Kraft said. "This is not one of those jobs where 'if you do this, turn it in on time, this will happen.'"

6

Organizational Profile
San Diego Padres

In 1998, the San Diego Padres cruised to a division title and won two playoff series before getting swept by the New York Yankees in the World Series. Despite getting trounced in the Fall Classic, it was still a banner year. The Padres hoisted their second National League pennant in franchise history. After the season, the small-market Padres chose to let go many of the high-priced veterans who helped fuel the run to the World Series. Among the players who signed with other teams as free agents were starting pitcher Kevin Brown, third baseman Ken Caminiti, and outfielder Steve Finley. Between them, these players had eight All-Star appearances and an MVP award up to that point. The departure of other stars, including slugger Greg Vaughn, who belted 50 home runs in 1998, sent the clear signal that the Padres were about to go from the class of the National League to a club in full retrenching mode.

The 1999 draft offered San Diego a major opportunity to build for the future. Per the rules of free agency, the losses of Brown, Caminiti, and Finley resulted in compensation from the teams that signed these players. For the Padres, that meant *five* first-round draft choices in addition to their own selection.

The first of San Diego's six opening-round picks didn't come until nineteen amateur players, including Josh Hamilton, Josh Beckett, and Barry Zito, had come off the board. With the twentieth pick, the Padres chose outfielder Vince Faison, a high schooler from Vidalia, Georgia. With their next three picks, they took right-handed pitchers Garik Baxter (28th overall), Omar Ortiz (29th overall), and Casey Burns (41st overall).

With the forty-ninth and fifty-first picks, respectively, they took left-handed pitcher Mike Bynum and catcher Nick Trzesniak.

The Padres and Kevin Towers, who served as the team's general manager from 1996 to 2009, were successful in signing all six top picks, but that was about the extent of their effectiveness.

The first round of the 1999 draft worked out terribly for the Padres. Only Bynum reached the majors, staying there for parts of three seasons, over which he went 2–5 with a 7.73 ERA. Faison and Trzesniak plateaued at Triple-A. Ortiz only made it as far as Double-A. Burns never made it past Single-A. And Baxter was killed in an automobile accident in 2001.

Reflecting on his fourteen years as Padres general manager, Towers acknowledged the long-term impact of first-round draft busts: "Two or three bad drafts can set your organization back for years, because you won't have players to fill the voids left by free agents you can no longer afford. That goes extra for small-market clubs. It also hurts because the best prospects have high trade value. If you whiff on two or three first-rounders, it's hard to recover from that."[1]

In 1999, San Diego whiffed six times in the first round. But the fifteenth round of that year's draft almost made up for that failure. It was then that the Padres chose Jake Peavy, an Alabama high school pitcher, with the 472nd overall pick of the draft. Of all the players selected and signed by the Padres in the 1999 draft, only Peavy went on to have a "serviceable" major league career, which we define as one in which a player was or has been active in the majors for at least five years and had or has had an overall positive wins-above-replacement value as determined by Baseball-Reference.com. In 2012 and 2013, Baseball-Reference.com slightly modified its formula for calculating WAR. This book uses a combination of the old and new formulas.

By any definition, Peavy has had far more than just a serviceable career. He won 92 games and a Cy Young Award in San Diego before being traded to the Chicago White Sox during the 2009 season. Thanks to Peavy, the Padres averted a disastrous draft in 1999.

Not surprisingly, the team experienced lean years following its 98-win season in 1998. Over the next five seasons, it averaged just 72 wins. But by 2004, with Peavy firmly established as the ace of the rotation, the Padres rebounded to win 87 games, the first in a string of four consecutive winning seasons. But how good would the Padre teams of the mid–2000s have been had just a couple of the first-round picks from 1999 become productive major leaguers?

The Padres' experience in 1999 demonstrates several points. First, a team's success or failure in any given draft cannot only be measured by looking at its top picks. Second, and more significant for the purposes of this book, the single word that best describes the baseball draft is "capricious." While statistically speaking, first-round picks are far more likely to go on to enjoy successful major league careers than players selected in any other round, baseball is littered with success stories involving players selected late in the draft. The baseball draft has far more rounds than its football and basketball counterparts, and as the Padres learned in 1999, a great find later in the draft can help ease the pain of miscalculating the potential of players selected in the first round.

This section of the book chronicles the draft histories of three major league organizations from 1990 to 2006. The teams—the Padres, Cardinals, and Twins—were chosen based on research suggesting the experiences of each can impart different lessons about the drafting and developing of young talent.

As we discussed earlier in the book, two-thirds of players drafted in the first round between 1990 and 2006 went on to make the major leagues. For comparison purposes, we also noted that players drafted in the fifth and tenth rounds made the majors at a rate of about 30 and 20 percent, respectively.

For these profiles, we examined every pick of each team from the first through fifth rounds of the draft from 1990 to 2006. In these rounds, we memorialized a pick, regardless of whether the team was successful in signing the player or not. We then tracked all players drafted later than the fifth round who eventually reached the big leagues. In order to avoid giving teams undue credit for selecting players in lower rounds who had no intention of going professional that year, we only included future major leaguers chosen later than the fifth round who signed contracts with the team that drafted them that year.

Additionally, we calculated the cumulative WAR value of all players drafted and signed in a given year, arguably the single most revealing statistic about a team's overall draft success. Based on this measurement, there were four years in the 1990s when the Padres would have been better or equally served by drafting *no players at all.* In 1992, San Diego drafted and signed only one player who went on to make the majors, a right-handed pitcher named Todd Erdos, who finished his five-year major league career with a WAR of negative 0.2. Three years later, the Padres drafted and signed six future major leaguers, but only second overall pick Ben Davis finished his career in the positive WAR realm. The other five cost teams 4.9 wins over the course of their careers. Journeyman catcher Wil Nieves, a forty-seventh round pick in 1995 who was an active major leaguer in 2013, had the lowest WAR of players in that group: negative 2.6.

In 1996, as in 1992, only one player selected and signed by the Padres went on to make the majors. Jason Middlebrook, a right-handed pitcher drafted in the ninth round out of Stanford University, played three seasons in the big leagues and registered a WAR of 0.0. Middlebrook's situation is noteworthy, because he received a signing bonus of $755,000, which at the time was the largest amount paid to a player taken after the first round.[2]

The 1997 draft yielded five future big leaguers who combined for a cumulative WAR of negative 0.1 as of the end of the 2013 season.

The caveat to the argument that the Padres would have been better off sitting out the draft in these years is that the cumulative WAR metric does not take into account future major leaguers acquired by the Padres in trades for career minor leaguers obtained through the draft.

To date, the best draft results for the Padres between 1990 and 2006 came in 1993, when the club selected and signed three players whose career WARs were above ten. Derrek Lee paced that group with a WAR of 31.5. Although these players started their major league careers in San Diego, all three enjoyed their greatest successes elsewhere. Only sixty-three of Lee's 7,963 career plate appearances came with the Padres. Five years after the Padres took him with the fourteenth overall pick of the draft, Lee was part of a trade with the Florida Marlins that brought Kevin Brown to San Diego. As discussed earlier, the Padres did not cash in on the compensatory first-round pick they received after losing Brown to free agency a season after acquiring him. The other two players with 10-plus WARs from the Padres' draft in 1993, Matt Clement and Gary Matthews Jr., also played the vast majority of their careers in cities other than San Diego. Rodney Wells, the reliever who went from the Cubs to the Padres in 2000 in exchange for Matthews, compiled a 0.0 WAR in three seasons with San Diego. The Padres dealt Clement to the Marlins in 2002, receiving utility man Cesar Crespo and outfielder Mark Kotsay in return. Crespo hit just .203 in two seasons with the Padres. Kotsay, a first-round pick of the Marlins in 1996, had three solid years in San Diego before being traded to Oakland.

The conclusion: With the exception of Peavy, no player drafted by the Padres in the 1990s significantly affected the club's fortunes.

The Padres' overall struggles are best illustrated by their persistent attempts to find a backstop of the future in the draft. Between 1990 and 2006, the Padres selected thirteen catchers in the first five rounds of the draft, including two in the first round. To put that number in perspective, the team drafted only nine outfielders in the fifth round or earlier during this timeframe. Of the eleven catchers signed by the club, four reached the majors, including Davis, the second overall pick of the 1995 draft.

Though Davis registered the lowest career WAR of any of the first five picks of the 1995 draft, he was still a resounding success by Padres standards. Each of the five catchers selected by the team between 1996 and 2001 plateaued in the minors. That group included a first-round, a third-round, a fourth-round, and two fifth-round picks. Trzesniak, a member of that ill-fated 1999 draft class, was the third catcher taken in the draft as a whole that year, ahead of backstops including Ryan Doumit and Justin Morneau, whom the Minnesota Twins converted into a first baseman in the minor leagues.

With Davis struggling to find his way in the majors, the Padres tried again in 2000 to land a catcher for the new millennium. Once more, they failed. Omar Falcon, a third-round pick out of Miami Southridge High School, toiled for eight seasons in the minors, where he compiled a career batting average of .227 before retiring without making it to the bigs. In the fourth round of the 2000 draft, the Cardinals nabbed Yadier Molina. In the seventeenth round, the Angels picked Mike Napoli.

Finally, in 2005, San Diego drafted and signed a catcher who went on to make a significant impact in a Padres uniform. Nick Hundley, the seventy-sixth overall pick and fifth catcher selected in that year's draft, had accrued a 5.0 WAR value through the 2013 season. To date, that makes him the most successful backstop of a draft class in which two catchers went in the first thirteen picks.

The 2005 draft is on pace to become the Padres' most successful of the years we studied. Nine players from that class had reached the majors as of 2013, including six whom San Diego selected in the first four rounds. Hundley and another second-round pick, third baseman Chase Headley, along with Will Venable, an outfielder from the seventh round, all rose through the Padres' farm system and won starting jobs with the big league club. Still early in their respective careers, they had a cumulative WAR of more than 30.0 at the end of the 2013 season.

The 2006 draft was nearly as impressive. The Padres drafted two players whose careers started to blossom by the start of the next decade. The ninth round yielded third baseman David Freese, who emerged as one of the organization's best minor league hitters. But looking to fill a short-term need, San Diego traded Freese to the Cardinals after the 2007 season for veteran outfielder Jim Edmonds. The trade didn't pan out for San Diego. Edmonds hit an abysmal .178 in 103 plate appearances with the Padres, prompting his release. Freese, meanwhile, has blossomed in St. Louis, winning the 2011 World Series MVP award and making his first All-Star Game in 2012.

In 2006, the Padres also nabbed right-handed pitcher Mat Latos in the eleventh round. Latos won twenty-seven games in a Padres uniform before being dealt to the Reds after the 2011 season for a package including Yonder Alonso and Edison Volquez. Alonso, the eighth overall pick of the 2008 draft, had an impressive debut season with the Padres in 2012, placing sixth in National League Rookie of the Year voting.

The drafts of the mid–2000s provide hope for the Padres' future. Between 1990 and 1999, San Diego drafted and signed forty-six future major leaguers. Through the 2013 season, the 2000 to 2006 drafts had already yielded thirty-eight major leaguers and an overall positive WAR value every year.

Towers attributes the improved performance at least in part to advancements in technology: "There were no computers when I ran my first draft in the mid–'90s. There were handwritten reports. We didn't have cell phones or Skype. Our scouts were hand-writing reports and sending them into our office. We then had to read that information and get it out to our crosscheckers, who would get second looks at the players. We weren't all that efficient. In the draft room, we didn't have 'smart-boards.' Without computers, we had boxes of files that had to be read through very, very quickly. We just weren't very efficient back then. We still look at players the same way, but because of technology, the infor-mation we have on players, and the showcases we're able to go to, not only on the West Coast but on the East Coast, too, we're getting better looks at the top players and are probably able to make better decisions on draft day. In the '90s, you had to rely on area scouts, because you couldn't get too deep on an area scout's list of players. Nowadays, area scouts are still valuable, but because of video and technology, I can sit in my office and watch clips of all the top players and get a pretty good idea of their arm action, swing, and defense before I ever get out and see them in person."

It's also worth noting that the Padres hired Bill Gayton as their new scouting director at the end of the 2000 season, a job he held until 2009.

Because the focus of this book is top draft choices, it is instructive to evaluate how the Padres fared in selecting players in the first round.

Just fifty-six percent (fourteen of twenty-five) of San Diego's first-round picks from 1990 to 2006 reached the major leagues. Take away the abject failure of 1999 and that percentage rises to sixty-eight percent. Seven of the fourteen first-round picks who got to the majors went on to have serviceable careers. But through 2012, only one, Lee, became an All-Star.

The Padres drafted twelve high school and thirteen college players in the opening round. Through 2012, only four of the high school draftees had reached the majors, compared to ten who came from the college ranks.

In the first five rounds of the draft, San Diego selected and signed thirty-four future major leaguers, compared to thirty-nine the organi-zation picked in the tenth round or later.

Between 1990 and 2006, the Padres drafted seventy-seven players in the first through fifth rounds of the draft. The team signed all twenty-five of their first-round picks and failed to come to terms with only nine others in the second through fifth rounds. Of the players San Diego did not sign, only second-round selections Todd Helton (1992) and Troy Glaus (1994) can be classified as ones that got away. Helton went to the University of Tennessee and was selected in the first round of the 1995 draft. Through the 2013 season, he was a five-time All-Star with a WAR of more than 60.0. Glaus attended UCLA before being drafted in the first round by the Anaheim Angels in 1997. A four-time All-Star, he wrapped up his career in 2010 with a WAR of 38.0.

Between 1990 and 2006, the Padres didn't draft a single player in the fourth or fifth rounds who has had a serviceable major league career. And only one of the organization's third-round picks, Clement, played at least five big league seasons and accumulated a positive WAR value. By contrast, eight players selected in the thirteenth round or later, including Peavy and Matthews, have had serviceable careers.

Two of San Diego's unsigned draft picks offer cautionary tales about the perils of waiting for a better offer to come along. In 1993, the team spent a fourth-round pick on right-handed pitcher Tim Miller, who had recently been named Pennsylvania's high school player of the year.[3] A round earlier, the Padres chose that state's runner-up for the honor, pitcher Matt Clement, who signed with the team and made his major league debut five years later.[4] Miller chose not to sign and instead accepted a baseball scholarship to Florida State University. An inability to crack the starting rotation in Tallahassee prompted him to transfer to the University of Tennessee. In Knoxville, continued injury woes and a personality clash with head coach Rod Delmonico led to the revocation of his scholarship.[5] Miller ended up at Cumberland University, an NAIA school in Tennessee. No major league team took a chance on him in later drafts.[6]

Miller is an example of a highly drafted player who remained an amateur and was never drafted again. Matt Harrington, selected in the second round by San Diego in 2001, is the only player in baseball history to be drafted five times without ever signing a contract.[7]

In 2000, the Colorado Rockies took Harrington out of Palmdale

High School in California with the seventh overall pick of the draft. Rather than accept $4.9 million spread out over a period of eight years, Harrington sat out a year and waited for an opportunity for even greater riches.[8] Enter the Padres, who took a chance on him in 2001. The right-handed pitchers chosen after Harrington in the second round of that year's draft included future major leaguers Dan Haren and Brandon League. Again not satisfied with the money offered him, Harrington jilted the Padres and opted to play for an independent league team in Minnesota.[9] There, he went 0–2 with a 9.47 ERA in six starts. From there, his stock continued to drop. Over the next three years, he went in the thirteenth, twenty-fourth, and thirty-sixth rounds of the draft. In the end, as discussed in Chapter 3, Harrington became the rare player to start and finish his career in the independent leagues, where he finished with a career record of 16–18 and a 4.49 ERA. Following his baseball career, Harrington found work at a California Costco store, where he earned $11.50 an hour.[10]

No evaluation of the Padres' draft fortunes between 1990 and 2006 would be complete without a discussion of Matt Bush, the top overall pick of the 2004 draft.

In a year when eighty-three percent of first-round picks eventually reached the majors — the highest percentage during the time frame of our study — Bush stands out as one of the most high-profile flops in draft history. Barring an astonishing reversal of fortunes, one that cannot take place until he finishes a lengthy prison sentence stemming from a DUI hit-and-run conviction, Bush will join Brien Taylor and Steven Chilcott as the only first overall picks who failed to make the majors.

From the time San Diego native Bush entered the Padres' minor league system out of Mission Bay High School, he failed to play — and behave — up to expectations. His first year in the pros was marred by an arrest stemming from a bar fight in Arizona, where Bush had been assigned to the Padres' Rookie League team.[11] After serving a suspension for that misdeed, Bush split his first season between Rookie and Low-A ball, hitting just .192 in 119 plate appearances. Despite that performance, the Padres promoted him to the Class-A Midwest League in 2005. There, he hit just. 221.

Bush's offensive struggles in the minor leagues prompted the Padres to reevaluate his future in the organization. Looking beyond his hitting woes, the Padres maintained hope that he could still develop into a productive player. The way he rocketed throws from shortstop to first base piqued the curiosity of Towers and his staff, who wondered whether his strong right arm might be equally impressive on a pitcher's mound.[12]

The experiment got off to a successful start. In a limited slate of seven pitching appearances during the 2007 season, Bush gave up just one run in seven and two-thirds innings. But soon after getting promoted from the Arizona League to the Midwest League, he tore a ligament in his pitching elbow, an injury that sidelined him for the next two seasons. During his recovery period, Bush assaulted two high school lacrosse players in San Diego. The Padres had seen enough. In 2009, Bush was dealt to the Toronto Blue Jays for future considerations. Bush never played an inning in the Blue Jays organization. At the end of spring training, Bush flew into an intoxicated rage at a party and threw a baseball at a woman's head.[13] Though he wasn't arrested, Toronto decided to immediately part ways with Bush, who had agreed to adhere to a strict conduct policy upon joining the organization.[14]

By this point, Matt Bush was officially adrift. But the Tampa Bay Rays were willing to give him yet another chance. After missing the entire 2009 season, Bush began a steady progression through the Rays' system that took him from rookie ball to Triple-A. He was scheduled to start the 2012 season at Triple-A when his improbable comeback came to a screeching halt. In March of that year, an intoxicated Bush struck a seventy-two year-old motorcycle rider with his SUV.[15] In December 2012, he pleaded guilty to DUI with serious bodily harm and received a fifty-one-month prison sentence, minus 272 days of time served.[16]

Towers said both at the time[17] and in a recent interview that Bush's playing ability never appealed to him very much. But two of the three players he coveted more, shortstop Stephen Drew and pitcher Jered Weaver, were represented by superagent Scott Boras, whose asking price was out of the Padres' range. The Boras factor scared off other suitors as well. Weaver and Drew were taken with the twelfth and fifteenth overall picks, respectively. Another player Towers coveted, pitcher Jeff Niemann, was the fifth selection of the draft.

"We were on the right guys that year," Towers said. "It came down to Drew, Niemann, and Weaver. Then we narrowed it down to Drew and Weaver. Then we narrowed it down to Drew. Drew was going to be our guy. It didn't happen, and I take total blame for that, because my owner [John Moores] asked me about our slot dollars. I told him it was $3 million. He asked if we could sign Drew for $3 million. I told him we couldn't. He asked what it was going to take. I said we would have to give him a major league deal for $6.5 million. He asked me if Drew was worth it. I said, 'No amateur's worth it. They're unproven talent.'" I learned a lesson from that. When a business-minded owner hears something like that from a GM, he thinks, 'Then why would we give him that?' We had the right guy, but we chose the signable guy. From a scouting standpoint, we were right. Matt Bush was probably not even in our Top 10 in terms of talent that year. Hindsight is twenty-twenty. I should have done a better job selling my owner on the idea. Is Drew worth it? No, but three or four years down the road, he may be worth it much more so than Matt Bush. You either have to spend the money now or spend it later."

7

Organizational Profile
St. Louis Cardinals

This chapter was written before the 2013 postseason.

It was a transaction that even the most dedicated baseball minds might have overlooked. The Cardinals took junior college third baseman Terry Evans in the forty-seventh round of the 2001 draft, using the 1,409th overall pick. It's the point in the draft when only the team executives holed away in draft war rooms are paying much attention to the proceedings. Even a few of them begin to lose interest at this point, as evidenced by the handful of vanity picks over the years, when the son or nephew of a longtime front office hand may have his name inscribed in the record books as a favor.

Still, teams occasionally uncover gems at this stage of the draft, and 2001 was an example. The Braves took a chance on a high schooler named Dallas Braden in the forty-sixth round. Though he didn't sign, and was held only in marginally higher regard when the A's drafted him out of college in the twenty-fourth round of the 2004 draft, he eventually joined the Oakland rotation and pitched the nineteenth perfect game in major league history on Mother's Day in 2010.

The Cardinals took Evans as a draft-and-follow player, exploiting a rule that existed until 2007 allowing teams to wait to sign draftees up until a week before the next draft. That way, Evans could use another year of his remaining college eligibility while the Cardinals evaluated whether it was worth signing him. They brought him aboard in 2002 and switched his position, making him an outfielder as they dispatched him to Johnson City of the rookie-level Appalachian League to begin his long shot at making the majors. Evans muddled along the next few years, batting .224 and .221 in consecutive seasons at High-A Palm Beach in 2004 and 2005, and seemed destined to become as inconsequential as most forty-seventh-rounders. Back at Palm Beach for a third straight season, he suddenly found his groove. He hit .311 with fifteen homers in 263 plate appearances, and stole twenty-one bases while getting caught just once. That earned him midseason promotion to Double-A Springfield, where he continued to sizzle, batting .307 with seven homers and five steals in eighty-four plate appearances. Suddenly, Evans was a commodity, and Cardinals general manager Walt Jocketty executed his *modus operandi* with such up-and-coming talents, selling high. The Cardinals sent Evans to the Angels on July 5, 2006, for Jeff Weaver, and Jocketty convinced Angels counterpart Bill Stoneman to throw in some cash to offset Weaver's $8,325,000 salary. Weaver, a former first-round pick, had struggled that season, but returned to top form by the 2006 postseason. He started five playoff games for the Cardinals that year, winning three and compiling a 2.43 ERA. He drew the starting assignment in Game Five of the World Series and outpitched Tigers star Justin Verlander, going eight innings to deliver a championship-clinching victory to St. Louis. Evans continued to make his move toward the majors, batting .316 with fifteen homers and twenty-four steals in a full season at Triple-A in 2007, and earned a pair of brief call-ups to the big club. A torn labrum cost him significant time in 2008,[1] and appeared to rob him of his momentum. He hit twenty-six homers and stole twenty-eight bases at Triple-A in 2009, but again only saw brief action at the major league level. He regressed in 2010, the year he made one final plate appearance in the bigs, and has bounced around with three organizations since.

Had they stuck with Evans, the Cardinals would have had little to show for their late-round pick, as is the case most of the time with players selected at the end of the draft. Instead, Jocketty made something out of next-to-nothing with the type of maneuver the organization frequently used to offset its inability to produce stars with its top picks. The Cardinals, perhaps as much as any team from 1990 through 2006, demonstrated that an organization's draft record need not be defined by high-profile misses. Instead, St. Louis has built much of its success over the past decade and a half on late-round gems and canny trades involving prospects.

No find paid more dividends than Albert Pujols, whom the Cardinals drafted in the thirteenth round with the 402nd overall pick in 1999. On the surface, it looks like perhaps the most ingenious move in all of baseball over the last quarter century, as Pujols cut a beeline to Cooperstown while delivering a pair of World Series titles to St. Louis. John Mozeliak, Jocketty's successor as general manager, was in his first season as scouting director the year Pujols was taken, but he admits the fateful selection wasn't the result of some kind of proprietary magic.

"I do think Pujols, to some degree, was fortuitous," Mozeliak said.[2] "Because so many other teams could have picked him at some point, but we did, and that's great, but it wasn't because we had a sophisticated way of thinking about it. It was fortunate."

Pujols wasn't the team's only mid-round draftee from that year to make an outsized impact. Mozeliak and his staff also nabbed Coco Crisp in the seventh round. The Cardinals missed out on bringing Crisp to the big leagues only because they traded him as part of a midsummer 2002 deal to acquire thirty-nine-year-old Chuck Finley. The veteran came to St. Louis and finished his last season with a flourish, going 7–4 with a 3.80 ERA and 1–0 with a 3.18 ERA in a pair of postseason starts. The Cardinals ultimately came up short against the Giants in the National League Championship Series that year, and the trade looked progressively more regrettable as Crisp served as the primary center fielder for the Red Sox 2007 World Series titlists and swiped a league-leading forty-nine bases for the A's in 2011.

Yet the Crisp deal proved to be the exception to the rule that the Evans-Weaver swap exemplifies.

The groundwork for the Cards' strategy of maximizing the value of their prospects via trade was established in the mid–1990s, when wholesale changes to the franchise took place. It began after the 1994 season, when longtime A's executive Jocketty succeeded Dal Maxvill as general manager. He fired manager Joe Torre in June of 1995 and replaced him after the season with Oakland skipper Tony LaRussa, who had managed many of the players Jocketty had brought along as A's farm director to three consecutive pennants and a World Series title in 1989. The same offseason that LaRussa came aboard, Bill DeWitt bought the club from the Busch family, owners since the 1950s. And, in a move that was much less heralded but equally important, Mozeliak joined the team's scouting department.

St. Louis fans could be excused for thinking their familiar Redbirds just didn't look the same. Indeed, it seemed much of their plumage had taken on the distinctive green-and-gold hue of the A's.

A January 1996 trade typified many the Cardinals would make in the years to come. St. Louis acquired starting pitcher Todd Stottlemyre from the A's for three prospects the Cardinals took in either the first or second round, plus a former tenth-round pick. Stottlemyre was a sub–4.00 ERA pitcher the next two and a half seasons, totaling 35 regular season wins and helping St. Louis to within a game of the World Series in 1996. More importantly, the deal allowed the Cardinals to extract value from draft picks who largely did not pan out. Bret Wagner, the first-rounder in the deal, never made the majors. Carl Dale was a second-round pick who pitched in just four big-league games. Tenth-rounder Allen Battle saw 288 plate appearances in two major league seasons. Only 1993 second-round pick Jay Witasick was anything more than an after-thought in The Show, with a 12-year career as a journeyman reliever who compiled a 4.64 ERA for seven different teams. The combined major league WAR of the draftees the Cardinals sent away for Stottlemyre was 0.8, dwarfed by the 6.1 WAR Stottlemyre produced over his brief time in St. Louis.

A month after the Stottlemyre trade, Jocketty sent another high draft pick to his former team. St. Louis turned third-rounder Steve Montgomery, he of seventy-two career big league games, into future Hall-of-Famer Dennis Eckersley, who still had enough over the next two seasons to give the Cardinals sixty-six saves, the last of which came just two weeks shy of his forty-third birthday.

Another mid–1990s trade with Oakland gave the Cardinals a man who briefly became the game's biggest star, a key figure in baseball's nightmare with performance-enhancing drugs, and later the team's batting coach during the 2011 World Series championship season. Mark McGwire was, if nothing else, a transcendent force whose 1998 pursuit and eclipse of the single-season home run record brought prestige to the franchise and fans into seats and in front of television screens. Many was the night when ESPN's *SportsCenter* led with another of

McGwire's bombs landing in the Busch Stadium left-field seating area that fast-food titan McDonald's had slickly branded as Big Mac Land.

For all that McGwire would bring in return, the Cardinals sent Eric Ludwick, T.J. Mathews and Blake Stein to Oakland at the July trade deadline in 1997. Ludwick, the older brother of future Cardinal Ryan Ludwick, was a second-round pick the Cards had acquired in a previous trade with the Mets. Stein was the Cardinals' sixth-round selection in 1994. Mathews, who had the longest major league career of the three, was a thirty-sixth-round find by the Cardinals in 1992. McGwire's 2.0 WAR in two months with St. Louis at the end of the 1997 season outstripped the combined career WARs of the three men he was traded for, never mind the 7.2 WAR the slugger put up in his defining 1998 campaign.

While the Cardinals excelled at trading prospects for productive major league talent, the McGwire trade was atypical in one regard. St. Louis didn't send away a single player it had picked from the top five rounds. Usually, when the Cardinals traded their draftees, they were high selections, while the team kept its late-round sleepers and watched them develop into productive major leaguers. Indeed, much of the Cards' draft success from between 1990 and 2006 came from the later rounds. The forty-six players the team selected and signed between rounds one and five who went on to become major leaguers collectively totaled a major league WAR of nearly 200. The Cardinals drafted and signed another sixty-two eventual major leaguers in round six and beyond, and they compiled a WAR of 199.1. Even though the average WAR for early-round picks was about a point higher than their late-round counterparts, as could be expected, it's remarkable that the Cardinals found significantly more major league players in later rounds than they did in the early part of the draft, and that the late-rounders turned out to be slightly more productive collectively.

"I think from a simple economic standpoint, you try to be right on those top picks, because there's such a higher cost," Mozeliak said. "But having said that, we value every draft pick we have, in the sense of, the minute we make those choices, it's because we think we see something in that player that could potentially allow them to play in the big leagues.

Clearly the odds are not good, but when we think about the draft rounds, we feel there's a value pick in each one of those."

The Cardinals have made their fair share of value picks. They uncovered Placido Polanco in the nineteenth round in 1994 and Jack Wilson in the ninth in 1998. Both became All-Stars, though they did so in other teams' uniforms. St. Louis instead benefited from more subtle contributions by late-round picks in the 2000s. Kyle McClellan, a twenty-fifth-round pick in 2002, won eleven games while splitting time between the bullpen and the rotation for the 2011 World Series championship team. The team took catcher Jason Motte in the nineteenth round in 2003, converted him to a relief pitcher, and watched him lead the National League in saves in 2012. Jaime Garcia, a twenty-second-round pick in 2005, finished third in NL Rookie of the Year voting in 2010. The team's 2006 eighth-round selection, Allen Craig, became a super-utility player for the 2011 champions and an All-Star in 2013.

And though Yadier Molina was drafted relatively early, in the fourth round in 2000, there were still 112 players selected that year before the catcher who went on to start for two World Series winners, earn five consecutive Gold Gloves and make four straight All-Star Games, all before he turned thirty. No one could have imagined on draft day in June 2000, with Pujols just two months into his first minor league season at Class-A Peoria, that he and Molina would become cornerstones on a pair of championship teams. But their selection in the mid-to-late rounds defined the team's draft success in the 1990s and 2000s.

Pujols, Molina and the "value picks" helped offset the team's mistakes in the first round. The Cardinals picked thirty-one players in the first round between 1990 and 2006, and only four compiled career WARs of greater than 10. Dmitri Young barely gets over the line at 10.1, but compiled a WAR of negative 0.1 during his brief time in St. Louis prior to his trade to the Reds. Matt Morris was the only one of the first-rounders to make an All-Star Game in a Cardinals uniform. J.D. Drew had by far the best career of the group, but never proved to be the superstar he was purported to be when agent Scott Boras engaged in a game-changing fight with Major League Baseball over his draft eligibility.

The team's first-round failures tell the story even more effectively than its mild successes. The Cardinals began the decade of the 1990s by drafting a serviceable starting pitcher in Donovan Osborne, but whiffed on their pair of compensation picks in the 1990 first round, taking Aaron Holbert and Paul Ellis. Holbert's paltry contribution to the major league team, a single game in 1996, was the better of the two only because Ellis failed to advance beyond Triple-A. Tom McKinnon, one of a pair of Cardinals first-rounders in 1991 to fail to make The Show, didn't get past High-A. Aside from Young, the most decorated selection among the five first-round choices the Cardinals had in 1991 turned out to be Allen Watson, who compiled a 1.9 career WAR and a 5.03 ERA in eight unremarkable seasons as a back-of-the-rotation starter and middle reliever. St. Louis made six first-round picks between 1999 and 2001, and the only one of them to make the majors was Chris Duncan. In spite of Duncan's twenty-two homers as a fourth outfielder on the 2006 World Series championship team, he never equaled the impact on the organization made by his father, longtime pitching coach Dave Duncan. The year before that World Series win, the Cardinals made four first-round picks, two of whom never made it out of the minors. Tyler Greene arrived in St. Louis in 2009, but hit so poorly that the fans booed him during his final game at Busch Stadium before he was traded away.[3]

Colby Rasmus was the most successful of the 2006 first-rounders, but clashed with LaRussa, rankled Pujols, and was traded to the Blue Jays.[4] Shortly after the Rasmus trade, the Cardinals went on a historic tear, rallied from ten and a half games behind to pass the Braves for the National League wild card on the season's final night, and beat three teams with superior records in the postseason to win the 2011 World Series title. The players St. Louis received in the deal played a significant role in that championship run. Edwin Jackson went 5–2 with a 3.58 ERA down the stretch in the regular season, and Marc Rzepczynski and Octavio Dotel provided serious bullpen depth in the postseason, combining for nine holds and a 3–1 record.

As many times as the Cardinals made a mistake with a first-round pick, they seemed to come up with just as many trades to get themselves out of trouble. Bret Wagner, the team's lone 1994 first-rounder, didn't make the majors, but was sent away in the Stottlemyre deal. Braden Looper, taken with the highest pick the Cardinals held between 1990 and

2006, only briefly showed why he had been the third overall selection in 1996. He was the closer for the 2003 Marlins and winner of nine games in middle relief for the 2006 Cardinals, both World Series champions, yet had a largely pedestrian career. Long before his return to St. Louis in 2006, the Cardinals traded him in December 1998 as part of a package for Edgar Renteria, a twenty-two-year-old shortstop who blossomed in St. Louis, earning three All-Star nods, three Silver Sluggers and two Gold Gloves during his six years with the Cardinals. The Cards' only first-rounder in 1997, Adam Kennedy was the second baseman for the 2002 World Series champion Angels, but few St. Louis fans will fault Jocketty for packaging him with Kent Bottenfield in a trade for popular center fielder Jim Edmonds. Kennedy's 18.2 career WAR is precisely half that of the 36.4 WAR Edmonds produced during his eight years in a Cardinals uniform. Justin Pope was the twenty-eighth overall pick in 2001 and never advanced past Triple-A, and neither did Ben Julianel, the team's twelfth-rounder that year. Nonetheless, they were the only players the Yankees took back in a 2003 deal that brought in Sterling Hitchcock, who had enough left in his arm to go 5–1 with a 3.79 ERA down the stretch for St. Louis that year.

In total, the Cardinals received much better production from the players they traded for than the draft picks from the first five rounds they traded away. Seventeen of their picks from the first five rounds between 1990 and 2006 were traded away either before they reached the majors or when they had three or fewer years of big league service. Put together, they compiled a major league WAR of 79.9 through 2012, which excludes the brief time some of them spent in St. Louis. In return, the Cardinals received nineteen major league players. Collectively, they produced a WAR of 92.7 through 2012 in their time as Redbirds.

Not every trade worked out. The A's and general manager Billy Beane got their revenge on Jocketty in December 2004, sending him Mark Mulder, who won sixteen games for the Cardinals in 2005 before quickly fading first-round pick Daric Barton, 2001 second-round pick Dan Haren, and Kiko Calero, a reliever who was originally a late-round pick of the Royals. Together, they've produced a 42.4 WAR through 2012, compared to Mulder, who managed a WAR of just 0.3 in four years with St. Louis. Cardinals 2006 first-rounder Chris Perez made the All-Star team in back-to-back seasons as the Indians' closer in 2011 and 2012 after he was traded to Cleveland for Mark DeRosa, who barely made a ripple in half a season as the Cards' third baseman. Mozeliak probably regrets the day in March 2009 when he included Luke Gregerson as the player to be named to complete a trade with the Padres for Khalil Greene from the previous December. Gregerson broke in as a middle reliever for San Diego in 2009 and posted a respectable 3.24 ERA. That number became progressively lower each of the next three seasons, as he established himself as one of the best right-handed setup guys in the game. Greene, a former first-round pick, never regained the form he exhibited early in his career, batting .200 in 193 plate appearances for St. Louis before leaving the game for good.

Still, the Cardinals took more steps forward than backward in trades involving their early-round draftees. Mitigating, if not eliminating, the need to erase those drafting miscues is what Mozeliak has set out to do in recent years.

Looking back on the team's top picks who failed to produce, Mozeliak doesn't think the team vetted many of them as thoroughly as it should have. One incident in particular, with a first-round pick he declined to identify, helped convince him and others in the team's front office that they had to do their homework all the way to the end.

"We saw him early, very well," he said of the failed draftee, a pitcher. "When you check boxes in terms of fastball, command, all those things looked very good early. And then through the course of the season, we didn't really go back and spend time understanding exactly what we had here. So we drafted him. I literally fly up to the College World Series to see him pitch, and the head coach doesn't even use him."

Just a few days too late, Mozeliak and the Cardinals had their first indication that their draft pick wouldn't turn out as expected.

"That was striking, because here's a player that went in the top thirty in the country, and for some reason their head coach didn't want to trust him," Mozeliak said. "One of the things we learned from that is that our due diligence and making sure that we have eyes on a player throughout the entire draft period is important. But I think what's evolved is that we try to extend that draft period now. So we go out not only the summer before a player is draft-eligible, but we start tracking these players as freshmen and sophomores, and try to have a better feel for, when they are ready, what we are actually getting."

Rather than rely upon scouting or statistics alone, Mozeliak's front office uses them in tandem to piece together the fullest picture possible of the amateurs in whom they're about to make multimillion-dollar investments.

"So I think it was a real call for us to understand that we have to do this deeper, and longer, and spend more time getting looks. And of course the analytical world helps with that because it would identify trends of player success or failures," he said.

Using the tools of today to help refine the way the team evaluates draft prospects, Mozeliak, aided in part by former scouting director Jeff Luhnow, who became general manager of the Astros before the 2012 season, has overseen the development of a thriving organization. Keith Law of ESPN.com named the Cardinals baseball's best minor-league system in 2013,[5] three scant years after he ranked them twenty-ninth out of thirty organizations.[6] Mozeliak hasn't relied as heavily upon trading his prospects as his predecessor, though he hasn't hesitated to pull the trigger when appropriate, as the Rasmus trade demonstrated. The twenty-five-man roster the Cardinals carried into the 2012 National League Championship Series was an example of the team's recent emphasis on homegrown talent. Only six of those players came entirely from outside the organization.[7] Two were acquired via trade before they made their major league debuts, so they were products, at least in part, of the Cardinals' system.[8] Mexican-born relief pitcher Fernando Salas was an international signee, and the other 16 players on the roster were all drafted by St. Louis.

Perhaps no event better juxtaposed where the Cardinals organization had been with where it was than what took place on a mild Tuesday evening in St. Louis during the final week of the 2013 regular season. Right-hander Michael Wacha was making just his fifteenth major league appearance as he got the start for the Cards, who were nursing a two-game lead on both the Reds and Pirates for the Central Division title. Wacha had grown up a Cubs fan in Iowa City, Iowa, not far from Chicago's Triple-A affiliate in Des Moines.[9] The Cubs and Cardinals may have the Midwest's most venerable baseball rivalry, but it didn't curb the elation Wacha felt when St. Louis drafted him nineteenth overall out of Texas A&M in 2012.

"It was unbelievable," Wacha said about his experience on draft day. "My family came down to College Station, and I had a few teammates who were still in town. We were just watching on the TV, just anxiously waiting for the name to be called. My little sister, she's got her video camera out on her phone, just filming from about pick 10, every single one of them all the way up to 19. I just went crazy in the house. It was a lot of fun, having family there, having them be able to enjoy that feeling with me."

Fans at Busch Stadium and around the country watching via bonus coverage on MLB TV that Tuesday night in September came tantalizingly close to seeing Wacha burst into another celebration. He had no-hit the Nationals through eight and two-thirds innings when Ryan Zimmerman slapped a pitch into the dirt in front of home plate. The ball bounced high into the air and began its descent to Wacha's right. It hung the air just long enough to do no more than graze Wacha's outstretched glove as he reached across his six-foot-six frame. It bounced three more times on the infield grass before charging shortstop Pete Kozma finally fielded it with his bare hand and flung it toward first base, where Matt Adams came off the bag to field it. Adams failed in his attempt at a whirling swipe tag and Zimmerman was safe. Both Wacha's no-hit bid and his night on the mound were over. Reliever Trevor Rosenthal took it from there and recorded the final out, preserving a win for Wacha and the Cardinals. Kozma, Adams and Rosenthal were Cardinals draft picks age twenty-five or under, just like Wacha. Yet even though the tall right-hander was an infield single shy of a no-hitter that night, he was the reason the Cardinals highlight led *SportsCenter* just minutes after the game ended. Wacha also carries a distinction that will stay with him for much longer than an ESPN news cycle. The Cardinals received the draft pick they used to take the ex-Cubs fan as compensation for Pujols signing with the Angels before the 2012 season.

"I wasn't aware of it until probably ten minutes after I got picked," Wacha said in August 2012, when he was still in High A ball, barely more than a year before the near-no-hitter.

"People were like, 'Hey, you know that was the Pujols pick.' I was like, 'That's pretty sweet,' but I just hope that I can get up there and help out the big club as soon as possible."

Mission accomplished. Wacha went 8-2 with a 2.74 ERA in 95 and one-thirds major league innings between the playoff and the regular season in 2013 as he inherited the legacy of Cardinals past.

The Cardinals are one of the most well-regarded major league franchises, and have been postseason regulars since 2000, missing the playoffs just four times in the new millennium. The 1990s had been a dry spell for the club, the only postseason appearance of the decade ending in a 15–0 seventh-game loss to the Braves in the 1996 National League Championship Series. The starting pitcher for St. Louis that night was Donovan Osborne, the team's first draft pick of the 1990s, and he was shelled, giving up six runs, all earned, in two-thirds of an inning. He then handed the ball to LaRussa, in his first year as Cardinals manager, who had come out to the mound to remove him from the game. It was a moment that symbolized the direction of the team, even if the only emotion St. Louis fans could feel at the time was disappointment that a promising season's end was nigh. Soon, the legion of Cardinals faithful would recognize how the ex–A's revitalized their team, as Jocketty flipped draft duds that might well have extended the club's 1990s malaise for many years to come in trades that brought back productive major leaguers. Jocketty and his staff continued to struggle to draft stars in the first round, but they learned from their mistakes, found buried treasures in later rounds, and built a consistent winner. The Oakland interlopers seemed fully inculcated as Cardinals by the time Jocketty turned his job over in October 2007 to Mozeliak, a homegrown front-office talent who's not only continued the major league team's success but fortified the minor league system as well. LaRussa's final act before retiring after the 2011 season was to bring the Cardinals a second World Series title under his watch, one more than he had won with the A's. While Oakland turned into ground zero for *Moneyball*, the vestiges of its last championship employed a less-heralded but more-decorated approach that won the hearts of St. Louis.

8

Organizational Profile
Minnesota Twins

Twins fans had been spoiled. At the end of the 1991 season, they had just watched Jack Morris pitch a ten-inning shutout in Game Seven of the World Series to clinch their team's second World Series championship in five years. No team since the vaunted Yankees, who won back-to-back World Series in 1977 and 1978, had captured the title twice in such a short span. Unbeknownst to those fans, the team had just pulled off an eighth-round steal in the 1991 draft, nabbing right-hander Brad Radke, a future twenty-game winner who compiled a WAR of more than 40.0 in over a dozen seasons as a major leaguer, all of them spent in Minnesota.

It's not surprising that many fans lost interest in the team when it fell into a malaise of eight consecutive losing seasons from 1993 to 2000 amidst the changing economic realities of the game that, paradoxically, punished clubs that were without overwhelming fan support and cachet. The Twins finished last in attendance in the American League three years in a row, from 1998 to 2000. Through no fault of his own, those were the same three seasons Radke led the team in WAR.

Such a backslide would have prompted legendary Yankees owner George Steinbrenner to replace the "baseball people" in his front office many times over. Carl Pohlad, his Twins counterpart, took the opposite approach. From the time he bought the team from Calvin Griffith in 1984 until his death in 2009, Pohlad never fired a general manager — son Jim Pohlad made the call to fire Bill Smith in 2011.[1] During the years of our study, 1990 to 2006, the Twins had two general managers, two managers, and one farm director. The position with the greatest upheaval was scouting director, as three men occupied the post, but that's somewhat misleading, since Mike Radcliff, now the team's vice president of player personnel, served in that capacity from 1994 through 2007, covering most of our study. His predecessors, Terry Ryan and Larry Corrigan, remained with the organization throughout Radcliff's tenure as scouting director, with Ryan serving as general manager for much of that time.

That cohesive front office oversaw the lean years of the 1990s as well as a renaissance in the 2000s, when the team won the AL Central four out of five years. The Twins tacked on another pair of division titles in 2009 and 2010. Minnesota began its string of nine winning seasons in ten years in 2001, but in many ways the 2000 season represented as much of a turning point as any. In a year the Twins relied heavily on home-grown talent, the shortcomings and promise of the 2000 squad faithfully depict how the organization's draft work manifested itself at the major league level.

The year 2000 was the nadir of the team's attendance woes, as the club sold only 1,000,760 Metrodome seats, the fewest under Pohlad's ownership. The payroll, which Baseball-Reference.com estimates peg at about $17.5 million, was the lowest in all of baseball.[2] The product on the field was an improvement from the year before, when the team piled up ninety-seven losses, but it still couldn't crack seventy wins, finishing with a 69–93 record.

That Radke was the team's best player that year speaks to the team's struggles. It was a below-average season for the right-hander, as he went 12–16 with a 4.45 ERA. Control was more of struggle in 2000 than usual for him. He compiled the second-highest number of walks and hits per innings pitched, or WHIP, of his career. He struck out 2.76 batters for every walk he issued, well off the 3.63 rate he maintained during his 20-win season and roughly half of his league-leading 5.27 strikeout-to-walk ratio in 2001, a year he issued a major-league-low one walk every nine innings.

In 2000, Radke put up numbers similar to the only Twins first-round draft pick in the rotation that year. Mark Redman was the thirteenth overall pick from 1995, and went 12–9 with a 4.76 ERA in 2000, his first full season in the majors. While it was an off year for Radke,

Redman never really improved on his rookie campaign, and only exceeded a dozen victories once, in 2003, when he went 14–9 in a career year for the World Series champion Marlins. He was one of ten players the Twins signed from their drafts from 1990 to 2006 to make an All-Star team, but his selection was misleading, as it came in 2006 amid an 11–10, 5.71-ERA season for the 100-loss Royals, and was largely the result of baseball's rule that each team must have an All-Star representative.

The bullpen was the strength of the staff, and three of the team's top relievers were fruits of the draft. In particular, the 1991 draft had paid dividends for the team, but in a much different way than the Twins had originally scripted. Third overall pick Dave McCarty had long since departed for a journeyman career as a bench piece, never to compile three hundred at-bats in a season again after racking up 350 in his rookie year with Minnesota in 1993. Fellow first-rounder Scott Stahoviak played his final major league game in 1998, capping an undistinguished five-year career. That was still better than the one-year, 40-game stint second-round pick Mike Durant enjoyed. The team's next four draft picks failed to make the majors. Still, the Twins found three regulars in the middle rounds of that draft — Radke, right fielder Matt Lawton, and LaTroy Hawkins, a seventh-rounder who, as of 2013, was still pitching in the major leagues. In 2000, the Twins shifted Hawkins to the bullpen from the rotation, where he had put together an ominous 6.66 ERA in 1999. Hawkins immediately improved, cutting his ERA almost in half, to 3.39, and earned a team-leading fourteen saves as part of a three-man closing committee. Hawkins endured a regression in 2001, but the next two seasons he kept his walks to a minimum and served as the primary right-handed setup guy for Eddie Guardado, another of the team's draft successes.

"Everyday Eddie" was a hard-earned nickname for the twenty-first-rounder from 1990. He led the majors in appearances with a whopping eighty-three in 1996, and he nearly matched that total in 1998, pitching in seventy-nine games. Through 1999, he was much more noteworthy for his durability than anything else, having compiled a career 5.22 ERA. Once the Twins started tamping down his workload, he began to pitch better. In 2000, his last season of seventy appearances or more, he opened a string of four consecutive sub–4.00 ERA seasons in a Twins uniform, sneaking under the line with an ERA of 3.94. It was his second consecutive year with an ERA lower than the season before, a streak he eventually ran to seven years after leaving for the Mariners as a free agent in 2004. He recorded nine saves in 2000, and when he finally took over as full-time closer in 2002, he led the league in saves and made the first of back-to-back All-Star Games for a pair of Twins playoff teams.

The other Twins draftee to spend the 2000 season in the bullpen was a first-rounder, but Travis Miller, the thirty-fourth overall pick in 1994, didn't make much of a ripple in his seven major league seasons. His only three sub–4.00 ERA years, 1998 to 2000, coincided with the franchise's nadir, and 2000 was the season in which he recorded his only save. He was one of two first-round picks the Twins made in 1994, and while eighth overall selection Todd Walker was more productive, it's hard to argue the team received a fair return with either of those draft choices. Walker became a full-time player in 1998, taking over the second base job after the Twins traded Chuck Knoblauch. Walker responded with a .316 batting average and .845 OPS, a year better than all but two of Knoblauch's seven seasons as a Twins mainstay. Walker came back to earth in 1999, losing more than a hundred points off his OPS, and after starting with a .234 batting average and .612 OPS through the first month of the season in 2000, the Twins traded him in early May to the Rockies for Todd Sears, a third-rounder who never panned out. Walker's high-level production returned in the thin air of Colorado, but he spent only a season and a half there and never fulfilled the promise the Twins entrusted in him with a top-ten pick.

Another Twins first-rounder joined Walker in the 2000 opening day lineup for his major league debut. Just like Walker, Matt LeCroy was an occasionally proficient hitter, but ultimately proved a disappointment, given his high draft position. To be fair, LeCroy was a compensatory pick, at fiftieth overall, so the Twins didn't have quite as much riding on him as with other first-rounders. Still, they couldn't have been encouraged when he, like Walker, struggled out of the gate in 2000, batting .170 with five homers into late June. At that point, the Twins sent him back to the minors for more seasoning. LeCroy returned for a few September at-bats, but he didn't become a full-time major leaguer again until 2003, when, at age twenty-seven, he knocked in seventeen homers and compiled an .832 OPS, helping the Twins to the division title. He hit the same number of home runs in 2005, but those were the only two seasons of double-digit long balls for LeCroy, who finished with a career WAR of negative 0.3.

Still, of the seven former Twins draftees in the opening day lineup in 2000, LeCroy and Walker represent the only two whose careers were marked by underachievement. And there were a pair of relatively high draft picks who were bit players that season, but soon became key contributors when the Twins turned into playoff regulars. Catcher A.J. Pierzynski, a third-round pick in 2004, and first baseman Doug Mientkiewicz, who went in the fifth round the next year, emerged as starters in 2001, when the Twins finally broke through with a winning season. Each of them were .300 hitters twice between 2001 and 2003, with Mientkiewicz earning a gold glove while Pierzynski made an All-Star team. The Twins traded them both away within nine months of each other, returning little for Mientkiewicz but fleecing the Giants for Francisco Liriano, Joe Nathan and Boof Bonser in the Pierzynski deal.

Of all the successful draft picks on the Twins roster in 2000, none were better than Torii Hunter, the twentieth overall pick in 1993, who became a star in center field as the Twins returned to prominence. In 2000, he was a season removed from his 2001 breakout campaign, when he recorded the first of ten twenty-homer seasons in eleven years. That most of that production came in a Twins uniform was the result of a transaction that took advantage of three methods of player acquisition — trades, free agency, and the draft.

John Smiley had his finest season in 1991, when he compiled a 3.08 ERA, made his first All-Star team and was one of four pitchers to rack up twenty wins. He was one of three lefties in an imposing Pirates rotation that, along with a star-studded lineup of Barry Bonds, Bobby Bonilla, and Andy Van Slyke, guided the team to the best record in baseball that year. Pittsburgh was a game away from meeting the Twins in the World Series, and Minnesota's advanced scouts surely had their eyes on Smiley. As was the case with many of those Pirates, free agency loomed, and Pittsburgh knew it couldn't keep its team together in the long run as baseball's economics slanted away from small markets. The Twins were facing a comedown, too, after having won the World Series;

and as the Pirates looked to cash in Smiley for prospects a year in advance of his free agency, Minnesota wound up with the best of both worlds. During spring training in 1992, Twins general manager Andy MacPhail sent 1990 first-rounder Midre Cummings and Minnesota's third-round pick from 1989, Denny Neagle, to Pittsburgh for Smiley, who helped the team to another ninety-win season. The Pirates and new general manager Ted Simmons cast their lot with a pair of high draftees, and in the long run, it was by no means an unsuccessful trade on their side. The highlight of the deal for them was bringing in Neagle, who finished with a higher career WAR than Smiley. Cummings never developed into more than a fourth outfielder, and in a twist of fate, wound up with the Twins in 2000.

The Pirates came just as close to the World Series in 1992 without Smiley as they had with him the year before, losing in the seventh game of the National League Championship Series to the Braves, while the Twins went from winning the World Series to missing the playoffs in Smiley's lone season with the team. But MacPhail did not mortgage the future in the deal. When Smiley signed as a free agent before the 1993 season with the Reds, Cincinnati was forced to give up its first-round pick to the Twins as compensation. With that selection came Hunter, whose career WAR of 50.1 through the 2013 season was better than that of Smiley, Neagle and Cummings combined.

The Smiley trade had been a calculated risk. Trading a first-rounder and a third-rounder to wind up with only a first-rounder a year later doesn't seem like a fair deal on the surface. And had Smiley not delivered a strong season for the Twins in 1992, going 16–9 with a 3.21 ERA, he wouldn't have warranted such a high compensation pick when he left as a free agent. Nonetheless, it was a way for the club to manipulate its drafted assets to remain competitive in the short term while still looking out for the future.

As it happened, the Twins had their own selection at twenty-first overall in 1993, one slot after they took Hunter with the Reds' pick. The difference between turning one pick into a perennial All-Star and watching the other become an iconic figure elsewhere may simply have come down to a choice of representation. Unlike Hunter, Jason Varitek went with Scott Boras as his agent, and elected to return to Georgia Tech for his senior season. The Mariners took him with the fourteenth overall pick in 1994, and as a negotiating ploy, Boras had Varitek sign in Minnesota — not to play for the Twins, but for the independent league St. Paul Saints.[3] Varitek wound up with signing with Seattle for a $650,000 bonus,[4] $200,000 more than Hunter received from the Twins.[5]

It wasn't the only time Boras burned the Twins, and on one occasion, it even happened with a player whom Boras wasn't representing. Boras discovered a loophole in 1996 that allowed client Bobby Seay, whom the White Sox took twelfth overall that year, to become a free agent simply because Chicago had not tendered a contract offer within fifteen days after the draft.[6] The same was the case with the Twins and second overall pick Travis Lee, and so Minnesota lost its rights to the second-highest draft pick it made during our study, and watched Lee sign with the Diamondbacks for an eye-popping $10 million.[7]

Still, the top of the 1996 draft worked out for the Twins. Lee had a serviceable but unspectacular nine-year career, compiling a 5.3 career WAR and exceeding an .800 OPS in only one season. Second-round pick Jacque Jones, the thirty-seventh overall selection in 1996, fared better, particularly during his seven major league seasons as a Twin, when he totaled a 9.9 WAR. He played ten years in all, putting in a career similar to that of the other man who joined Hunter in the Minnesota outfield on opening day in 2000. Matt Lawton played six and a half seasons with the Twins, compiling a 9.8 WAR in that time. Jones finished his career with a batting average just ten points higher than Lawton's, while Lawton had a career OPS ten points higher than Jones'. Yet few would have predicted they'd wind up with so much in common when the Twins drafted them. Jones, the second-rounder, was already an outfielder when he came out of the prestigious baseball program at the University of Southern California. The Twins drafted Lawton in the thirteenth round of 1991 as a junior college second baseman, and they turned him into an outfielder during his second professional season at Class A Fort Wayne.

Lawton's draft profile has more in common with another product of the Twins system who made the team's opening day lineup in 2000. Corey Koskie didn't have to undergo a position switch, but he faced exceedingly long odds to become a major leaguer when the Twins drafted him in 1994's twenty-sixth round, 715th overall, out of a junior college in his native Manitoba. He steadily climbed the minor league ladder, earning a promotion each year, and finally received a September callup to Minnesota in 1998. He never looked back, and racked up a WAR of 22.6 in a relatively brief nine-year major league career as an efficient hitter who drew more than his share of walks. Aside from Hunter and Radke, Koskie's career WAR was the highest of any Twin in the lineup on opening day in 2000, and exceeded that of two-time first-rounder Varitek, who went to the Mariners 701 picks before the Twins nabbed Koskie that year.

Koskie's major league success was probably as predictable as Denny Hocking's ability to make the bigs at all. The Twins took Hocking with the next-to-last selection of the fifty-second round in 1989, a round that doesn't even exist in today's drafts. Though he wound up with a negative WAR, he hung around for thirteen major league seasons, eleven with Minnesota, as a utility man. He saw a career-high 433 plate appearances for the 2000 Twins, a year when he appeared at every position except pitcher and catcher.

Longtime Twins farm director Jim Rantz cites Hocking as an example of a late-round gem, but he could have just as easily pointed to one of the team's many unexpected discoveries in the 1990s. What lies between the draft and the majors is the point at which a player becomes a professional, and one of the most difficult tasks for a baseball executive is to predict how a prospect handles that transition.

"There are so many different things that take place once you sign a professional contract," Rantz said.[8] "Number one, a kid might have all the skills, but you don't know what's in his heart.

"You think he's a competitor, but when you get into a situation where there are a lot of players who fall into that category, he's coming from a small town or a program where he was the number one guy, but now he's competing with a lot of number one guys. You get to see if he's a competitor, and what's in his heart. Sometimes, players go the other way after you select them, but the fact is it's a tough grind being in this game. You play every day. There's no days off; at least scheduled days off are very few."

The same unpredictability that can turn an afterthought of a draft pick into a major leaguer can turn a first-rounder into a costly bust. But that's not what happened when the Twins made their most important pick during the years of our study.

Minnesota finished tied with Tampa Bay for the league's worst record in 2000, but since the Twins had an inferior record in 1999, the draft position tiebreaker went their way. The same had been the case in 1995, when a tiebreaker gave them the nod over the Blue Jays. At the time, the top pick was awarded to the worst team in each league on alternating years, and in 1996, it was the National League's turn. The Twins wound up with the number two pick and Travis Lee, who vanished from their hands thanks to Scott Boras. Minnesota had the worst record in the American League outright in 1999, but again the National League had first dibs, and instead of a crack at top overall pick Adrian Gonzalez, the Twins took Adam Johnson, a right-handed pitcher who made only nine major league appearances. In 2001, the Twins finally got a crack at the first pick, and they took full advantage of it.

There's always a certain amount of risk involved with drafting high schoolers, in part because there's less of a dossier on them than their college counterparts. The Twins had an advantage with Joe Mauer, since the catcher was a local who attended high school at Cretin-Derham Hall in St. Paul. Even without that advantage, the Twins proved proficient at identifying high school talent. They signed sixty-six picks right out of high school from the drafts between 1990 and 2006, and those players combined for a 217.5 WAR over their careers. Seventy-one of their signed draft picks in that time span had some college experience, but they only mustered a total WAR of 142. In 1998, when none of the team's first five picks would go on to make the majors, four of them were college players.

The Twins narrowed their choices for the top pick in 2001 to Mauer and a pair of collegians—pitcher Mark Prior and third baseman Mark Teixeira.[9] The question of whom would be the easiest to sign loomed over the organization. The previous year, the team had three first-round picks, and Johnson was the only one to sign. The last time Minnesota had the number one pick, in 1983, they took Tim Belcher and couldn't sign him.[10] The consensus among major league scouting directors that year was that Prior was the best player available, but teams worried it might take $15 million to sign him.[11] Scott Boras represented Teixeira, who was considered the best hitter in the draft, and the Twins knew all too well how Boras could disrupt their plans.[12] Mauer, the first player that *USA Today* ever named high school player of the year in both baseball and football,[13] had a scholarship waiting for him to play quarterback at Florida State.[14] That drove estimates of the kind of baseball money he could command up to as high as $7 million, but his two-sport status also allowed the Twins to spread his bonus payment out over five years under a rule designed in part to mitigate the leverage of multitalented athletes.[15]

The Twins went with the least expensive option, and they haven't regretted it. Minnesota gave Mauer a $5.15 million bonus, the highest ever granted to a first overall pick at that point.[16] The Cubs took Prior second, and gave him a $10.5 million major league contract that included a $4 million bonus.[17] He made an All-Star team and pitched four quality seasons before injuries forced him out of the major leagues after just five years and 106 starts. Teixeira fell to fifth, where the Rangers drafted him and inked him to a deal similar to Prior's. It was a major league contract worth $9.5 million, $4.5 million of which came in the form of a bonus.[18] Two years later, the aptly nicknamed "Tex" arrived and immediately began slugging. He never hit fewer than twenty-four homers in any of his first ten major league seasons, but he spent only four and a half of those years with the Rangers. Anticipating his free agency, the Rangers swapped him in a landmark trade that brought back three prospects who turned into All-Stars.

Meanwhile, Mauer became an icon in his native Minnesota. He won three batting titles and the 2009 American League MVP award in his first six major league seasons, and, together with Justin Morneau, a third-rounder from 1999 and the 2006 AL MVP, formed half of a fearsome one-two punch at the heart of three division-winning teams.

The same year the Twins drafted Mauer, they also drafted his older brother, Jake, in the twenty-third round. Jake Mauer didn't make it to the majors, but he joined his brother for their first three stops in the minor leagues and had one-of-a-kind insight on his ability.

"When we got sent to the Appalachian League together, playing against guys who I played against in college ... Joe was way better than all of them," Jake Mauer said.[19] "You don't see that. I know he was pretty good in high school, obviously. He put up all the huge, gaudy numbers, but to see him, the guy hit .400 against supposedly the best college pitching around, and you start to realize he's going to be pretty good. It was pretty neat to watch him develop and obviously have the success up there [in the majors]."

As Joe Mauer spent his first three pro seasons torching the minor leagues, the major league team improved thanks in large measure to their draftees of the '90s. The Twins continued to have success drafting in the early rounds for a couple of years after landing Mauer. Though Minnesota's first pick in the 2002 draft didn't come until twentieth overall because of the team's improved record from the year before, the Twins still landed Denard Span, a speedy outfielder who led the league in triples in 2009. He compiled a 16.5 WAR in five seasons with the Twins before they cashed him in for another first-round pick via trade in late 2012. Scott Baker was the team's second-round pick in 2003, and he was a fixture in the team's rotation from 2005 through 2011, notching a 3.44 strikeouts-to-walks ratio and a 14.6 WAR.

On their way to a third straight division title in 2004, the Twins were set up to reload in the draft that year with five first-round picks. Four of them made the majors, but only twenty-second overall pick Glen Perkins had a WAR of greater than 1.0 through 2012. Perkins, with a 4.2 WAR through 2012, won twelve games as a starter in 2008 before the Twins converted him into a reliever, later making him the team's closer. Trevor Plouffe, the team's highest pick in 2008 at twentieth overall, had the lowest WAR of the bunch at negative 1.9, but caught fire in June 2012, hitting eleven home runs. He hit just seven more in the season's final three months, reverting to form though the Twins made him their everyday third basemen in 2013. Right-handed pitchers Kyle Waldrop and Matt Fox have combined for just twenty-eight major league appearances, still better than Jay Rainville, who never made it past Double-A and was out of baseball by 2010.

The Twins bounced back in 2005, taking Matt Garza with the twenty-fifth overall selection, but after he'd put in just 133 major league innings, Minnesota traded him as part of a six-player deal with Tampa Bay that brought back 2003 top overall pick Delmon Young. Garza helped the Rays to the 2008 pennant and has an 11.1 career WAR, far outstripping

Young's 0.6 mark. Still, Young has occasionally shown flashes of his promise, and finished tenth in American League MVP voting in 2010 when his career-best .826 OPS helped the Twins to yet another Central Division title.

The problem in 2010, as was the case throughout most of the preceding decade, was that the Twins failed to capitalize on their regular season success. The playoffs are often a crapshoot, but not once in six appearances between 2002 and 2010 did Minnesota break through to the World Series. The Twins only won a single series in that span, beating the A's by one run in the deciding game of the 2002 Division Series, and were swept in their last three trips to the postseason.

The final division title was immediately followed by the crash of 2011, when the club was beset by frustrating injuries to Mauer and Morneau, among others. Both of them came back for full seasons in 2012, but the Twins jumped only from sixty-three wins to sixty-six. Even without injury, some of the team's players just seemed to unravel. Brian Duensing, whom the Twins took in the 2005 third round, went 15–5 with a 3.02 ERA in 2009 and 2010. The next two years, he was 13–26 with an ERA of 5.19. Danny Valencia appeared on his way to becoming a steal out of the 2006 nineteenth round, batting .311 with a .799 OPS in half a season as the team's first baseman and finishing third in Rookie of the Year voting. He hit just .246 the next season and was batting .198 midway through 2012, when the Twins traded him to the Red Sox for a rookie-leaguer from the Dominican Republic. The team's new outdoor home, Target Field, probably doesn't have much to do with its struggles, since the Twins moved there in 2010, a year when they equaled their second-best win total since winning the 1991 World Series.

Minnesota surely could have benefited if Valencia had been able to come close to what fellow third baseman Corey Koskie had done. Koskie, taken in 1994, was the last Twins draftee from outside the fifth round to compile a double-digit career WAR. J.C. Romero, a twenty-first rounder from 1997, was the only late-round draftee in that span to exceed a 5.0 WAR. The Brad Radkes and Matt Lawtons were absent from the team's profile over the last decade of our study, and that's one reason for Minnesota's recent struggles. Another appears to be the team's lack of production from its drafts in 2003 through 2006. Baker is the only one of the team's signed 2003 draftees to compile a positive career WAR, and he departed via free agency after missing all of 2012 because of Tommy John surgery. Garza is the only other double-digit career WAR player the Twins have produced thus far from those drafts, and only 0.5 of Garza's WAR came in a Twins uniform. Perhaps the Twins have been hurt by drafting late in each round, thanks to nine straight seasons with winning records. It's too early to judge the team's picks from more recent years, but only three players the Twins have drafted in the top five rounds from 2007 on had made the majors by the end of the 2012 season.

The Twins produced plenty through the draft from 1990 through the early 2000s, but their machine appears to have slowed of late. The team's success and failure at the major league level over the past two decades appears to correlate with the team's draft fortunes of a few years prior, and that lends credence to the importance of the draft, particularly for small- to mid-market clubs like Minnesota. The Twins made outfielder Brian Buxton the second overall pick in 2012, and took right-handed pitcher Kohl Stewart fourth overall in 2013. They'll have a top-five pick in each round of the draft for the second straight year in 2013, and the club's return to contention may rely on how well it fares in turning these draftees into productive major leaguers.

9

The Latin Factor

In the summer of 1974, a decade and a half before Puerto Ricans became eligible for the Major League Baseball draft and a decade before the imposition of a minimum age requirement for international players, the Philadelphia Phillies signed fourteen-year-old Jorge Lebron to a minor league deal, making him one of the youngest professional baseball players ever.[1]

The wiry but powerful teenager caught the eye of Ruben Amaro, Sr., the Phillies' coordinator for Latin America, at a tryout camp on the island. Despite Lebron's young age, Amaro felt Lebron's physique, bat speed, and instincts as an infielder made him worth the risk. His superiors in Philadelphia agreed and paid Lebron a $30,000 signing bonus.[2]

At the time of the signing, Amaro spoke of the competitive nature of scouting players in Latin America: "Baseball doesn't let you sign a kid in the United States until he's graduated from high school. But that rule doesn't apply in Puerto Rico, so we signed him. I think the Pirates and Expos were aware of him, but they thought they'd follow him for another couple of years. He just finished eighth grade, but part of his contract is that we will supply private tutors for him so that he will go through high school."[3]

Though Lebron wasn't subject to the rules of the baseball draft, he and the Phillies still had to adhere to U.S. child labor laws that forbade children under the age of 16 from working after 7:00 p.m. That meant young Jorge was mostly limited to appearances in afternoon games with the Low-A Auburn Phillies in 1974.[4]

Lebron is a minor footnote in baseball history, a player whose youth garnered him immediate attention from the likes of the *New York Times* and *People* magazine. He never panned out as a ballplayer, however, lasting just three seasons in the Phillies' farm system before exiting professional baseball in the United States at the age of sixteen.

Lebron hit .244 in 225 at-bats in the minors, a respectable performance for a non–English-speaking kid not yet old enough to apply for a driver's license. It was changes to his body that led the Phillies to cut ties with him. At the time of his signing, he was a lean 150 pounds. By the end of his time in the Phillies organization, he was "fat as a pig,"[5] according to Dallas Green, the Phillies' minor league director in the 1970s.

The few-holds-barred world of baseball scouting in Latin America since the institution of the major league draft in 1965 has provided teams with a secondary track for acquiring young talent. And as with drafted players, there has been no guarantee of future success for amateur free agents from Latin America.

Lebron didn't reach the major leagues, but the Phillies' aggressiveness in Latin America ended up paying off with the signing of future major league All-Stars George Bell and Julio Franco in 1978 and Juan Samuel in 1980. All three players hailed from San Pedro de Macoris in the Dominican Republic, which quickly gained a reputation as a hotbed of baseball talent.

The inception of the draft in 1965 fundamentally altered how major league teams built for the future. No longer could scouts go out and sign amateur players, regardless of age and location. Instead, they and their front office bosses had to wait their turn on a day in June to engage in a variation of the old schoolyard practice of picking sides. The new process was more orderly and gave teams with sagging fortunes first crack in each round of the draft. Rather than traversing the country in search of a strong arm or powerful bat and hoping enough bonus money could be offered to bring a player into the fold, teams now had exclusive negotiating rights with the amateur U.S.–born players they drafted. In 1989, the draft was expanded to include high school and college players from Puerto Rico. But that still left players in countries including the Dominican Republic a signature away from embarking on a professional baseball career with whatever team they chose. For decades, pre–1965 conditions have still largely applied to these players. That may soon change, however. With new spending caps on international free agents already in place and an expanded international draft under discussion, the identification and signing of amateur talent in a fertile swath of the baseball-playing world is likely to shift once again.

But from a historical standpoint, many aspects of baseball in the 1990s and 2000s, including the fate of top draft picks, were heavily influenced by how teams worked outside the parameters of the draft to sign Latin American players.

Latin American influence in Major League Baseball pre-dated the draft. In the 1950s, Puerto Ricans Roberto Clemente and Orlando Cepeda, as well as Venezuelan Luis Aparicio, embarked on what eventually became Hall of Fame careers.

It was in the post-draft years, however, that Latinos started entering the majors in significant numbers.

A July 1979 article in the *(Toronto) Globe and Mail* about the Dominican Republic's passion for baseball provided an inventory of all the Latin American players populating major league rosters: "At last count, 41 Dominicans graced major-league rosters.... Puerto Rico, a 40-minute flight across the blue water, can claim only about 20 current big-leaguers; Venezuela, Panama, Nicaragua, Cuba, Mexico and Canada have sent a handful, or fewer."[6]

The number of Latin players in the major leagues doubled between 1974 and 1979, a period during which big league teams expanded scouting operations and cultivated relationships with Winter League teams in the Caribbean.[7] This region represented a largely untapped market of young talent, and in the face of escalating payrolls and bonus payments to drafted players, major league teams flocked to places stocked with less expensive alternatives.

It wasn't all about the money, either. The outcome of international competition has revealed the high quality of baseball in Latin American countries. Between 1951 and 2011, the United States won only one gold medal in baseball at the Pan American Games. Cuba dominated the sport at the quadrennial event, winning twelve gold medals, including ten in a row between 1971 and 2007. The United States, the Dominican Republic, Venezuela, and Canada each captured gold once. The fact that Major League Baseball players have never participated in the Pan Am Games left unanswered the question of how the baseball elites of this country would fare against Cuba and other nations. That changed with the creation of the World Baseball Classic in 2006. Despite a major league–laden lineup, the United States failed to medal in the first three competitions, in 2006, 2009, and 2013. Japan won gold the first two times, and the Dominican Republic took the top prize in 2013.

With Cuban players off limits to Major League Baseball following Fidel Castro's revolution in 1959, big league organizations turned their focus to other Latin American countries with rich baseball traditions. Some baseball executives cited the talent and drive of Latin American players as the primary reason for bringing them to the United States to play.

"[The Latin players] are not as spoiled, not as pampered, they're hungrier than the American players," Tal Smith, then general manager of the Houston Astros, told the *Miami News* in 1979. "They play baseball year-round, and the interest in baseball in the Dominican Republic, Puerto Rico, and Venezuela is extraordinary."[8]

The Astros' sorties into Central America paid dividends. In the late 1970s and early 1980s, Houston fielded competitive teams, thanks in part to the contributions of Latin-born players including first baseman Cesar Cedeno, a Dominican signed by the team in 1967 at the age of sixteen.

The success of Latin players during the 1970s paved the way for an even greater proliferation of non–U.S.-born talent in future decades. In 2006, 23 percent of all major leaguers were from Latin American countries.[9] This growth was fueled by the opening of major league training facilities in the Dominican Republic and Venezuela, where big league teams have recently spent around $100 million a year to run forty baseball academies.[10] In Venezuela, however, many teams have scaled back on operations due to the country's high crime rate and unstable political situation. The number of teams with academies in Venezuela decreased from twenty-one to six between 2002 and 2011.[11] The kidnapping of Washington Nationals catcher Wilson Ramos in the town of Valencia in November 2011 helped underscore the nation's hazardous reputation. Still, the nurturing of athletes from Latin America continues to bear fruit. In 2011, 40 percent of players picked for the Major League All-Star Game were from the region.[12]

A core question of this book is why about one-third of first-round draft picks from 1990 to 2006 failed to reach the major leagues. While injuries altered or ended the careers of many players who plateaued in the minor leagues, it is a given that the influx of Latin-born players has created more competition for major league roster spots. This may explain why 72 percent of first-round selections ascended to the majors in the 1980s, compared to just 64 percent in the 1990s.

To bring some semblance of order to what was increasingly becoming a free-for-all, in which players as young as 13 were being signed to contracts, Major League Baseball enacted a rule in 1984 requiring international free agents to be at least seventeen years of age before the completion of their first professional season.[13] But this reform spawned the rise of *buscones*, talent agents who woo boys in their early teens to baseball schools that provide them with grooming until they are old enough to sign major league contracts.

A 2011 article in *Quarterly Americas* explored the growing influence of *buscones*:

> For some of the aspiring players, a *buscon*'s intervention is the best thing that ever happened. The *buscon* will facilitate a player's development, create a market for their talents and drive up bonuses. Few *buscones*, though, see to it that their young charges remain in school; many are more like hustlers than surrogate fathers. They might steal from a boy, enmesh him in career-damaging fraud (several boys have been suspended or had contracts revoked after being caught lying about their age) and even administer performance-enhancing drugs (PEDs) in the guise of B-12 shots to add pop to a player's bat or speed to his fastball.[14]

The experience of Carlos Alvarez is a cautionary tale. In 2006, Alvarez, age twenty, posed as a sixteen-year-old by the name of Esmailyn Gonzalez and received a $1.4 million signing bonus from the Washington Nationals. Three years later, his deception came to light, sparking an FBI investigation and vigorous debate about the conduct of *buscones* and whether Major League Baseball was party to an unseemly state of affairs in Latin American countries.[15]

Despite concerns about the Latin American pipeline, the flow of players from the region continues unabated. And from a financial standpoint, the involvement of *buscones* means the best Latin American prospects now sign lucrative contracts. In 2008, the Oakland Athletics gave a $4.25 million signing bonus to a sixteen-year-old player from the Dominican Republic named Michael Ynoa. And during a one-year period ending July 2012, major league teams spent $76.9 million in bonus money on players from the Dominican Republic and Venezuela, a 34 percent increase from the previous year.[16] During that same time frame, bonuses paid to draft picks dropped 11 percent.[17] The dip in draft-pick bonuses is likely as much a product of new cap rules as increasing spending on international players. With the imposition of international spending limits in 2012, we are likely to see further shifts in how major league organizations allot funds.

Joanna Shepherd of Clemson University and George Shepherd of the Emory University School of Law concluded in a 2002 research paper that Latin America had become a more desirable location to seek and groom baseball talent than the United States.

In 1965, professional baseball instituted labor-market regulations that, although purporting to protect young domestic players, instead penalized domestic players in favor of foreign players. Because the draft only applied to domestic players, teams soon shifted their scouting and development resources to foreign countries, especially Venezuela and the Dominican Republic. As our data show, the shift has led to a large growth in the number of foreign born players and a similar decrease in the number of U.S. players, especially African-Americans.[18]

Indeed, at just over 8 percent, the percentage of African-American players in the major leagues fell to historic lows in 2012; in 1975, 27 percent of all big leaguers were African-American.[19]

As *USA Today* noted in a 2012 article about this phenomenon, "Ten teams opened the year with no more than one African-American on their opening-day roster. There are nearly 30 more players from the Dominican Republic than the total of African-American players. Foreign-born players account for 28.4 percent of members of opening-day rosters."[20] Various estimates put the percentage of Latin-born minor league players at 40 percent.

Explanations for the sharp decline of African-Americans in baseball have ranged from a lack of widespread urban interest in and access to the sport to the reluctance of major league teams to promote the game and recruit players from the inner city. African-American star players, including Gary Sheffield and Torii Hunter, have made controversial remarks about Latino usurpation of roster spots.

Recent history suggests African-American participation in the game might be rising once again. In the 2012 draft, seven African-American players were selected in the first round, the most since 1992, when 10 went in the opening round. According to Major League Baseball, twelve alumni of its Reviving Baseball in Inner Cities (RBI) program were selected in the 2012 draft.[21] In 2013, six African-Americans went in the first round.[22]

It is impossible to put an exact number on how many additional first-round draft picks would have reached the majors in the absence of stiffer competition from foreign-born players. But it is logical to surmise that at least some highly drafted players were leapfrogged in the minor leagues by players from outside the country.

In a 2011 article for ESPN.com, Tim Keown wondered aloud whether American high school and college players realize the challenge of transitioning to the professional ranks of a sport increasingly populated by international athletes. "A question occurred Monday around the time Juan Cruz was pitching to Nelson Cruz, which was a half-inning after Alexi Ogando got the Rangers out of a seventh-inning jam and one inning before Neftali Perez came in to close out the Rays. The question was this: Do young American baseball players understand what they're up against?"[23] Citing the scarcity of foreign-born players in college baseball, Keown goes on to describe the culturally diverse minor leagues as an entirely different proving ground for players reared in suburban America.

In theory, the signing of non-draft-eligible amateur free agents has no bearing on the drafting of high school and college players. The draft pool and the number of picks allotted to teams remain the same regardless of how many players a team acquires from outside the country. The signing of an international player could, however, influence who a team takes in the draft. Suppose a team signs a pair of hard-throwing right-handed pitchers from the Dominican Republic. It stands to reason that that team would be less likely to choose a similar pitcher in a high round of the draft. The issue is not whether a player will be drafted, but rather how his future in the game will be influenced by increased competition for a major league roster spot.

One way to test the theory that major league teams' Latin American emphasis has had a deleterious effect on the careers of drafted players is to examine the situation of players from Puerto Rico, a U.S. commonwealth whose players have been eligible for the draft since 1989.

Shepherd and Shepherd cite the example of catcher Ivan Rodriguez, a Puerto Rico native signed at the age of sixteen by the Texas Rangers shortly before his countrymen became draft-eligible. Rodriguez was already a major league All-Star at twenty, an age when American college players would still be a year away from qualifying for the draft.[24]

When the same rules governing U.S. players started applying to Puerto Ricans, a dramatic shift occurred. In 2001, 4.3 percent of major leaguers hailed from Puerto Rico, but by the start of the 2012 season, that figure fell to 2.6 percent.[25] Government officials in Puerto Rico have blamed its inclusion in the draft for minimizing its citizens' chances of making the majors and, as a result, diminishing the game's popularity on the island. They cite the temporary demise of the Puerto Rico winter league, which was forced by financial problems to go on a one-year hiatus in 2007. The suspension of league play came after sixty-nine years of continuous existence, and four years after the Montreal Expos staged the first of 43 home games over a two-year period in the capital city of San Juan.[26]

"Why invest in Puerto Rico if 70 miles west and 500 miles south, in the Dominican Republic and Venezuela respectively, I can invest directly in the detection and development without going through the draft process?" Puerto Rico's Secretary of Sport David Bernier asked Evan Brunell of cbssports.com in 2007.[27] "The investment in Puerto Rico is not a cost-effective one for Major League teams and has lost charm for the recruiter. This reality is substantiated by the decrease in numbers of players selected through the draft and active in the Major Leagues. For example, in 1989, 47 players were signed, compared to only 21 in 2003. This creates a domino effect, less players at the top, less enthusiasm at the base. In the same way, organizations like our winter league, which could be associated with Major League teams in order to strengthen its structure, have suffered from the post-draft limbo state. To sum up, it is not the draft itself, it was the sudden way it was established and to have limited it to Puerto Rico that has affected the development of our baseball."

To address the perceived competitive disadvantage for Puerto Rican ballplayers, Bernier recommended a 10-year moratorium on the drafting of players from the country.[28]

Between 1990 and 2006, eight Puerto Ricans were drafted in the first round. Half of these players made the majors, most notably Alex Rios, who went on to become an All-Star with the Toronto Blue Jays. Arguably the best player out of Puerto Rico in recent years, former American League Rookie of the Year and multi-time All-Star Carlos Beltran, was a second-round pick of the Kansas Royals in 1995. In 2012, Carlos Correa became the first player from the island nation to be selected first overall in the draft. No one school has become a baseball factory in the Puerto Rican draft era; the eight first-round picks from '90 to '06, Beltran, and Correa attended ten different high schools.

Despite criticism from Bernier, Puerto Rican players have remained draft-eligible. And the country has tried to adapt to its circumstances. Correa attended the Puerto Rican Baseball Academy, which was founded in 2002 to showcase the country's best baseball talent. Jose Berrios, who also attended the academy, was the fifty-first overall pick in the 2012 draft. Beltran has opened a similar school on the island.[29]

Significant change is on the horizon for the current system of signing amateur international free agents. Increased public awareness of a Dominican baseball culture that sportswriter Jeff Passan calls "a festering pond of sleaze,"[30] the rising cost of signing Latin American players, and the complaints of the Puerto Rico faction have all combined to make the idea of an international draft look more attractive for Major League Baseball.

The first step toward reforming the current system came in 2011, when baseball owners and the players union agreed to levy a tax on teams whose spending on international free agents exceeds a certain limit. More significantly, that collective bargaining agreement led to the creation of a panel to study the efficacy of holding a single worldwide draft, or short of that, a separate draft for international players.

Not surprisingly, the baseball community in the Dominican Republic expressed disdain for either idea. Felipe Payano, the country's sports minister, went as far as to challenge the notion of a single draft for all players on the grounds that it would violate the Dominican Republic's free trade agreement with the United States. For their part, a group of *buscones* have staged anti-draft protests.[31]

In a 2012 interview with *Baseball America*, MLB commissioner Bud Selig said an international draft, in one form or another, is a great concept as well as a near-guarantee. "It is inevitable. I would like to see it. We have made some significant progress to that end. When we went to the draft in 1965, it was to create a more level playing field. We've done that, and the same thing will have to happen internationally."[32]

In a follow-up to their earlier research paper on the implications of the draft, Shepherd and Shepherd warned of the negative consequences of an international draft. "A worldwide draft would likely cause the [major leagues] to become even less diverse. The 1965 draft squeezed out African-Americans; the draft eliminated teams' incentive to train them. The worldwide draft will additionally squeeze out the Latin blacks and Hispanics."[33]

Jim Callis of MLB.com is among the baseball observers who have expressed doubt about the feasibility of an international draft. Logistics, Callis wrote in 2011 while with *Baseball America*, are among the impediments to such a draft. "MLB has made strides in verifying the identities and ages of Latin American players, but it's still a laborious process," he wrote. "An international draft would force MLB to investigate numerous players in a shorter period of time. The commissioner's office also would have to monitor teams conspiring to hide players or depress their stock, and it already has trouble preventing deals getting made before the current signing period officially starts on July 2 each year.... An international draft will create many more problems than it will solve."[34]

10

A Ballplayer's Story

Between 1990 and 2006, nearly seven hundred players were selected in the first round of baseball's amateur draft. Some ascended to major league greatness. Most weren't so fortunate. This is the first-hand account of David Yocum, a pitcher who fell short of his dream.

In 1989, as a freshman at Christopher Columbus High School, an all-boys Catholic school in Miami, I tried out for the junior varsity team. So did my classmate, future major league All-Star Alex Rodriguez, who played two years at Columbus before transferring.[1] Prior to tryouts, every player filled out a questionnaire stating his preferred position. I put down "right field" and "first base," because I felt I had the best chance of making the team at one of those positions. I wasn't the biggest or fastest guy at the tryouts, but given the opportunity, I felt I could hold my own against JV pitching. The tryouts lasted an entire week, and I ended up making the cut by the skin of my teeth. Considering the school's rich baseball tradition, that felt like a major accomplishment. The next step was proving I belonged on the team. But after nearly two seasons, it became apparent I was never going to be a stud first baseman or outfielder. Playing time was increasingly hard to come by, and I started to feel the pressure. To continue playing baseball at Columbus, I had to make the varsity by my junior year. If I didn't, my playing days there were numbered.

I needed a skill that would set me apart from the crowd. And I needed it fast. That's when I started flirting with the idea of trying to establish myself as a pitcher. Or re-establish myself, if you took into consideration the times I pitched in Little League. Unlike some of my teammates, I hadn't been groomed to pitch at the high school level. As a kid, I had developed a decent curveball, but at six feet tall and 145 pounds, I didn't have a whole lot of power behind my fastball.

Fortunately, I possessed a physical attribute that gave me an edge: I threw left-handed. Being a southpaw was a godsend. Like most pitching staffs from Little League to the majors, my high school's was comprised almost entirely of righties. I was a left-hander who could throw strikes, at least most of the time. After watching me pitch in practice, my JV coach, Jerry Streit, decided to give me a shot on the mound. The experiment worked out well. In the summer following my sophomore year, I threw a no-hitter in a tournament in Orlando. An older gentleman introduced himself to me after that game. It was Joe Arnold, the head baseball coach at the University of Florida. He shook my hand and congratulated me on my performance. The no-hitter boosted my confidence going into my junior year. I didn't feel like I was scraping by anymore. I was ready to take pitching very seriously.

I won a spot in the varsity rotation and stepped up as our ace after our best left-handed pitcher got hurt and missed the entire season. I went 9–0 my junior year, and in the process, added twelve miles per hour to my fastball. Even better, I pitched the Christopher Columbus Explorers to victory in the district championship. My dad told me after the game that Florida State coach Mike Martin had been watching from the stands.

The varsity coach, Brother Herb Baker, put a high priority on fitness and instructed me and the other pitchers to run cross country or join the swim team in the fall. None of us was going to be caught dead in a Speedo, so we all became long-distance runners. As a member of the squad, I ended up running fifty or sixty miles a week. I don't think any of my results played a role in whether we won or lost a meet, but I most definitely got into the best shape of my life. As the season went on, I started to view the regimen as fun. Above all, it taught me discipline.

It wasn't unusual to see major league scouts and college recruiters at my high school baseball games. Columbus had a long tradition of sending players to Division I programs in Florida. My plans were to attend college, whether or not I played baseball there. But going to college on an athletic scholarship had always been a dream of mine. During my junior year, I started receiving recruiting letters. One of the first came from Florida State, where my sister was attending school at the time. Soon, I was getting materials from Clemson, Georgia, Oklahoma State, Long Beach State, Notre Dame, Duke, Stanford, and every other Division I baseball powerhouse. I think my 3.0 grade point average probably had something to do with the widespread interest. After a few months, I had hundreds of letters. I put them all in a box, where they all remain to this day.

Florida State was particularly aggressive in recruiting me. At the start of my senior year, I signed a letter of intent to attend FSU on a baseball scholarship. That took a lot of pressure off me, because I got to play my senior season without worrying about where I was headed after graduation. My only loss that season came in a 1–0 game, in which the winning run scored on a passed ball. I also showed I could handle myself with the bat, so my coach played me at first base in some games. Near the end of the season, while playing that position, I broke my left wrist in a collision with a base runner. When I called Jamey Shouppe, FSU's pitching coach and recruiting coordinator, to let him know about the injury, he thanked me for the heads-up but didn't seem at all fazed by the news. It was then I realized that the Florida States of the college baseball world didn't have to panic if a top recruit got banged up. They had a lot of top recruits. That's why Florida State was one of the best programs in the country.

Yocum's commitment to attend Florida State likely scared off major league teams that might have considered drafting him out of high school. Still, he monitored the results of the 1993 draft, which took place the week he graduated high school, with more than a passing interest. He rushed home from school each day and listened to an AM radio broadcast of the draft. His former teammate Alex Rodriguez, who played his final two years of high school ball at Westminster Christian High School, was selected by the Seattle Mariners with the first overall pick. Another of Florida State's top recruits, pitcher Troy Carrasco, got picked in the third round by the Minnesota Twins. At the completion of the four-day event, Yocum believed he had gone undrafted. In reality, the San Diego Padres had taken him in the seventy-sixth round, long after most teams had stopped making picks.

After getting the news, he jokingly asked whether he was the last pick of
the entire draft. Not quite. That distinction belonged to Shawn Summers,
an outfielder from the University of Tennessee who went in the ninety-first
round, forty-four picks after Yocum, to the Florida Marlins, making him
the 1,716th and final selection in 1993.[2]

A day after the draft ended, I got a Western Union telegram inform-
ing me that the Padres had picked me. Then I got a call from a Padres
official asking me whether I still planned to attend college. The conversation was brief. After I told him I hadn't changed my mind about
Florida State, he wished me luck, and that was that. I couldn't help but
wonder what the Padres would have offered me as a bonus if I had
decided to sign. Maybe a pair of shoes, a new glove, and a bus ticket to
San Diego.

I never second-guessed my decision to go to college. It created a
perfect situation for me. The scholarship meant my parents, who had
put a lot of financial resources into my high school education, didn't
have to spend much money to send me to college. And from a baseball
standpoint, I had an opportunity to play for one of the best teams and
coaches in the nation.

It was extremely intimidating to walk out onto the field at Dick
Howser Stadium for the first time. In high school, I made first-team
All-Dade County my senior year and was a finalist for Dade County
Athlete of the Year. But as proud as I was of my accomplishments at
Columbus, they meant nothing now that I was in college. All my team-
mates could boast of having won similar accolades in their hometowns.
And I quickly realized each of them was as good, if not better, than me.
During my freshman season, my teammates included future major
leaguers Paul Wilson and Doug Mientkiewicz. There was a reason Florida
State was the top-ranked college team in the country going into the 1994
season.

My wrist was totally healed by the time I enrolled in school. At one
of our first practices, FSU coach Mike Martin Sr., or "11" as he's still
known, because that's the number he has worn on his back for three
decades, stood behind the second-base bag with a fungo bat and rocketed
balls off the right- and left-center field walls. It was part of a relay drill

for our outfielders, who had to play the carom off the wall and throw the ball to a cutoff man. As I watched the drill, I couldn't believe my eyes. The outfielders were throwing the ball into the infield harder than I could throw it from the pitcher's mound to home plate! I felt a huge lump in my throat at that moment. I got through practice that day and called my dad the moment I got back to my dorm.

"I don't know what I got myself into, Dad," I told him. "I think I may have bitten off more than I can chew."

"Keep your head down and do whatever they ask you to do," he replied. "Just stay with it."

No one in my family could directly relate to my situation. My dad had played college basketball at a small school in Georgia. And my sister was a competitive gymnast whose career ended prematurely due to an ankle injury. But I was the first in the family to compete at the Division I college level. I felt alone. And I felt scared. Even some of the other freshmen on the team seemed light years ahead of me in terms of development. There was a guy named Tim Miller, who had been drafted in the fourth round by the Padres but chose to attend college. The guy was an absolute beast, with a fastball in the mid–90s. If I wanted to get my innings in, I would have to show 11 that I was as good an option as Tim and the other young pitchers on the team.

From my first day in Tallahassee, I had trouble throwing my curveball for strikes. Controlling that pitch was vital to my success. I knew it, and 11 knew it, too. And he went to extreme lengths to drive that point home.

During fall practice, he would sit about ten feet behind the pitching mound in a folding chair, with his legs crossed thigh over thigh and watch me throw curveball after curveball. Well, he did more than just watch me. As I pitched, he screamed at me through a megaphone so that everyone within a square-mile radius could hear him.

"D.Y," he barked at me, "you're never going to play at Florida State if you can't hit with the curveball! You have to be able to throw it at 2–2 and 3–2. You have to throw it for a strike!"

Right behind our field was a busy thoroughfare called Apalachee Parkway that was well-traveled by students on their way to class. That meant it was well-traveled by the many pretty girls at Florida State.

There's no way that anybody walking past our field failed to hear the blare coming from 11's megaphone. My worst fear was that they might stop to find out who was 11 was berating. I was shy enough as it was. The last thing I needed was to approach a girl who might say, "David Yocum? Oh, you're the one that was getting yelled at by the baseball coach."

If I was ever going to have a chance to meet these girls, 11 had to stop screaming at me through the megaphone. And for that to happen, I needed to throw my curveball for strikes. So after several days of extreme embarrassment, that's what I learned to do. I learned something else from the experience, too. My coach looked so comfortable barking orders from that chair that I adopted the older-man style of sitting with my legs crossed.

Before the start of my freshman season, we found out we were going to Viera, Florida, for an exhibition game against the Florida Marlins, who were entering their second season in the big leagues. Our guys were super excited to make the trip to Space Coast Stadium to play against a major league team. A couple days prior to the trip, 11 came up to me with news that blew my mind.

"D.Y.," he said, "you're going to get the start against the Marlins. Just go out there and throw strikes."

This piece of information was almost as funny to me as being drafted in the seventy-sixth round by the Padres.

"This can't be right," I thought. "How has an unproven freshman earned the privilege to start this game? Why me? Is he serious?"

Of course, I didn't share these musings with 11. I simply nodded my head and let him know I was up to the task. Truth be told, I was ecstatic about the opportunity. I felt like I had won the lottery.

My dad drove up from Miami for the game. He wasn't going to miss the chance to see his son pitch against major leaguers. During warm-ups, our guys joked around with the Marlins players a little bit. Richie Lewis, a Marlins pitcher who had played for 11 at Florida State, had a little fun with our catcher, Mike Martin Jr., who was a batboy back when Lewis was a Seminole. The atmosphere was loose and relaxed. Only one guy acted like he was about to take a long walk to the gallows. And that was me. Warming up in the bullpen, I was a complete mess. I was all over the place with my pitches. My only saving grace, I thought, would be if the Marlins decided to take it easy on us by fielding a team of mostly minor leaguers. But that didn't happen. They sent out their big guns. I feared I might be in store for a long evening.

The first Marlins batter I faced was future All-Star Carl Everett. Thinking he'd want to take a pitch to see if I could hit the strike zone, I decided to start him off with a fastball down the middle of the plate. It would have helped immensely to get that first strike under my belt, but Everett foiled that plan. He swung and sent the ball right back through the box for a single. The ball was hit so hard I didn't even see it pass me. Now, I was in full panic mode. On top of trying to get hitters out, I now had to make sure I kept Everett from stealing a base or two on me. I looked up in the stands and could tell my father was nervous, too.

I didn't have much time to collect myself before facing the next hitter. In those moments, I reminded myself to just have fun. I had yet to pitch an inning of college ball, and here I was facing a major league team. The odds were already stacked against me. No good could possibly come from losing my mental focus.

Bret Barberie, Florida's second baseman, stepped to the plate. Throwing a combination of fastballs and curve balls, I got ahead of him in the count. A couple pitches later, he struck out swinging. I wanted to stay calm, but I couldn't help but think, "Oh my God, I just struck out a major leaguer!" That gave me a much-needed confidence boost. And it came at a good time, because I was about to face the Marlins' best hitter, Jeff Conine. I don't recall what pitches I threw or where I threw them, but I'll always remember the outcome of that at-bat: another strikeout. Was I excited? Yeah, just a little. "This is going all right," I thought to myself. "This is actually working out for me."

I had two outs and Everett still stood on first base. But I was hardly out of the woods. To get out of the inning I needed to retire Dave Magadan, the Marlins hitter I feared most. I had seen enough of his at-bats on TV to know he wasn't a guy who got himself out. He was similar in approach to Pete Rose in the way he watched pitches go into the catcher's mitt to make sure he didn't swing at a ball. In short, the guy was a professional hitter. After getting two quick strikes on him, I ran the count full. I'm sure at that point that he expected me to come at him with a fastball. Instead, I threw a curve. It hit the outside corner for a called third strike. After giving up a lead-off hit, I had struck out the side.

I gave up a run in the second inning before hitting the showers. We hung tight, but Florida ended up winning the game. Afterwards, my teammates and I posed for a bunch of pictures with the Marlins. Orestes Destrade, who attended the same high school as me, gave me a signed bat that read, "Not bad for a fellow Explorer." My dad joined me in the visitors' clubhouse, where we talked to Magadan and Marlins manager Rene Lachemann. As I was icing my shoulder, Marlins general manager Dave Dombrowski walked up and shook my hand. "You should be proud of yourself," he told me. "We're going to keep our eye on you."

I never asked 11 why he gave me that start, but I realized it probably happened for a combination of reasons. Following our exhibition against the Marlins, we hit the road for the start of our regular season. He had three other pitchers slated to go in that opening series, which made me a logical choice to pitch in the exhibition game. I also think he wanted to see what I was made of. I hoped my performance let him know I was ready for the challenges of Division I baseball. I know it helped convince me of that.

After the Marlins game, I didn't feel scared anymore. At a tournament in Hilo, Hawaii, I struck out ten hitters in a win against the University of Hawaii. I became the guy 11 sometimes turned to for a mid-week start against a non-conference opponent. I did okay in that capacity. But near the end of my freshman season, I was handed a different role. My ability to strike hitters out made 11 think I'd be a good closer.

Suddenly, I felt intimidated again. I didn't feel I had the stuff or classic closer mentality you hear so much about. And I wasn't used to entering games in such high-pressure situations. One particular appearance out of the bullpen stands out in my memory. It was an ACC conference matchup against Georgia Tech in Tallahassee. We were in a tight race with Tech for the conference championship and had split the first two games of the series. I entered the rubber match of the series with a one-run lead and three of the toughest college hitters in the country coming up: Jay Payton, Nomar Garciaparra, and Jason Varitek, all of whom were about to become first-round draft picks.

After I retired Payton for the second out of the inning, I was feeling pretty good. But Nomar hit a rocket off the thirty-foot-high wall at Dick Howser Stadium for a long single. That turned Varitek into the potential go-ahead run. The guy was a legend. He had been drafted in the first round the year before but went back to school instead of signing a pro contract. To this point, he was the best college player I ever had to face. I had yet to really prove myself at the college level, so I looked at it as a David versus Goliath matchup. My heart was beating hard. And after I got two strikes on Varitek, it was thumping even harder. I was a strike away from closing out the game and securing a series win. I tried to freeze Varitek with an inside fastball, but I missed my spot and left the pitch out over the plate. He jumped all over it and hit it off the scoreboard for a game-winning home run. In my memory, he hit it *through* the scoreboard. My heart sank. I put everything I had into that pitch. And I failed.

A strange thing happened to me after the Varitek home run. Even now, I still have a hard time trying to explain it. After my anger and frustration subsided, I became a different pitcher. In high school, my fastball peaked at eighty-five miles per hour. By the start of my freshman year at Florida State, I was throwing eighty-eight miles per hour. But within days of the Georgia Tech game, my fastball was clocked at 93 miles per hour. It was like a switch went off in my mind that enabled my body to perform in new and improved ways. I wasn't a guy with an average fastball anymore. Varitek must have heard about this new development, because he asked me about it before our second-round College World Series game against Georgia Tech. The Yellow Jackets beat us that day and ended up playing in the championship game, which they lost to Oklahoma.

If 11 wanted me in the bullpen, I was willing to embrace the role of closer. But before my sophomore season, he had a change of heart and made me his number two starter behind junior Jonathan Johnson. Part of that decision was based on Paul Wilson, our ace from the season before, getting drafted first overall by the Mets in 1994.

Prior to my second season at Florida State, I started hearing rumblings that I would be drafted in June. I didn't know what to make of that, because I was under the impression you couldn't get selected until the end of your junior year. But my coaches informed me that because my twenty-first birthday fell within forty-five days of the 1995 amateur draft, I was eligible for selection. That was all well and good, but it didn't mean I'd get drafted high enough to consider signing a professional contract. Like I said before, major league scouts were always at our games. I never stopped to think that they might be there because of David Yocum. My plan was to continue playing ball at Florida State. I took my dad's advice and focused on making the season as good as possible. "Whatever comes your way comes your way," he told me.

Baseball talent evaluators projected Seminoles ace Jonathan Johnson as a likely first-round pick.[3] As for Yocum, his stock soared during his sophomore season. He struck out a career-high 14 batters in a complete-game victory over number-one ranked Clemson, who, like Florida State, earned a trip to the 1995 College World Series.[4] Entering play in Omaha, Yocum led the Seminoles pitching staff in wins. A day before the tournament opened, the Los Angeles Dodgers took Yocum with the twentieth pick of the first round. In all, six current or former FSU pitchers were picked in that year's draft. That group included Johnson, who went seventh overall to the Texas Rangers, and Danny Kanell, who was picked by the Yankees in the twenty-fifth round despite having stopped playing baseball in order to focus on quarterbacking the Seminoles football team.

I was in my hotel room in Omaha when the ringing of the phone startled me. I knew it was draft day, but I was focused on the task at hand of trying to win an NCAA championship. The voice on the other end of the phone belonged to Bill Pleis, a Dodgers scout whom I had met a couple of times during the season. He was an old-school kind of guy who reminded me of my grandfather.

"I want to let you know that the Dodgers have chosen you in the 1995 amateur draft," he informed me.

"Thank you," I reflexively replied. "I'm very excited about the opportunity."

I guess my tone of voice didn't convey the kind of enthusiasm or curiosity Pleis expected.

"Son, don't you want to know where you were drafted?" he asked.

"Yes sir, I'd like to know, but right now, I'm just excited about the idea of playing for the Dodgers. It's an opportunity I've always dreamed of."

"Son, stop for a minute. I want you to understand what's going on. Son, you are the Los Angeles Dodgers' first-round pick."

That stopped me in my tracks.

"Excuse me?"

"You're our first-round pick, son."

"You're kidding me."

Two years earlier, the San Diego Padres called to say they had picked me in the seventy-sixth round of the draft. Now, this guy from the Dodgers was telling me I was one of the twenty best amateur players in the country. At that moment, two things ran through my mind: "This is unbelievable," and "I wish this guy would quit calling me 'son.'"

I thanked Pleis for the call and repeated how excited I was to become a Dodger. After hanging up the phone, I walked over to the bathroom and stared in the mirror. Then I started crying uncontrollably. It was one of those moments when time stops and you reflect on the people and events that got you to where you are. I mostly thought about my mom and dad, who had sacrificed so much to allow me to attend a private school with an elite baseball program. That opportunity helped pave my way to a baseball scholarship to Florida State. My dad worked as a master electrician at Miami International Airport. In high school, he couldn't make it to some of my Saturday games because he was out walking the picket lines with other employees of Eastern Airlines. During the strike, he went without a paycheck, which meant my family had to get by on my mom's earnings in a local orthodontist's office. My folks were the ones who set the groundwork for my success.

I couldn't stop crying.

I didn't make it to the team lunch that day. I told 11 I was sick. In reality, I wasn't sure I could make it through the event without breaking down in tears again.

When I finally caught up with my teammates later that afternoon, I was gripped by another feeling: guilt. Word spread quickly about who got drafted and in what round. I felt bad for some of the juniors and seniors who had busted their asses for three or four years, only to be passed over. I almost felt like I had taken a draft spot away from those guys. From the day I arrived in Tallahassee, I tried to be a team player. I was never an outspoken rah-rah type of guy. If I was a leader, I was a quiet one. It made me uncomfortable to think that any of my teammates might resent the attention I was now getting.

A day after the 1995 draft, Florida State beat the defending NCAA champion Oklahoma Sooners. Freshman J.D. Drew's two-run homerun in the bottom of the ninth inning led the Seminoles to victory.[5] Yocum took the mound two days later against the University of Miami. The Hurricanes scored three runs off him in the first inning and hung on for a 4–2 victory.[6] In its next game, Florida State was eliminated from competition by the University of Southern California.[7]

Before the start of his sophomore year, Yocum had traveled to Homestead, Florida, to try out for the U.S. National Baseball team. In the summer of 1995, he learned he had qualified for the squad. He had a decision to make. If he returned to Florida State for his junior year, he would get to play for the national team. But in order to compete in the 1996 Summer Olympics in Atlanta, he would have to stay in college through his senior year. Or he could sign with the Dodgers.

My folks and I had conversations with an agent prior to the 1995 draft, the same guy who had been advising for Jonathan [Johnson] since the start of the season. At some point, he realized my potential to go high in the draft, so he ended up advising me, too. He handled the legal side of things, but it was my mom who took the lead in negotiating with the Dodgers. She let it be known that I had two more years of college eligibility and the chance to pitch for the Olympic team. Terry Reynolds, the Dodgers' assistant director of scouting, came to our home in Miami to discuss the situation with us. We went to a Mexican restaurant near our house called Cisco's and listened to him talk about the long history of the Dodgers and how much the organization valued me. Then he got to his pitch. "We have every intention of signing you, and we want to make sure you stay happy and healthy," he told me.

About a week after his visit, I agreed to a deal with the Dodgers and received an $825,000 signing bonus. It was almost the exact amount paid to the team's lone first-round pick the year before, Paul Konerko, who had gone thirteenth overall, seven spots higher than me. In addition to the bonus, the Dodgers agreed to foot the bill for tuition if I decided to complete my degree in criminology at some point. I also made some baseball card deals with Topps, Donruss, and Fleer. All told, I was getting close to $1 million. That was more money than my family had ever seen before, and if my career worked out, it wouldn't really matter how much I signed for. It didn't seem worth haggling for a few more dollars.

Within ten minutes of signing the contract, I got a call from a secretary at Dodger Stadium.

"How soon can you be in L.A.?" she asked me.

"How soon do you want me there?" I replied.

"Can you be at the airport in three hours?"

The next thing I knew I was in the first-class cabin on a non-stop flight from Miami to Los Angeles. When I arrived on the West Coast, Reynolds was there to meet me at the airport. We took a town car to a five-star hotel in downtown L.A., and he told me he'd be back to pick me up at 10 o'clock the next morning for an introductory press conference. Before we parted ways, he handed me an American Express card with the Dodgers logo on it.

"Do me a favor," he said as I got out of the car, "and don't go too crazy with this."

Don't go too crazy? What did that mean? Did he think I was going to have a $500 meal and go out on the town? I went up to my room, ordered up some jumbo shrimp, watched TV, and hit the sack. The next morning at Dodger Stadium, general manager Fred Claire put a jersey on me, and I was paraded out in front of the cameras. After a physical exam and a drug test, I was back on a plane to Miami. It was quite the whirlwind. In a few days, I was due to report to the Dodgers' High Class-A team in Vero Beach.

On the day I showed up there, the team bus was waiting on me. During the ride to our road game, my new manager, Jon Debus, sat next to me and told me he wanted to see me throw on the side a little bit. "Why don't you give me 75 percent, and we'll see how you look," he said. My fifteen-minute bullpen session that day really impressed him. "Wow, if that's 75 percent, I'd like to see 100 percent," he commented.

In Vero Beach, I felt like the new guy, probably because I was. The scene around my locker didn't exactly help me blend in. There were boxes and boxes of stuff in front of it. Cleats, tennis shoes, gloves, and warm-up gear. Nike, Adidas, Reebok, and Rawlings. I guess each company wanted to stake an early claim to first-round draft picks. Looking around the clubhouse, I saw that everybody else had one pair of shoes and one glove. I had more stuff than I knew what to do with. The surplus of equipment ended up giving me a couple years' worth of Christmas gifts.

Looking back, I can say without hesitation that the best times I had playing baseball were in college. The moment you start playing for a paycheck, everything changes. In the minor leagues, you play on a team, but that doesn't mean your teammates are necessarily rooting for you. The reality of it is that you're in competition with your teammates to see who puts up better stats. When you're a Single-A pitcher, all you want to be is a Double-A pitcher. The Single-A manager you're playing for is dying to be a Double-A manager. And the Single-A trainer who wraps your ankle is dreaming of making big money in the majors. It took me a while to grasp this. When I showed up at Vero Beach, I tried to be everybody's friend. But not everybody wanted to be my friend. It wasn't anything personal, or at least I didn't think it was. To the other pitchers, I represented a potential obstacle to their promotion. Everybody at that level is looking over his shoulder. For this reason, you can cut the tension in a minor league locker room with a butter knife.

Another of my experiences during my first week in the minors deserves a mention, because it speaks to the era I played in. A teammate, whose identity I won't reveal here, approached me and asked whether I wanted to sample some of his human-growth hormone. I was taken aback by the offer, and of course I turned him down. I was raised to believe hard work and dedication to the game were the keys to success. But from that day forward, I realized that other guys felt differently and were looking for shortcuts.

I made my first appearance with Vero Beach in the eighth inning of a game we led by a bunch of runs. I felt really good warming up in the bullpen and came in to face the bottom third of the opposing team's lineup. In high school and college, the guys who hit lower in the lineup were usually speedy guys who liked to work the count. So I decided to try and blow away the first batter I faced. My first pitch was a fastball right down the middle of the plate. That turned out to be a mistake. He connected and hit the pitch to dead center for a home run. Lesson learned. I was a professional baseball player now, and easy outs were a thing of the past.

Yocum recovered from his rocky start and turned in a respectable season in Vero Beach. Since he was coming off a full college season, Dodgers officials had expected to use him sparingly in 1995.[8] But he ended up making seven starts and finished his first season of professional ball with a 2–1 record and a 2.96 ERA. That performance earned him an invitation to the Arizona Fall League, a showcase for the best minor league prospects.

As much as I wanted to play in the Arizona Fall League, I felt I would have benefited from some time off. I was tired, both physically and emotionally. But I wanted to live up to the Dodgers' high expectations of me. My arm was fatigued by the end of the 1995 season, but I wasn't in any real pain. So I pitched in Arizona, and as I recall, I did pretty well.

During the offseason, I got a chance to relax and spend some of my bonus money. For myself, I bought a truck and a house down the street from my folks. I also purchased vehicles for them, including a garnet-and-gold pickup truck for my dad. To this day, that truck remains his pride and joy. My parents also got wood floors to replace the nasty old carpeting throughout their house. Every single dog we ever owned had his way with that carpet, and it was time for it to go. While the floors were being installed, I sent my parents on a European vacation. Without throwing too much money around, I wanted to take care of the people who had taken care of me. I gave a nice donation to the Florida State baseball program and pitched in to help pay for a new community park in my neighborhood.

My contract with the Dodgers stipulated that I would get a non-roster invitation to big league camp for three seasons. Back at Vero Beach in the spring of 1996, I roomed with Konerko, who was coming off a season in the California League. I was immediately struck by how relaxed everybody and everything was at Dodgers spring training. It was a completely different atmosphere than I had experienced in my first year in the minors. The veteran players were as nice as could be. I guess guaranteed long-term contracts have a calming effect on guys. Mike Piazza came up and congratulated me on signing a contract. "I hope to see you in L.A. real soon," he said. I remember having breakfast every morning with Tom Candiotti, Brett Butler, and Raul Mondesi. I can still see Tommy Lasorda walking around in his shorts as the team worked out. All in all, it was a very cool experience. I was with the big leaguers for about six weeks. Near the end of spring training, Tommy called me into his office and told me I was going to start the season at Double-A San Antonio, where I would work with pitching coach Claude Osteen. It was a promotion, but it didn't feel like one at the time. I grabbed my stuff and walked a few hundred yards to the Dodgers' minor league facilities at Vero Beach. Having just experienced the laid-back nature of big league camp, I found that the minor league atmosphere felt even tenser than before.

I never made it to San Antonio. As camp broke, I started feeling pain in my left shoulder, and the Dodgers decided to shut me down for a little while to see if rest would cure the problem. It didn't. A few weeks into the 1996 season, I visited with Dr. Frank Jobe, the Dodgers' team physician and inventor of Tommy John surgery. He examined my shoulder and concluded I needed surgery to remove inflamed tissue. He performed the procedure and put me on a fitness program he hoped would get me back to 100 percent. Unfortunately, there were some complications with my rehab, and the pain remained. That resulted in a second arthroscopic surgery, in which Dr. Ralph Gambardella tried to tighten things up in my shoulder.

Hindsight is twenty-twenty, but if it had been left up to me, I would have signed a contract with the Dodgers and said, "See you next spring." I felt I was a little bit overworked in my first season in their organization. I was a small-framed guy not used to pitching so many innings. Then again, maybe I would have gotten hurt anyway. I don't know.

Following his two surgeries, Yocum returned to the Vero Beach Dodgers for the end of the 1996 season. In seven starts, he went 0–2 with a 6.14 ERA. For baseball writer Rod Beaton of USA Today, *Yocum's post-injury struggles evoked memories of other pitchers picked by the Dodgers in the first round who had suffered career-altering or ending injuries: Dan Opperman (1987), Bill Bene (1988), Kiki Jones (1989), Jamie McAndrew (1989), and Darren Dreifort (1993).[9] Of that group, only McAndrew and Dreifort saw major league action.*

After missing the entire 1997 season because of ongoing shoulder problems, Yocum told the Dodgers he wanted to seek the opinion of a doctor outside the organization. He traveled to Birmingham, Alabama, to meet with famed surgeon Dr. James Andrews. For the third time in less than three years, Yocum had a surgery to remove scar tissue from his left shoulder. Andrews told Yocum he was confident he would be able to resume his playing career in the near future.

After my third rehab, I still couldn't throw without experiencing tremendous pain in my left shoulder. But my competitive nature led me to believe I'd somehow, some way figure out how to salvage my career. The Dodgers had invested a lot in me and hoped I could come back from the injury. At the same time, they needed to know if I was damaged goods. During my spring training appearances in 1998, I was physically unable to perform at a level that would have shown the Dodgers I had a future in their organization. As badly as I wanted to hold on, I wasn't sure I could do it anymore. My body just wasn't right. And that made me feel helpless. I had two choices: Stay at it and hope I got better. Or step aside.

In June 1998, the Dodgers made the decision for me. I got a letter from them thanking me for my service and telling me I'd always be a part of their family. But the last sentence was the only one that mattered.

It read, "You are hereby released by the Los Angeles Dodgers organization."

Funny how the mind works, but after being let go, I became hell-bent on coming back to play. I didn't feel any ill will toward the Dodgers. In fact, I was grateful for everything they gave me. But that letter, especially the last line, motivated me to show the world that I could compete at the game's highest level. In retrospect, that was a pipe dream.

I gave rehab another shot, this time paying for it out of pocket, and worked out daily at the University of Miami. In early 1999, my family and I spread the word that I'd be throwing a bullpen session in Coral Gables. All interested teams were welcome to attend. A few teams, including the Marlins, showed up, but it certainly wasn't the turn out I hoped for. My entourage, which included my father, attorney, physical therapist, and some friends, outnumbered the scouts. I didn't do poorly that day. But I didn't wow anybody either. My fastball wasn't great, and my curve wasn't that sharp. And I was still pitching in pain. Maybe I should have postponed the bullpen session until I felt a little bit stronger. Or maybe I was just making excuses. I probably was good enough to throw a no-hitter against an average college team, but that's not the caliber of pitcher major league scouts are looking for. The fact is I didn't show I deserved to take a roster spot away from even a minor leaguer. There just wasn't a big market for an average pitcher who had been under the knife three times.

I sat around for a couple weeks waiting for my phone to ring. There was silence. When it finally did ring after about a month, I found myself talking to former New York Yankees catcher Rick Cerone, who owned the Newark Bears. A few other Independent League teams ended up contacting me, too. I thought over the situation before respectfully declining the invitations to join their teams. My heart just wasn't in it anymore. That's when I retreated into my own little world. I took all my baseball pictures off the walls of my house and stored them away in a closet. I didn't want to hear about baseball. I didn't want to talk about baseball. I didn't want to have anything to do with baseball. Not only that, I didn't really want to hear, talk to or have anything to do with other people.

It took some time, but once I accepted the dream was over, I was able to go on with my life. At the time I left baseball, I was like any young man looking to start a career. In 2001, I joined the City of Miami Beach Fire Department as a firefighter and paramedic. I love my job. Riding on the back of a fire truck isn't all that different from standing on top of a mound with a baseball. You feel the same rush of adrenaline as you go off to put out a fire or save a life.

For a long time, I couldn't help but think about what might have been. I don't do that as much anymore. In fact, there's a lot of stuff in this chapter I've never even told my wife or my parents. This is the way I look at it: No matter how good you are, eventually your day is going to come. That's not just in baseball. That's in life. I wish I had reached the majors, but that's not how it worked out. My experience in the game has given me a greater appreciation for guys like R.A. Dickey, who overcame great adversity and showed incredible resiliency. R.A. was drafted a year after me, and before ever throwing a pitch in the minors, he learned he was missing a ligament in his pitching arm. Unlike me, he decided he loved baseball too much to give it up. He completely changed his pitching style and willed himself into becoming a Cy Young Award-winning pitcher.

I got out of baseball before I was twenty-five. I can't help but worry about the players who knock around the minors for a lot of years, only to receive their release papers one day. What happens to the thirty-year-old guy who hasn't earned much money, only knows baseball, and now has to readjust to a life outside the game?

In 2012, I was inducted into the Christopher Columbus High School Sports Hall of Fame. Despite falling short of my ultimate goal, I had a wonderful time playing baseball. My years on the field far exceeded anything I ever expected. I enjoyed the highest of the highs and endured the lowest of the lows during my career, but I wouldn't trade my experience for anything. The game of baseball has truly blessed my life. As I said before, no one gets to play forever. So whether you're playing in a big league ballpark with a well-manicured field, or on a community diamond overgrown with weeds, enjoy every moment of it. Baseball is a special game.

With each passing year, fewer and fewer people remember David Yocum the baseball player. And with each passing year, I'm more and more able to focus on the good times I had on the baseball field.

First round of the 1995 MLB June Amateur Draft

Darin Erstad	OF	Univ of Nebraska	Angels	MLB
Ben Davis	C	Malvern Prep	Padres	MLB
Jose Cruz	OF	Rice Univ	Mariners	MLB
Kerry Wood	RHP	Grand Prairie HS	Cubs	MLB
Ariel Prieto	RHP	N/A	Athletics	MLB
Jaime Jones	OF	Rancho Bernardo HS	Marlins	AAA
Jonathan Johnson	RHP	Florida State Univ	Rangers	MLB
Todd Helton	1B	Univ of Tennessee	Rockies	MLB
Geoff Jenkins	OF	USC	Brewers	MLB
Chad Hermansen	SS	Green Valley HS	Pirates	MLB
Mike Drumright	RHP	Wichita State Univ	Tigers	AAA
Matt Morris	RHP	Seton Hall Univ	Cardinals	MLB
Mark Redman	LHP	Univ of Oklahoma	Twins	MLB
Reggie Taylor	OF	Newberry HS	Phillies	MLB
Andrew Yount	RHP	Kingwood HS	Red Sox	A+
Joe Fontenot	RHP	Acadiana HS	Giants	MLB
Roy Halladay	RHP	West HS	Blue Jays	MLB
Ryan Jaroncyk	SS	Orange Glen HS	Mets	A+
Juan Lebron	OF	Carmen Bozello Huyke	Royals	AAA
David Yocum	**LHP**	**Florida State Univ**	**Dodgers**	A+
Alvie Shepherd	RHP	Univ of Nebraska	Orioles	AA
Tony McKnight	RHP	Arkansas HS	Astros	MLB
David Miller	1B	Clemson Univ	Indians	AAA
Corey Jenkins	OF	Dreher HS	Red Sox	AA
Jeff Liefer	3B	Long Beach State Univ	White Sox	MLB
Chad Hutchinson*	RHP	Torrey Pines HS	Braves	MLB
Shea Morenz	OF	Univ of Texas	Yankees	AAA
Michael Barrett	SS	Pace Academy HS	Expos	MLB
Chris Haas	3B	St. Mary's HS	Cardinals	AAA
Dave Coggin	RHP	Upland HS	Phillies	MLB

*— did not sign

11

Bad Breaks

In 2008, the Washington Nationals epitomized futility, finishing with 102 losses and the worst record in the major leagues. But the Nationals' dismal performance that season had a significant upside; it landed them the first overall pick of the following year's draft. The history of the draft teaches us that no player, no matter how highly touted and drafted, is guaranteed future stardom. But Stephen Strasburg, the right-handed wunderkind out of San Diego State, carried the consensus label of being, by far, the best amateur player available in 2009. With deep pockets and the hope of a better future, the Nationals drafted Strasburg and handed him a record-setting $15.1 million contract.[1] Strasburg's signing brought a much-needed jolt of excitement to Beltway baseball fans who were watching the hometown team flounder in 2009. The Nationals lost a major-league-high 103 games, but as a result, they got to pick first in the draft again. This time, they took seventeen-year-old Bryce Harper, whose high school exploits had landed him on the cover of *Sports Illustrated* a year earlier. With Strasburg and Harper down on the farm, the Nationals were two steps closer to shedding their reputation as also-rans.

Strasburg lived up to the hype in his first minor league season. Splitting time between Double-A Harrisburg and Triple-A Syracuse in the spring of 2010, he registered a 7–2 record, a 1.30 ERA, and averaged more than a strikeout per inning. He had dominated the best the minor leagues had to offer, so the Nationals opted to promote him to the bigs in June 2010. In the nation's capital, he continued his mastery of opposing lineups. In his major league debut, he struck out fourteen batters in seven innings to earn a win against the Pittsburgh Pirates. The mid-week game drew more than 40,000 fans to Nationals Park, the stadium's largest crowd of the year since Opening Day.[2]

For the next month, every Strasburg start became a much-anticipated national media event, an unusual situation for a team well on its way to another last-place finish. But the party didn't last long. Prior to his tenth start, Strasburg complained of right shoulder pain, an ailment that sidelined him for the next three weeks.[3] Upon his return, Strasburg pitched less effectively, and his season came to a premature end when he tore a ligament in his pitching elbow. That injury required Tommy John surgery and kept him out of the majors for more than a year.[4] Upon returning to the Nationals in September 2011, he once again dazzled, but as he was coming off surgery, the Nationals exercised caution with him. He threw a season-high seventy-nine pitches in his final start of the season, a six-inning, one-hit outing against the Marlins. More importantly, the Nationals came within one game of .500 in 2011.

An almost uninterrupted string of dreary seasons between 2004 and 2010 gave the Nationals ample opportunity to benefit from the draft. Strasburg and Harper became the biggest prizes, but they were by no means the only selections to help put the team on a winning track. Washington's other first-round picks between 2005 and 2010 included third baseman Ryan Zimmerman (fourth overall pick in 2005), pitcher Ross Detwiler (sixth overall pick in 2007), and reliever Drew Storen (tenth overall pick in 2009). Washington also showed a knack for identifying talent in later rounds of the draft. Pitcher Jordan Zimmermann (second round in 2007) and second baseman Danny Espinosa (third round in 2008) also ascended quickly to the majors.

These draftees all played key roles in the Nationals' metamorphosis from also-ran to contender.

With Strasburg, Jordan Zimmermann, and Detwiler holding down three-fifths of the starting pitching rotation and Ryan Zimmerman keying a balanced offense, the Nationals went 98–64 in 2012, cruising to the National League East title.

But the team whose miserable past helped pave the way for a brighter present decided even better days lay ahead. In an attempt to protect the sizeable investment in 24-year-old Strasburg, Washington announced in early September 2012 that he would not pitch again for the rest of the season or the playoffs. The decision was controversial, if not totally surprising. Before spring training, Nationals general manager

Mike Rizzo told reporters the team would impose a 160-inning limit on Strasburg to guard against the possibility that the young star could overexert a right arm that had undergone elbow-ligament replacement surgery in 2010. "There's not going to be a whole lot of tinkering going on," Rizzo said. "We're going to run him out there until his innings are gone and then stop him from pitching."[5]

Of course, that proclamation came before the Nats established themselves as a World Series-caliber team.

But Rizzo remained true to his word. Strasburg exited the rotation with a 15–6 record, a 3.16 ERA, and 197 strikeouts in 159 and one-third innings pitched. Despite these impressive numbers, he wasn't the best pitcher on the team; that honor belonged to former A's first-round pick Gio Gonzalez, who won twenty-one games in 2012. No one disputed, however, that the Nationals' rotation was better with Strasburg than without him.

The decision to shelve a key player in the thick of a pennant race was met with disbelief by those who felt Rizzo was sabotaging his team's chances of winning a World Series. Strasburg's opposition to the decision only added fuel to their argument. "I don't know if I'm ever going to accept it," Strasburg said. "It's something I'm not happy about at all."[6] Rizzo still didn't budge. He viewed the Nationals' successful 2012 campaign as the beginning of a long period of prosperity. "We'll be back and doing this a couple more times," he said on the eve of the team's first postseason game.[7] Whether those words reflect arrogance or prudence remains to be seen.

Without the value of hindsight, some pundits weighed in with support of Rizzo. Jake Simpson of *The Atlantic* noted that the imposition in 2011 of a similar innings limit on Zimmermann, another veteran of Tommy John surgery, had paid off for the Nationals. Zimmermann came back in 2012 to throw nearly two hundred innings in helping Washington win a division crown. "Baseball history is littered with pitchers who flamed out at a young age because they either were overworked in their early 20s or rushed back from a career-threatening injury too early," Simpson wrote.[8]

What we will never know is if the Nationals would have advanced farther into the playoffs had Strasburg pitched in the National League

Division Series. As it stands, Washington lost a heartbreaking five-game affair to the Cardinals, a club whose postseason roster included nineteen players who were drafted or signed as amateurs by the St. Louis organization or came up through its system after being acquired as minor leaguers.[9] The Cardinals rallied for four runs in the top of the ninth inning of decisive Game Five to knock the Nationals out of the postseason. The starting pitching didn't fail the Nationals in that game; Storen, the team's closer, did, giving up all four runs in the ninth. But fairly or not, the absence of Strasburg in the series became widely viewed as an enormous and unprecedented flub. Even *The Nation*, the venerable purveyor of Beltway politics, weighed in on the controversy. "I have no problem with caring about his health," wrote Dave Zirin. "I do have a problem with the Nats tanking this season out of arrogance and the media whipping a new, unsteady, colt-like baseball fan base into going along with the ride."[10]

Would Strasburg's career have been put in jeopardy by pitching additional innings? That question falls into the realm of the unanswerable. For the purposes of this book, the debate over whether the Nationals used poor judgment in shutting down their young ace is secondary. However anyone may feel about the decision, it provides evidence that major league teams are serious about protecting their investments in young players.

Maybe Strasburg will pitch in a World Series someday. The second overall pick of the 2001 draft never did. And no discussion of Stephen Strasburg is complete without at least a mention of Mark Prior.

At twenty-two, Prior became a superstar. His 18–6 record for the Cubs during the 2003 season included 245 strikeouts in just 211 and one-third innings. As the ace of the Chicago rotation, he helped lead the team to the National League Championship Series. Throughout the season, Cubs manager Dusty Baker routinely allowed Prior to stay in games long after he exceeded the hundred-pitch mark. By 2005, Prior suffered from major elbow and shoulder problems. He hasn't pitched a game in the major leagues since 2006.

Rightly or wrongly, Baker is blamed for wrecking Prior's career and severely damaging Kerry Wood's career.[11] Lost in the collective memory of baseball fans is that Jim Riggleman, Baker's predecessor, was loudly booed whenever he removed Wood from a game in 1998.[12]

Then there are the hundreds of pitchers who can only wish they had been the subject of Strasburg-like debate or experienced a few seasons of Prior-like success. While it's difficult to quantify precisely how many highly drafted pitchers failed to make the major leagues due to arm or shoulder problems, our research shows that many of those who plateaued in the minors experienced a career-ending or -altering injury early in their professional careers. Some of these injuries were sudden and largely unavoidable, while others were likely the result of overexertion.

Of the nearly seven hundred players drafted in the first round between 1990 and 2006, 370 were pitchers. Through the 2012 season, about one-third of these pitchers were career minor leaguers. That group includes about three dozen pitchers who never made it past the Single-A level. Using those figures, we can conservatively estimate that at least ten percent of pitchers drafted in the first round experienced career-ending injuries in the minor leagues.

Chris Stowe, the thirty-seventh overall pick of the Montreal Expos in 1997, was the only pitcher between 1990 and 2006 selected in the opening round who signed with a major league organization but never made it past rookie ball. His story, though far less publicized than Strasburg's, is equally instructive for young phenoms and the teams that draft them.

More than twenty major league scouts showed up to watch the first start of Stowe's senior year at Chancellor High School in Fredricksburg, Virginia. The tall right-hander did not give up a hit until his third start that season and finished with an unblemished record for the second consecutive year.[13]

The Expos handed Stowe a $500,000 bonus[14] and assigned him to West Palm Beach of the Gulf Coast League. A 1997 profile in the *Washington Post* described an eighteen year-old country boy who was trying to overcome bouts of homesickness as he tried to make a name for himself in the minor leagues.[15]

In that article, Expos minor league pitching coordinator Jim Benedict heaped praise on Stowe: "In the Gulf Coast League, we're just trying to make sure he gets acclimated to pro ball, learns what it's like to be in an every-fifth-day rotation, throws on the side between starts, does the conditioning and learns how to be a professional. Making the jump from high school to pro ball is a big one for a lot of guys, and it hasn't been for him."[16]

In nine starts for West Palm Beach, Stowe posted a 2–1 record and 3.23 ERA, striking out thirty-six batters in thirty-nine innings.

In 1998, Stowe left Expos spring training after becoming embroiled in a dispute with team management over the condition of his arm. Stowe believed he was hurt and needed time off. The team felt he could pitch through the soreness.[17]

Stowe apparently was right. Though few people outside of his hometown noticed, he never pitched another inning of professional baseball.

Our research shows that Stowe's situation might have been handled differently if he had been drafted ten years later. A significantly higher percentage of pitchers drafted in the first round in the early to mid–2000s have reached the majors than their counterparts of the previous decade. During the 1990s, 59 percent of left-handed pitchers drafted in the first round reached the major leagues. For top-picked southpaws between 2000 and 2006, that percentage jumped to 76 percent. The percentage of right-handers ascending to the majors has remained stable, but it is likely to rise as draftees from the mid–2000s continue to gain promotions to the big leagues.

There are several possible reasons why more highly drafted pitchers are making the majors than before. The fact that nine of thirteen left-handers selected in the first round of the 2007 draft had ascended to the majors by the end of the 2013 season suggests, at least for lefties, it is more than just a fluke.

Could it be that organizations have simply become more eager to promote left-handed pitchers to the majors? This theory deserves attention, even if it falls short of providing an adequate answer. In an era of extreme bullpen specialization, in which relief pitchers sometimes enter a game to face just one batter, it is advantageous for teams to have at least a couple of left-handed arms on the roster. Zachary Levine of *Baseball Prospectus* notes the 2012 major league season "saw a new record with 697 left-handed relief appearances lasting exactly one batter, up from 584 such outings in 2000."[18] It is a widely held belief that left-handed pitchers are more effective against left-handed batters, just as right-handed pitchers fare better against right-handed batters. But while the percentage of batters taking swings from the left side of the plate has steadily increased over the past forty years, the percentage of left-handed pitchers on the mound for those plate appearances was lower in 2012 than it was in 1972, 1982, and 1992, according to Levine.[19]

A second theory: Baseball organizations deserve the credit for doing a better job of identifying pitching stars of the future and selecting them at the top of the draft. The early and mid–2000s provide fodder for this argument. Through the 2012 season, six left-handed pitchers taken in the first round between 2000 and 2006 have already become major league All-Stars, and many from that group are just hitting their stride, including Clayton Kershaw, who won the 2011 and 2013 National League Cy Young award. David Price, the first overall pick of the '07 draft, won the AL Cy Young in 2012. Meanwhile, only nine lefties drafted in the first round in the 1990s became All-Stars, and unless one of them makes a late-career All-Star debut, that number won't change. Similarly, thirteen right-handed pitchers who were opening round picks between 2000 and 2006 have become All-Stars. That is only three fewer than achieved this status in the entire 1990s.

Then there is a third theory, one that may best explain this phenomenon.

Major league teams are more aware than ever before of the need to protect the health of young pitchers, especially left-handers, who researchers say are more susceptible to injuries than their right-handed counterparts.

Relative to other sports like football, in which bone-jarring hits are an accepted part of the game, and basketball, in which collisions and awkward falls can sideline players for months and even end careers, baseball is considered a safe alternative. A football player with a bone protruding through his skin or a basketball player with a bloodied face evokes a more visceral reaction from fans and stakeholders. In baseball, many injuries are of the beneath-the-surface variety, usually involving muscle pulls and strains.

11. Bad Breaks

Baseball safety issues tend only to become a major topic of conversation when the effects of an injury are clearly visible, as in 2012 when Brandon McCarthy of the Oakland A's and Doug Fister of the Detroit Tigers were hit in the head with batted balls. The images of line drives ricocheting off heads prompted calls for all pitchers to wear caps with protective linings. Similarly, a season-ending injury to San Francisco Giants catcher Buster Posey in 2011 led to baseball's vow to end violent confrontations at home plate between base runners and catchers.

The sight of a pitcher knocked unconscious by a line drive or an All-Star catcher writhing on the ground with a broken leg provide easy entry points for debate about increased safety measures.

Protecting a pitcher's long-term health by monitoring the number and type of pitches he throws and providing him with adequate rest are preventive measures. To most fans, these precautions are "inside baseball" and, over the years, have been less likely to inflame passions in the public arena.

Then Strasburg came along, and that all changed.

In a debate that pitted those who felt the Nationals exercised sound judgment in shutting down Strasburg against those who felt the team frittered away its chances at a championship based on junk science, Rany Jazayerli of *Grantland*, writing prior to the Nationals' playoff loss, framed the discussion in a different way.

"But there is middle ground, which comes from the understanding that the only sure way to eliminate injuries in baseball is to eliminate baseball," Jazayerli wrote. "There is some baseline risk of injury that exists every time a player takes the field. That risk is elevated for pitchers, whose value derives solely from the kinetic chain that is centered in the shoulder and elbow of their pitching arm."[20]

Jazayerli notes that pitch counts weren't an official Major League Baseball statistic until 1988, which left hurlers in the pre-pitch-count era at risk of injuries associated with overuse. "The Nationals are making Strasburg pay for sins inflicted on pitchers from a different generation," he argues.[21]

To clinch his point, Jazayerli cites the folly of the Nationals' placing a strict limit on the young Washington star's innings and not his number of pitches.[22]

The Strasburg situation generated so much buzz because it was historic. Never before had a team competing for a championship opted to bench an ace pitcher for precautionary reasons.

The decision raised the hackles of critics who felt the Nationals were coddling Strasburg. But the factors that led to the decision were decades in the making. From the adoption of the five-man pitching rotation to the popularization of the pitch count stat, baseball is no longer the game it was when Nolan Ryan threw 235 pitches for the California Angels in a fifteen-inning win over the Boston Red Sox. That happened in 1974, the same year Dr. Frank Jobe, the Dodgers' team physician, performed ligament-transplant surgery on Tommy John.

Former major league pitcher Orel Hershiser, who underwent shoulder surgery in 1990 after pitching an average of 250 innings in three consecutive seasons, considers himself lucky.[23] He won ninety-nine games before surgery, and 104 after making it back. It is the baseball fate that befell his brother Gordie that moved Orel to lobby as a broadcaster for the protection of young arms. Gordie Hershiser reached the Double-A level in the Dodgers organization in the late 1980s, but according to Orel, Gordie was never the same pitcher again after blowing out his elbow at the University of Alabama. Orel blamed his brother's injury on overexertion.[24] "I'm going to get on the soapbox this year, and you're going to hear it," Orel told the *Chicago Tribune* in a 2006 interview. "It's going to be about pitch counts and protecting pitchers' arms—from Little League through college."[25]

Well-placed and respected advocates like Orel Hershiser can help a cause, but it is telling that he omitted minor and major league pitchers from the group of arms that need protecting. It was an implicit concession that in the big-money world of professional baseball, only managers and general managers have authority to decide how much is too much for a pitcher. But the pre–Strasburg era provides evidence that big league executives had already come around to Hershiser's way of thinking.

In the 2000s, many organizations adopted staggered pitch limits for pitchers as they climbed each rung of the minor league ladder.[26] At the major league level, the days of Nolan Ryan-like pitch counts seemed like a distant memory by the turn of the millennium. In 1998, major league hurlers exceeded 120 pitches in a game 475 times; by 2003, that number had dropped to 228.[27]

An increased awareness and understanding of the delicate nature of elbow and shoulder ligaments has trickled down to the lowest levels of the game. In 2007, Little League Baseball modified its rules for pitcher eligibility by creating mandatory pitch-limit rules for young hurlers. Dr. James R. Andrews and Dr. Glenn S. Fleisig, heads of the American Sports Medicine Institute, were vocal proponents of Little League pitch counts. In a written introduction to a Little League handbook that explained their point of view, Andrews and Fleisig offered evidence of a growing problem among young pitchers. From 1995 to 1999, twenty-one of the 190 Tommy John surgeries performed at the institute involved youth pitchers. In the first five years of the 2000s, however, 124 of the 627 procedures were performed on pitchers of high school age or younger.[28]

Behind those numbers are real young men.

In December 2007, Hayden Hurst was a fourteen-year-old in Jacksonville, Florida, hoping to make the high school varsity baseball team as an eighth-grader.

"I was throwing and felt a pop in my elbow but didn't think much of it," Hurst said.[29] "At the time, I was throwing in the mid–80s. I told my dad it hurt it a little, but it wasn't so bad that I couldn't throw."

A month after first feeling discomfort in his throwing elbow, Hurst made varsity at Bolles High School, whose alumni included Chipper Jones, the first overall pick in the 1990 draft, and whose baseball coach, Storm Davis, had pitched in the major leagues for thirteen seasons. Hurst tried to block out the pain, but it only got worse. Jerry Hurst mentioned his son's problem to longtime University of North Florida baseball coach Dusty Rhodes, who had helped groom more than thirty players taken in the draft.

"With his potential, don't mess around," Rhodes told Hurst's father. "You need to take him to Dr. [James] Andrews." Rhodes handed him a piece of paper with what turned out to be Andrews' cell phone number.

The elder Hurst put in a call to Andrews, who recommended that his son stop pitching in games and concentrate for the next eight weeks on rehabilitating his elbow.

"If things don't improve, call me back," Andrews instructed.

Hayden Hurst spent the next couple months trying to strengthen his elbow. By the end of April, he was back on the mound pitching his team to victory over crosstown rival Englewood High School. But his elbow was still bothering him. He didn't need to share that news with his father; Jerry Hurst could tell his son wasn't throwing with the same velocity he had before. He was back on the phone with Andrews the next morning.

In May 2008, father and son drove to Birmingham, Alabama, to meet with Andrews. When the doctor set eyes on Hayden, who was 6'3" and 200 pounds at the time, he exclaimed, "When you told me he was fourteen, I wasn't expecting you were going to bring me a big ol' boy like this!"

A first magnetic resonance imaging exam on Hayden's elbow was inconclusive, but a second test gave Andrews a better idea of what was wrong. Unlike many young pitchers who tear elbow ligaments because they throw a lot of curveballs, Hayden, a fastball pitcher, suffered his tear because of his size and arm strength. Simply put, his ligament couldn't keep up with the rest of his arm.

That same day, Hayden went in for Tommy John surgery. After the procedure, he started a year-long rehabilitation process. By April 2009, his freshman year of high school, he was ready to pitch again. His coach eased him back into the rotation, gradually elevating his pitch count over the course of three starts, in which he pitched a total of four innings.[30] In his fourth start, the district championship game against Fernandina Beach, Hurst set down the first fifteen batters and took a no-hitter into the seventh and final inning of a game Bolles won 4–0.[31]

For the rest of his high school career, Hurst avoided further arm problems and, in 2009, earned a spot on the under-sixteen national team.[32] By his senior year, he was garnering interest from major league scouts. In 2012, the Pittsburgh Pirates selected him in the seventeenth round of the draft and gave him an unusually high $400,000 signing bonus.[33]

Hurst suffered a serious pitching-related injury before even starting high school. It remains to be seen how Hurst's arm will hold up long-term. A dead arm, MRSA infection and caution on the part of the Pirates organization combined to limit him to just a single professional appearance through 2013.

For decades, baseball organizations treated players like commodities. The vestiges of that can still be heard every time a player is referred to as the "product" of this or that university. The ability of players to move freely between teams represented a seismic shift. Only recently has Major League Baseball adopted more progressive policies regarding playing with injury, physical or emotional. Major leaguers can now avail themselves of mental health and bereavement leaves; Joey Votto, Aubrey Huff, and Zack Greinke were among the first major leaguers to publicly acknowledge that they battled psychological ailments. And the seven-day disabled list exists to help protect players suffering from concussions.

In this context, the Nationals' decision to sit Strasburg for the final weeks of the 2012 season and the postseason is less shocking. It remains to be seen whether greater protections of players' health continued to translate into a rise in the percentage of highly drafted pitchers who make the majors.

12

The Boras Effect

Perhaps the most enduring criticism of the fairness of a draft in any professional sport is that it artificially imposes a value on incoming talent, instead of allowing the market to dictate what a prospect is worth. If players had the chance to negotiate with every team in the league, instead of just one, a true price would emerge, as the theory goes. One year in baseball, thanks to Scott Boras, that's more or less what happened.

At the heart of the matter was an outdated definition of what professional baseball is. In the 1930s, Major League Baseball clubs began widespread formal adoption of minor league outfits as farm teams, bringing just about every professional baseball league into some sort of cooperative agreement, save for notable exceptions like the "outlaw" Carolina Baseball League of 1936–38. When the modern draft was established in 1965, major league executives reserved eligibility for amateurs, whom they defined as players who hadn't signed a professional contract.[1] At the time, professional baseball was tantamount to major league baseball teams and their affiliates. Even as independent leagues might try to compete with the baseball establishment, the mid–1960s was hardly the time for it. Minor league attendance was on its way down from nearly forty million fans in 1949 to a low of 6.9 million in 1967.[2] There wasn't a demand to support competition. That had changed by the early 1990s, when a pair of independent leagues formed to try to capitalize on revitalized attendance and renewed interest in the minor league game, and several other new non-affiliated circuits followed. The Frontier League and, more directly, the Northern League, soon had an effect on the game that no one in the baseball establishment saw coming.

Boras, always looking for an advantage, seized upon the trend years before baseball would catch up. The Mariners took Boras client Jason Varitek with the fourteenth overall pick in 1994 and stuck to their offer of $400,000.[3] Normally, if the Mariners were committed to that figure, the only recourse for the player would be to re-enter the draft the next year, and likely be taken with a later pick and receive an offer for even less money. Boras was not so easily boxed in. He convinced Varitek to sign with the St. Paul Saints of the Northern League, and asserted that he was no longer subject to the draft, since he had become a professional.[4] That meant that rather than go into the 1995 draft, Varitek would become a free agent a week before the draft took place. Recognizing that new-found leverage, the Mariners increased their offer to $650,000, enough to satisfy Boras and Varitek, and avert the cataclysm that would occur later with another Boras client in a similar situation.[5]

Just the threat of impending free agency had prompted a team to increase its offer by nearly two-thirds. Boras had exploited the game's failure to vigilantly keep up with its own rules, and, in continuing to understand the bylaws better than most, he continued to find loopholes.

Teams had months to sign their draft picks, but only fifteen days to submit their first offers. No one paid much attention to this rule, but Boras knew it, and in 1996, he used it to have Bobby Seay, the twelfth overall pick that year, declared a free agent when the White Sox failed to offer him a contract before the deadline.[6] Three of the top ten picks that year followed the same path. Matt White never made the majors, but he signed with the Devil Rays organization for $10.2 million, approximately six times what he could have otherwise expected when the Giants took him with the seventh pick.[7] The Twins selected Travis Lee with the second pick, and he wound up getting $10 million from the Diamondbacks, an amount four or five times greater than the bonus number one pick Kris Benson drew from the Pirates.[8] While Tampa Bay and Arizona, talent-needy expansion franchises that were still two years away from fielding major league teams, signed all four of the free agents and perhaps inflated their value, the stunning discrepancy between what the liberated draftees signed for and what they might have otherwise received made it clear a Pandora's box had been ripped wide open.

Baseball amended the rules that had deposited those draftees on the open market, but curiously left its definition of a professional unchanged in spite of the proliferation of independent leagues.[9] That allowed Boras, armed with the precedent of the Varitek saga and the player valuations set in 1996, to strike arguably his most notorious blow against the draft.

J.D. Drew was a sensational college player, drawing consideration from scouts as the best outfielder ever to play at that level.[10] He entered the draft having just completed a junior season of thirty-one home runs and thirty-two stolen bases for Florida State, making him the first thirty-thirty man in NCAA Division I history.[11] There was little doubt he would make it to the majors and become an All-Star, and he did, even if he never became the transcendent, Hall-of-Fame caliber player his college career suggested.

The Tigers, picking first, passed him over for Matt Anderson, a pitcher who finished an undistinguished seven-year major league career in 2005 with an ERA of 5.19 and a negative WAR. Detroit's front office wanted no part of the price tag that Boras, Drew's agent, had set for him, rumored at the time to be between ten and twelve million dollars.[12] The demand wound up being eleven million, a figure Boras claimed Giants officials told him they'd be willing to give Drew if he were still available when they picked fourth overall.[13] The team denied the conversation took place.[14] There were also rumors that Boras would use Drew as a test case in an attempt to have courts declare the draft illegal.[15] Instead of reaching into that bee's nest, the Tigers sat back and signed Anderson for $2.5 million.[16]

Phillies general manager Lee Thomas was wary of drafting another Boras client after tense negotiations with client Carlton Loewer in 1994.[17] The Phillies, who had the second pick, wanted to make an initial offer to Drew of between $2.5 million and $3 million, commensurate with what the Tigers and Anderson agreed to, but it was clear as the draft began that such a lowball bid would not bring Drew aboard.[18]

Still, the Phillies took the plunge, hoping to grab the big fish. Instead, they came up with nothing.

They went into the process figuring it would take nearly a year to sign Drew, but they didn't think he needed much minor league seasoning and thought he'd be in Philadelphia before long.[19] So, they dug in for a protracted fight. Since they thought of him as almost major-league ready, they might have met Boras' demands by giving him a major league contract, as other teams had done with top draft picks. That would have allowed them to spread the money out over time, instead of delivering it all at once with a bonus. But with the Diamondbacks and Devil Rays set to join the majors in 1998, there was an expansion draft set to take place later in 1997. Giving Drew a major league contract would have forced the Phillies to protect Drew or risk losing him to one of the new teams, and since they could only protect a limited number of players, that would have forced them to leave another major leaguer exposed. Thus, the Phillies were reluctant to pursue that option, making them victims of poor timing.[20]

Boras also appeared to engage in a bizarre game of hide-and-seek in an effort to ensnare the Phillies in the same non-tender scenario that led to free agency for the handsomely rewarded group of 1996 draftees. The Phillies sent their offer to Drew's family home in Georgia using the address provided when Drew became eligible for the draft, but Boras said that Drew no longer lived there.[21] The Phillies tried unsuccessfully to find and deliver to addresses listed for Drew in Florida.[22] At one point, someone who identified himself as "Mr. Niles," believed to be Florida State assistant coach Jack Niles, refused to sign for the package containing the team's offer.[23] The Phillies wound up sending Drew a fax, but Boras claimed that a faxed offer did not constitute a formal contract. Therefore, Boras contended, the Phillies had failed to give Drew his required tender within fifteen days after the draft, making him a free agent.[24] Ultimately, an arbitrator ruled against Boras, concluding that the Phillies made reasonable attempts to meet the deadline, and if Drew was not living at the last address he gave to Major League Baseball, that was negligence on his part, not the team's.[25]

Those were just the initial salvos in a yearlong fight. Drew still had a season of college eligibility remaining, so he could have returned to Florida State. Doing so would have ended negotiations with the Phillies and put him back in the draft in 1998, likely with another round of tense negotiations looming. Drew could do little to improve upon his college résumé, and if he failed to once more achieve the unprecedented standard he had set, or suffered an injury, his draft stock might slip. That would make it harder, if not impossible, for Boras to secure an eight-figure bonus for his client. So Boras did with Drew just what he had done with Varitek and convinced him to sign with the Northern League's St. Paul Saints.[26] It meant he forfeited his college eligibility, but his contract with the Saints allowed Drew to sign with the Phillies at any point if he and Boras had a breakthrough in negotiations, unlike Florida State, where he would have been stuck until the next year.[27]

Much more significantly, signing with the Northern League also gave Boras the hammer of Drew's impending free agency a week before the 1998 draft, which was a much greater negotiating tool than the mere threat of going back into the draft if the Phillies failed to sign him. Boras had used this to his advantage with Varitek, and he intended to do it again with Drew.

The rules that nearly put Varitek on the open market still remained unchanged. Suddenly, in the middle of Drew's negotiations with the Phillies, baseball decided to "clarify" its rule on draft eligibility and make independent leaguers subject to the draft.[28] Instead of the "Amateur Draft," the event would now be formally called the "First-Year Player Draft," a moniker that persists today.[29] Naturally, this sort of heavy-handed tactic didn't meet well with Boras, but he had little recourse other than to sue baseball, putting Drew's career on indefinite hold while trying to buck the precedent that had established the legality of pro sports drafts.[30] Boras didn't file suit, but the players' union instead decided to take up Drew's case through a grievance that would be heard by arbitrator Dana Eischen.[31] The pairing of Drew and the union was a strange marriage, considering his protracted holdout sparked ire from several Phillies veterans who expressed their feelings during Spring Training in 1998.[32] Indeed, baseball contended Eischen had no jurisdiction over the matter because Drew was not a member of the union, which restricted its membership to players on a team's forty-man roster.[33] The union built its case on the idea that baseball failed to give sufficient notice about its midstream policy change.[34] Eischen, in his last ruling before stepping down,[35] essentially punted on the issue. In May, with a week to go before the Phillies' negotiating window with Drew ended one way or another, Eischen overturned baseball's changes to draft eligibility, but referred Drew's case to the executive council, a group of owners chaired by the commissioner.[36] That body clearly would not rule in

Drew's favor. The Phillies, finally armed with the knowledge that Drew would not become a free agent, had a short window to bring Drew aboard before he would go back into the draft. As fate would have it, the Phillies had the first pick in 1998, but by rule could not have used it on Drew without his consent, which neither he nor Boras were about to give.[37]

Perhaps complicating negotiations was upheaval at the top of the Phillies organization. Owner Bill Giles handed over day-to-day management of the club to David Montgomery shortly after the draft in 1997.[38] In December, Montgomery replaced Thomas as general manager with Ed Wade, who had served as Thomas' assistant.[39] Wade's promotion didn't appear to change the tenor of the standoff between the club and Boras, perhaps because the Phillies hired from within, but fans may wonder what Thomas would have done in the face of a deadline and with the team's sudden leverage. Wade didn't publicly divulge his final offer, but Boras said it was a five-year deal that would have been worth a minimum of $5.3 million, including a $2.6 million signing bonus.[40] Boras would go as low as a $5 million bonus, but never went below a $7 million guarantee for the entire package.[41] The specter of an incoming No. 1 overall pick, and with it another sizable payout, seemed to have affected the Phillies' offer. Boras believed the team didn't want to set the bar too high for whomever it would take in the 1998 draft, and Wade didn't deny that was the case, as Jim Salisbury of the *Philadelphia Inquirer* documented at the time.

"We couldn't view J.D. in a vacuum," Wade said. "We had to look at a lot of circumstances. This draft was one of them. We have a finite amount of money and if we want to build and go forward we can't focus on just one guy. You have to consider what impact it will have on all areas, including being able to retain the talent you already have in your clubhouse." [42]

The deadline to close a deal with Drew came and went, and the Phillies lost the rights to the college phenom they'd taken second overall in 1997.

"I still believe we did the right thing," Phillies scouting director Mike Arbuckle told Salisbury shortly after the deadline. "We've gone beyond the realm of what any draft pick has ever received. If we gave this guy a run-of-the-mill offer, I'd say we didn't give this our best shot. But we have no regrets."[43]

As compensation, the team received the forty-second pick in the 1998 draft, and used it to select UCLA outfielder Eric Valent. He batted .234 with thirteen homers in 450 major league plate appearances, with a career WAR of negative one, but the Phillies fared much better with their first overall pick that year. Tempting fate with another college standout from the state of Florida, they took Pat Burrell from the University of Miami, a client not of Boras but of Jeff Moorad. They inked him in July to a major league contract with a signing bonus of $3.15 million, and by 2000 he was in Philadelphia's everyday lineup as a first baseman.[44] He switched positions that August with, as fate would have it, noted Boras client Travis Lee, and Burrell held the Phillies left field job through the Phillies' 2008 World Series championship season.

The Cardinals drafted Drew fifth in 1998 and signed him a month later to a deal that was worth nearly $9 million.[45] He was a September call-up that year and became a major league regular in 1999, making the early impact the Phillies once imagined he would have in their uniform. Late in his first full season with St. Louis, the team traveled to Philadelphia for Drew's initial brush with Philadelphia's notoriously antipathetic fans. His debut in Veterans Stadium was delayed for nearly ten minutes when fans began hurling batteries and other objects at him as he attempted to man his position in center field.[46] Only the threat of a forfeit seemed to halt the abuse. Years later, more than a decade after the saga began, and long after it was clear Drew would fall short of the promise he showed in college, Philadelphia still hadn't forgiven him, booing him each time he stepped up to the plate as a visitor.[47] Even J.D.'s brother Stephen, a shortstop who made his major league debut in 2006, was not spared the wrath of Phillies fans.[48]

The failure to strike a deal with Drew clearly had a lasting impact in Philadelphia, even though the Phillies enjoyed some of their most successful seasons while Drew pursued his major league career elsewhere. Eischen's ruling effectively put a stop to other players and agents who might have attempted to follow Drew's circuitous path to their desired bonus figures, but more than a decade later, Boras appeared ready to mount a similar challenge to the draft rules and baseball's interpretation thereof. In 2009, he privately dropped hints that he might use the Japanese league, rather than a domestic independent league, as a way around the draft for Stephen Strasburg.[49] Since the draft applies to residents of the United States and Canada only, Boras considered sending Strasburg to Japan, where he could establish residency as he developed in one of the world's premier professional circuits outside of Major League Baseball.[50] The superagent had briefly looked at stashing Drew in Costa Rica to pursue the same loophole. Japanese baseball seemed unlikely to play along with Boras' idea for Strasburg,[51] while Major League Baseball assured the Nationals that Strasburg wouldn't have the leverage of free agency if he went to Japan, and would have to re-enter the draft before he could pursue his career domestically if he didn't sign with Washington.[52] That was apparently enough for Boras to abandon his idea. Strasburg signed a major league contract with the Nationals worth more than $15 million, including a bonus of $7.5 million, far below his astonishing $50 million asking price.[53] Still, the idea had some legs, and Jim Callis, then of *Baseball America*, responded to a reader question in 2012 by acknowledging that going to Japan was an option for Boras client Mark Appel, who slid from a projected number-one overall pick to number eight that year as teams feared his bonus demands.[54]

More than fifteen years after Boras and Drew struck at the heart of the draft, the effects of their donnybrook with baseball's powers that be still ripple through the game. The most enduring outcome of Drew's drawn-out introduction to professional baseball is what it did to affirm the power of the agent, and Boras in particular. Baseball has seemingly always been on the run, at one speed or another, in its fight to control how talent enters the game, and no one gives more dogged pursuit than Boras.

13

Psychology of the Draft

Draft prospects are touted for golden arms, disciplined eyes, and legs that can turn singles into doubles. Yet it's the brain that might be the most important part of the body for a professional baseball player.

"You have your five tools, but I think the mental part is the sixth tool," says Dave Tollett, coach of the Florida Gulf Coast University baseball team.[1]

Tollett has mentored four major leaguers, including White Sox pitcher Chris Sale, who made the majors just months after being taken in the first round of the 2010 draft. The coach believes his peers spend too much time on physical development and not enough on the mind.

"So many people, when you ask them, 'How important is the mental side of baseball?' the lowest number you're ever going to get is 80 percent," he said. "And if it's 80 percent, then why don't we work on it more than we do?"

The math may have been different for Yogi Berra, who famously said, "Ninety percent of the game is half mental."[2] However you add it up, many people involved with the game believe the right frame of mind is a hidden weapon of sorts that helps distinguish successful players.

"There are a lot of kids who are physically gifted enough to play pro baseball," said Tim McIlvaine, a Brewers scout.[3] "What separates a lot of them is the mental side of it, being able to be mentally ready for that, and realizing that if you strike out, it's OK. You're going to be in there."

The lengthy professional season, usually 140 or more games at the minor league level, is usually full of peaks and valleys. One of the first challenges many newly drafted prospects face is learning how to deal with failure at a game that's always come easy for them.

"The kid who throws ninety-three [miles per hour] in a town with 2,000 people in it, he's going to strike a lot of people out," McIlvaine said. "But you go out and all of a sudden people are turning that around, and you go, 'Wow, what's going on? I'm getting hit.'"

The same is true for a hitter facing a higher caliber of pitchers than he's ever seen before. Johnny Rodriguez, a minor league manager for the Cardinals, has seen plenty of batters experience their first taste of adversity.

"Pitchers are better, they command the ball better, all their secondary pitches and fastballs. They've got sinkers. They've got cutters, and they expose your weaknesses," he said.[4] "How do you handle all the failure, mentally? Now you've got to be mentally tough, not only to perform in that moment of pressure, but now you've got to adjust."

Scouts can assess the ability of a hitter to react to a fastball or the speed of a base runner's reaction to a pickoff move. What's harder to measure is the ability to handle a tough break. Nonetheless, that's something McIlvaine attempts to do as he evaluates draft prospects and gets to know them away from the field.

"I met with a kid once, and I told him the best outing I've ever seen is the day he gave up five runs in two innings, and he looked at me like I was crazy," McIlvaine said. "And I said, 'Do you want to know why?' and he goes, 'Yeah, of course!' And I said, 'Because you didn't give up. You kept firing away, you kept at it, you didn't get down, you didn't drop your head and just pout about it, you kept going. That showed me a lot.' So, watching kids, how they react to the failure is just as important as figuring out how fast they are."

Many teams have players go through a battery of tests, including psychological assessments, but the key to understanding what goes on between a prospect's ears is spending time with him, McIlvaine said. Royals scout Alex Mesa draws a distinction between a player's mental ability and his personality as he sizes up potential draftees.

"The mental ability has probably more to do with their ability to make adjustments, and stuff like that," he said.[5] "The personality side of it has a lot more to do with getting to know the guy, and whether it's a personality that you think will succeed or not."

The scouts of today aren't the first to try to understand what makes players tick. Perhaps the earliest example of the use of psychology in baseball was a Columbia University study of Babe Ruth in 1920. The legendary Yankees slugger was brought to a laboratory so that researchers could measure his reaction time, attention span, memory, learning and coordination in the hopes of determining the psychological and physiological attributes that set Ruth apart from his peers.[6] In 1938, the Cubs hired Coleman Griffith, later hailed as America's first sports psychologist, as a consultant.[7] He produced a series of psychological reports for the team over the next three seasons, but met with a lack of cooperation from managers Charlie Grimm and Gabby Hartnett, and the project was widely regarded as a failure.[8] The St. Louis Browns hired psychologist David F. Tracy in 1950 in part because they believed the use of psychology to improve performance in other industries might translate to baseball.[9] Tracy's use of hypnosis garnered attention and led to more widespread use of the practice throughout sports in the 1950s and '60s,[10] but that was decades before major league teams applied psychology on any regular basis.

In the 1980s, the Yankees had a future All-Star pitcher on their hands who could have used someone to help him move beyond a few moments of trepidation early in his career. After a promising rookie year, he struggled in 1987, and the team traded him in the middle of the season as part of a package for a more experienced pitcher, Steve Trout, who never won a game in a Yankee uniform. It would take a few more years of struggle, but Bob Tewksbury finally broke through with the Cardinals in 1992, when he made the All-Star team, finished third in National League Cy Young Award voting, and posted a 2.16 ERA. It was the first of back-to-back years in which he led the majors in strikeout-to-walk ratio, but prior to that he had a sub-.500 record in parts of six major league seasons, having struck out fewer than twice as many batters as he walked. Perhaps it wouldn't have taken him until the age of thirty-one to have a breakout season if the Yankees had given him the access to psychological resources he now wishes he had.

"I had an elbow surgery when I was in the minor leagues, and it would have been nice to have someone to talk to through the rehab process,"[11] he said. "If someone was around, I would have picked his brain about how to be better, and I think had I done that, had I had it earlier, I would have been able to deal with some stuff that happened at the major league level a little quicker."

Tewksbury's first taste of the big leagues came in 1986, and it was no subtle entrance to The Show. Yankees owner George Steinbrenner was in the midst of eighteen managerial changes in seventeen years, though somehow Tewksbury played for just one manager, Lou Piniella, during his time in the Bronx. The right-hander had a strong rookie season spent mostly as a part of the starting rotation, and posted a 3.31 ERA with a 9–5 record. The next season, his ERA more than doubled, to 6.75, by the time of the trade.

Tewksbury had begun to worry about matters that were out of his control. He started to wonder what Piniella thought of him and tried to dissect general manager Woody Woodward's roster moves, fearing a return to the minors.

"It's one thing to be a successful minor leaguer, and you know that you can go there and you have the respect of your organization and your peers, and if you have a bad game, you have a bad game, but if you're a young pitcher in New York, and you go to New York and you have a bad game or two, the first thing you're thinking about is, you're going to get sent back down again," Tewksbury said. "So, those types of things really were overwhelming for me, and I would have definitely benefited from conversation."

Instead, Tewksbury didn't want to express the way he felt and risk showing weakness, long perceived as a cardinal sin in the world of professional sports. The memory of this inhibition stuck with him as he grew more mature personally and professionally, and it inspired the career move that followed his playing days.[12]

Perhaps no one has as much personal insight on the marriage of psychology and baseball as Tewksbury. After pitching in the majors for thirteen seasons, Tewksbury earned a master's degree in sport psychology and counseling from Boston University. Since 2004, he's been putting that degree to use with the Red Sox, for whom he works as a mental skills coach. His experience in the game allows him to connect with players in a way other counselors can't.

"I've had two surgeries, I got demoted seven times, I got traded, I got released, I made an All-Star team. I got knocked out of a game in the first inning. I've had situations that allow me to tell my own stories," Tewksbury said. "I've ridden the buses in the Southern League and I've been on the early morning flights in the International League. I've pitched in front of 50,000 people and dealt with media in big cities. I've done all that.

"So if someone comes to me with a situation, there's usually a story that I can pull out that says, 'You know what, I've been there before, and this is what happened to me, and this is how you should deal with it.' And then we talk about the strategies to kind of put that in place to try to deal with it in a better way."

Tewksbury said he "kind of lucked into" his position, when, after his playing career, he was doing some general consulting work for the Red Sox. Another consultant working for the team in sports psychology suggested Tewksbury do the same. The former pitcher was intrigued, but waited two years to go back to school and finish up the counseling degree he had begun to work toward years before. It only took Tewksbury a year to complete the degree, and the Red Sox hired him for his current position right after that.

Along the way, he was influenced by Ken Ravizza, a professor of applied sport psychology at Cal State Fullerton; Karl Kuehl, a coach, executive and player development specialist who briefly managed the Expos; and especially the renowned sports psychologist Harvey Dorfman.

"He was a great mentor and friend," Tewksbury said of Dorfman, who passed away in 2011. "I saw him on occasion, talked to him often. He was a colleague who was able to review cases of players whom he talked with and mentored me with regard to situations I was going through, and just reading his book, he did a lot of teaching just through his writing."

Together, Dorfman and Kuehl wrote *The Mental Game of Baseball: A Guide to Peak Performance*, a cornerstone book first published in 1989 and last revised in 2002, years that coincided with a rise in the awareness of cognitive factors in the sport. In 1983,[13] the A's hired Kuehl as director of player development, and he persuaded the team to bring Dorfman aboard as a special instructor the next year.[14] With Kuehl and Dorfman in tow, the A's won three straight pennants from 1988 through 1990, sweeping the Giants to win the World Series in 1989. Dorfman later moved on to the Marlins, helping them to the 1997 World Series title, and worked under superagent Scott Boras.[15] Dorfman's list of clients was star-studded, including names like Alex Rodriguez, Roy Halladay and Greg Maddux.[16]

With the success of Dorfman and Kuehl came more widespread use of psychology in baseball. Charles Maher, a sports psychologist who worked for the Indians, estimated that the number of major league teams that worked with a psychologist rose from 20 percent of all clubs to 70 percent over a four-year period in the late 1990s.[17]

Dorfman defied the stereotype of touchy-feely sensitivity that might have made some in the sport reluctant to embrace psychology. He pushed his clients to regard the brain as a muscle to develop and train just like any other part of the body. Right-handed pitcher Mike Pelfrey, the ninth pick of the first round in 2005 by the Mets, spoke to *Newsday*'s David Lennon around the time of Dorfman's death and recalled how the psychologist drilled him to concentrate more keenly on the mound.

"You were focused?" Dorfman asked Pelfrey, after the pitcher remarked how he had been particularly zeroed in for his last start. "Then what did the catcher's glove look like? What kind of glove does he have?"[18]

Pelfrey replied that he didn't know.

"Then you weren't — paying attention!" Dorfman snapped. "You're just feeding me full of BS right now."[19]

Dorfman prodded the players he counseled to set challenging yet reasonable goals for themselves, and value their own benchmarks over those set by others. That advice held for accomplished major leaguers as well as prospects trying to find their way in the game.

"Whether greater or less, whether real or imagined, the expectations a player senses his organization has for him compounds the pressure he puts on himself in his desire to prove he has what it takes to be a big leaguer," he wrote, along with Kuehl, in *The Mental Game of Baseball.*[20]

Tewksbury, with whom the Red Sox have enjoyed plenty of onfield success, believes one of the advantages an organization can reap by establishing a focus on mental health with its prospects is that those players will understand the benefits and continue to use those resources as major leaguers.

"You may not talk to a guy for a year, but if something comes up and you have to be reactive to it, you have a relationship and a trust built that allows that communication to happen," Tewksbury said.

The process begins as newly drafted and signed players adjust to becoming professionals for the first time, facing a new and more difficult level of competition.

"You have to be comfortable with being uncomfortable, and that's hard to do," Tewksbury told MLB.com in 2009.[21] "But it's necessary. You try to teach that early. The sooner they can learn with that, [the more] they increase their chances for success and getting to the next level — and hopefully to the big leagues."

Cody Stanley certainly knows what it's like to encounter an uncomfortable situation. The fourth-round pick of the Cardinals in 2010 was suspended for 50 games at the start of the 2012 season after testing positive for Methylhexaneamine and Tamoxifen, banned substances under the minor league drug program.[22] Stanley said his lack of thorough research into a nutritional supplement he took was the reason the test came up positive, adding that he was "completely blindsided" by the results.[23] In any case, the catcher got a late start to his third professional season, playing his first game for High-A Palm Beach of the Florida State League on May 30. Less than two weeks later, he was knocked out of action again, this time when he tried to block a curveball that bounced off the dirt and dislocated the middle finger on his right hand.[24] He missed more than a month, and after a short rehab stint in rookie ball, he returned to Palm Beach on July 15 for the final month and a half of the season. There were plenty of reasons for Stanley to feel unsettled, but he nonetheless regained his footing. Stanley returned to a level of production similar to his performance at Class A in 2011, and earned an invitation to the prestigious six-team Arizona Fall League at the end of the season. He credits mental toughness for his perseverance.

"You've just got to know that you can do it. You know that you have done it before, and you can do it in the future," he said. "Nothing changes. Just keep the same mental stability that you had before the suspension, and everything pans out. You've got to stay grounded."

He also points to his support structure.

"All these guys and the coaches and my family, they help me realize that things could be worse. And they could," he said. "So when you think about that, it's not that hard to deal with a suspension."

While at rookie ball in 2010, Stanley worked on the mental part of the game with Mike Matheny, who was promoted two years later to manager of the big club in St. Louis after having served as a roving instructor for the organization. Stanley also takes a cue from Palm Beach manager Johnny Rodriguez, with whom Stanley was paired for all or part of the first four seasons of his pro career.

"He knows me now. I know him. He knows the other players, and we all kind of have this camaraderie that it's hard for people to get," Stanley said.

It's clear Rodriguez has no shortage of professional admiration for Stanley. Rodriguez says they've been close ever since they were first put together in 2010, when Stanley was promoted to Rodriguez's Class-A team in Davenport, Iowa, just in time for the playoffs.

"He's more of a straight-line guy. He can have success, and he looks the same," Rodriguez said of his pupil. "He can have a great game, and he looks the same. He can have a real bad game, and he looks the same. He's mentally tough enough to make it to the big leagues, because he keeps it on an even keel."

Rodriguez is a longtime scout, coach and manager for several major league organizations, as well as college and high school teams. The door to his office adjacent to the Palm Beach clubhouse featured a sign that reads "Please Knock Before Entering," but Rodriguez is a welcoming fellow, and seems enthusiastic about sharing his collected wisdom about baseball and life with an eager listener. His desk resembled a table at a bookstore, topped with hardcover motivational tomes that marry sports and motivation, with Tony Dungy, Stan Musial and Tim Duncan among the faces on the covers. He's spent his life observing, evaluating, and helping players deal with the white-knuckle, sweaty-palmed at-bats that define winners and losers in baseball.

"That's the key. How does he react?" Rodriguez offers. "You find out a lot about players. Some have it right away. Some learn a little bit about it. Some never get it. The ones who don't get it really don't get past High-A. You've got to be able to perform at your best level at your toughest moment, or in other words, your toughest pressure moment. If not, you don't get out of High-A, because it just gets tougher from then on."

Many top-level draftees wrestle with the adjustment to playing professionally. Just as every new draftee may struggle with the step up in competition, the harsh reality of a slump hits home doubly hard for a No. 1 pick, who's that much less familiar with failure than a player taken in the later rounds.

"With a lot of first-rounders, that's happened. They had great success, and they get here, and they're just average," Rodriguez said. "And now how do they get above average? We thought they'd have the tools to be above average, and now they're not average. They're fringe or below [average], because they're not adapting or fighting through all the failures."

A player who suffers a career-altering injury, especially early in his professional career, faces perhaps the stiffest mental test. In addition to confronting the physical challenges associated with staying in the game, he has to grapple with the mental burden of adapting to a post-injury body.

Tewksbury believes learning to deal with adversity, whether it's injury, lack of performance, or another hurdle, is a necessary step in a player's development, and there's no way for organizations to speed up the process of getting through it.

"They just have to play, and the litmus test is the 144-game minor league season," he said. "And over the course of that time, you learn a lot about yourself, and what you can and can't do, and the players who move forward are able to take those lessons and apply the change the following year. And there are some players who can't. It's the inevitable process of professionalization, and it happens to everybody."

Yet for all the obstacles he's faced as a pro, Stanley observed that the mental challenge he encountered in college, at the baseball backwater of the University of North Carolina at Wilmington, was more difficult.

"The college level, I think, weighs on you more, mentally," he said. "When you get up here, you understand the game a little better, so it's not as tough, mentally, because you've grown."

Indeed, the mental and psychological challenge of baseball starts long before the draft. Anyone who's stood in the batter's box against the kid with the best fastball in Little League understands how important the right frame of mind is in the sport. Dave Tollett, the head baseball coach at Florida Gulf Coast University, suggests that mental toughness is something he's identified in some of his players before they turned pro.

"Every one of my big leaguers, I think, has had a mental approach that has separated him from the rest of the group," he said. "You take Casey Coleman, drafted in the fifteenth round [in 2008], and he'd tell you the reason he made it through [to the majors] is he just thought he was mentally tougher than a lot of the other guys he was up against."

It's part of what baseball executives call makeup, and there's a prototype they look for, as Tewksbury told David Laurila of *Baseball Prospectus* in 2007.

"High-achieving players play with confidence, have a short-term memory regarding past failures, keep their focus on the process of their actions rather than on the result, and minimize their achievements," he said.[25] "Those players have the ideal baseball personality."

Scouts look for players with the right makeup when they meet with prospects and try to get to know them before the draft. But sometimes the potential rewards of overwhelming physical talents outweigh the risks of questionable makeup. An example from another sport illustrates the allure of the skilled but psychologically troubled draftee. Going into the 2012 NBA Draft, the Houston Rockets regarded Royce White as one of the top five talents available in the entire draft, so they snapped him up when he was available with the sixteenth pick.[26] White's struggles with obsessive-compulsive disorder and generalized anxiety disorder had been common knowledge, and they had caused many other teams to pass on him. White took multiple leaves of absence from the team in his rookie year to sort out disputes over how the Rockets would accommodate his maladies. He never appeared in a regular season game for the Rockets, who traded him to the Philadelphia 76ers for little in return just a year after drafting him.

Baseball, too, has a long line of players whose psychological problems have manifested themselves either on the field or in a way that

181

directly affected their careers. Jimmy Piersall, Bill Blass, Steve Sax, Chuck Knoblauch and Rick Ankiel are just some of the more notorious figures who've stared down their demons and blinked. Ankiel, unlike many others, was able to overcome his issues. The Cardinals' second-round pick in 1997, he famously self-destructed in the third inning of a 2000 Division Series game against the Braves, sending multiple pitches to the backstop with a sudden and disturbing lack of control. He never recovered the pitching ability that had allowed him to finish second in National League Rookie of the Year voting that year, and to be named *Baseball America's* No. 1 prospect entering the 2000 season.[27]

Ankiel was demoted in 2001 to rookie ball, where he served as both a pitcher and designated hitter. He put up strong numbers, but carried a churlish attitude to the ballpark in Johnson City, Tennessee, making it clear to reporters that he didn't feel he belonged in such an obscure baseball outpost. Injury cost him all of 2002, and in 2003, he underwent Tommy John surgery that effectively ended his pitching career, save for five major league relief appearances at the end of the 2004 season. After the injuries, though, Ankiel was a changed man. Humble and accommodating to beat writers a few miles down the road in Kodak, Tennessee, the home of the Cardinals' Double-A affiliate, he began a slow climb back to the majors, where in 2007 he achieved the remarkable accomplishment of not only remaking himself from pitcher to outfielder, but also overcoming a psychological block in the process. As if to further emphasize the full-circle element of his tale, Ankiel was reportedly considering a return to pitching as of late 2012,[28] though he had recommitted to hitting by the time he agreed to head to spring training as a non-roster invitee with the Astros in 2013.[29]

In 2006, Zack Greinke, the sixth overall pick in 2002, missed time with a social anxiety disorder and depression.[30] His struggle shed new light on players with psychological issues, and soon several others were acknowledging their problems, including well-known figures like Joey Votto, Dontrelle Willis and Khalil Greene. A 2009 story by Jim Luttrell for the website of the *The New York Times* quoted psychiatrist Allan Lans, who was suspicious of the sudden preponderance of the social anxiety disorder diagnosis.[31]

Lans believed that such a disorder should be easily detectible before a player reaches the majors.[32] That suggests teams could at least have an idea of the problem before a player is drafted, too. Once a player is in a team's system, the emphasis turns to prevention and treatment. Tewksbury's aim is to foster day-in, day-out repetition, like the kind that Stanley relied on to carry him through his rough patches.

"That's the goal, is to have consistent routines, because consistent routines will lead to consistent performance," Tewksbury said. "The goal is to have consistent thoughts so that those thoughts lead to consistent performance, and consistent performance leads to movement through the system and hopefully a shot at the major leagues, where you learn routines and consistency both with your thinking and with your performance."

Taking a page from Dorfman and Kuehl, Tewksbury believes players achieve consistency through focus on the process of going about their business in the game rather than concentration on the numbers. That's easier said than done, of course, in a sport that's defined by numbers and, in the case of many front offices, driven by them. The Red Sox, under general manager Theo Epstein and his successor, Ben Cherington, embraced the Sabermetric revolution, but Tewksbury said he isn't the only one in the organization who tries to help players keep their focus on the process. Jonah Keri, in his book *The Extra 2%*, reveals how Rays manager Joe Maddon, another team with a decidedly "new school" approach, also tries to get his players to be more concerned about the process than the numerical results that are so closely studied in the executive suite.[33]

"I support the pitching coordinator, the hitting coordinator, the farm director, the individual coaches that are with these guys every day," Tewksbury said. "We're all in this as an extension of taking care of the player and the development of the player. They're the ones who are on the ground, so to speak, every day developing the routines. I'm kind of an additional resource to help reinforce those routines or to help a player talk through some mental obstacles that might be preventing him from playing his best."

The word "routine" in baseball is sometimes synonymous with "superstition." Hall-of-Famer Wade Boggs was almost as well-known for his habit of eating chicken before games, one of many parts of his daily ritual, as he was for his .328 career batting average. WGN cameras often depicted images of pitcher Turk Wendell brushing his teeth in the dugout between innings, a necessity after he chomped down on his beloved black licorice, two of his many bizarre practices. Lesser known is the story of Kevin Rhomberg, a bit player for the Indians in the early 1980s who felt a need to touch everyone and everything that touched him.[34] Teammates and opponents were keenly aware of this quirk, and on one occasion umpires called time out during a game in New York to tell Yankees players to quit touching Rhomberg and triggering his compulsion.[35] Baseball's lengthy lore includes all kinds of alleged curses, perhaps none more notorious than the supposed "Curse of the Bambino" that hung over the Red Sox until they won the World Series in 2004. Tewksbury joined the Red Sox that year, and while he's no believer in superstition, he doesn't try to get players to stop believing in whatever works for them.

"The superstition to think that if you don't eat chicken, you're going to have a bad day, that doesn't help you prepare to play," he said. "But if you think it's going to help you, go do it. But you have to understand that you might have a Whopper at Burger King and hit just as well. There are players who I've talked to about that. I'm sure there's more than what they talk about; I know there is because I played with a lot of guys who were that way. They would argue that it's part of their routine, and there's that fine line between routine and superstition. But it's definitely part of the game, and it's part of human behavior. I think that in some instances we all have some of those idiosyncrasies."

The difference between routine and superstition, according to Tewksbury, is that a routine is an action or set of actions that help you prepare to perform, while a superstition is the belief that if an action is not taken, you're bound to fail. Tewksbury teaches players to stick to routines but trust that their abilities can withstand a sudden momentary change of plans.

"You kind of talk about routines as part of a way of preparing yourself to play, but in the event that that routine gets broken, which happens occasionally in the game — the bus could break down, it could be a rain delay, there could be a variety of things that happen that are out of the player's control where their routines might get prohibited — they still ought to believe they're going to be ready to play," he said.

For decades, Major League Baseball organizations regarded the psychological troubles of their players much as they would a broken-down bus or a rain shower — unforeseen events about which little or nothing can be done. That attitude has changed over the past two decades, and a greater respect for the science of sports psychology has affected the way teams evaluate and develop prospects. The counseling available to players now helps ease the transition of amateurs into professional life. It gives a No. 1 draft pick an outlet for discussing his frustration, anger, fear or any other sort of feeling he gets when he meets with failure and doubt about his abilities in the game for the very first time. Baseball has long had an ideal makeup in mind, but continued research may allow clubs to further pinpoint a prospect's mental strengths and weaknesses, and develop a holistic approach that goes far beyond the psychological testing that's already in place to help teams better know whom they're about to draft. Just as with physical shortcomings, there may be no way to predict or prevent every mental obstacle that derails a baseball career. Instead, progress toward that end achieved through the sort of reasonable goals Dorfman encouraged his clients to set is just what baseball appears to be making.

14

Life Imitates the Draft

As baseball talent evaluators scour the country in preparation for the next draft, they are not alone. Countless others from a diverse range of industries are also assessing and recruiting the people they hope will be the next stars in their fields. And, just as in baseball, not everyone pegged to succeed actually does.

Consider the words of one of the nation's top talent evaluators, who recently spoke about the holistic review her "team" conducts to identify the stars of the future. "There's nothing formulaic about the process," she said. "At least two readers have read your file, and we go to committee to make all of our decisions...We care about who you are as a person."[1]

The speaker was Janet Rapelye, dean of admission at Princeton University. Of course, most day-to-day hirings aren't as thought-out, well-documented or glamorous as the baseball draft. Even the most selective grocery store doesn't hire a team of scouts and number crunchers to assess the merits of three candidates for an opening at cashier. Few, if any, industries other than professional sports are set up in a way that allows competing franchises to select candidates in an orderly, one-by-one fashion. Elite colleges and universities competing for the best and brightest students might offer the closest comparison. Even the long-dormant American military draft, probably the most notorious draft outside of sports, bore little resemblance to the way baseball draws its domestic talent. Still, there are common threads in the way every industry selects and evaluates personnel that can shed light on the efficacy of baseball's unusual system.

The game is certainly not unique in that there are far more job-seekers than jobs. But, just like any other industry, there is a scramble for the most highly regarded talent that gives the best in the field significantly more leverage. That's why Will Smith, for instance, is offered millions of dollars to appear as the leading man in a film, while an actor with a pair of commercials and a cable television cameo on his resume has to perform in countless auditions for a shot at a bit part in the same movie. It's debatable whether the extra effort a studio heaps upon a star is worth it, since, just as late-round draft picks often outperform their first-round counterparts, independent films with no recognizable names sometimes wind up making larger profits than big-budget, celebrity-driven projects. There are many similarities between professional sports and Hollywood, but the concept of lavishing significantly greater money and attention on the most sought-after performers is common across just about every industry. The matter of CEO pay versus the average worker's take-home is politically charged, but in 2012 the nonpartisan Economic Policy Institute pegged CEO compensation at between 209.4 to 231 percent of that of the average worker, depending on the measures used.[2]

Large corporations and government agencies often use search firms and recruiters to identify and seek out executives. It's an approach in contrast to baseball teams that, with the exception of the Major League Baseball scouting bureau, largely rely on internal operations to identify potential draftees and negotiate with them once they've been selected. Joe Walsh, a recruiter based in Asheville, North Carolina, believes that while baseball might benefit from outsourcing their talent search, it would be hard to improve upon existing front office practices.

"Most of these ball teams are going to have expertise in negotiating already, because they've done it so often, with so many players that they've recruited over the years, or brought in over the years," he said.[3]

Still, teams have priorities that extend beyond haggling with their draft picks. Front office types certainly do plenty of negotiating, but depending on the way a team delegates responsibilities, executives may have a lot more on their minds than outfoxing an agent. Player representatives usually have multiple clients, but spend every day concentrating on the back-and-forth required to strike a favorable deal.

That might help explain why agents held such sway over the draft during the 1990s and 2000s. It's just the opposite in the corporate world, where recruiters specialize in finding the best talent available at the lowest price, or within a preferred range specified by the company that hires them. Recruiters can give companies advantages that go beyond the deal, too. Walsh explained how, when he knows what a corporate client is willing to offer, he can bring the new hire on board with greater satisfaction than he or she might otherwise have.

"Generally what I do is try to close the candidate a little bit lower, so then when they get the offer, they're pleased," he said. "They're like, 'Oh, man, I thought I was going to get ninety-six [thousand dollars].' 'Well you know, they must have really liked you, because they did a hundred [thousand dollars].' I have to do that because I represent the company and have to get the most qualified candidate who's affordable."

The perception of the deal is the key. That's why Walsh doesn't think baseball's concept of assigning a slot value to draft picks is a smart idea.

"Then it just becomes a commodity to know how much they're worth," he said. "They know how much an ounce of gold is worth, and they think they're an ounce of gold. So they say, 'OK, now here's my value. Wherever I go, this is how much I want,' or, 'How much can you do that's better?'"

In his line of work, his corporate clients let him know a range of annual salaries they're willing to offer, such as $80,000 to $100,000, but the recruiting target is not made privy to those figures.

"I'm very reluctant to tell what the top of the range is, because once they know that, obviously that's what they want, even if they're making eighty [thousand dollars]," he said. "I generally don't even tell them the salary. I try to find out what they're making. I might say, "You're making eighty? Well, generally this company will do a ten to fifteen percent bump. It's pretty rare for them for them to go above that."

If Walsh encounters a savvy target who knows what the company usually offers, brinksmanship is again involved. Walsh shared what he might tell a potential recruit in this circumstance.

"They [companies] usually look at what the person's making. And yeah, they have a range, but the range is interesting because when people join the company, they're going to fall into the range. So they want to have enough upward mobility where you stay in the same job, but can still have a salary increase. So they don't bring people in at the top of the range."

In baseball, it would be hard to envision Scott Boras believing that a team wouldn't go to the top of its range to bring in his client. That's the advantage of having a dedicated negotiator on your side.

Perhaps no organization tries as hard to gain a psychological advantage in recruiting as the military, which poured $666.7 million in 2012 into advertising designed to convince young men and women to kill or risk being killed,[4] according to Defense Department estimates. There's no worthwhile comparison between the task of signing an eighteen-year-old up for a tour of duty in a war zone and what's necessary to convince an eighteen-year-old to join a professional baseball team. Years ago, young men went out of their way to avoid the military draft, and now they travel to showcases around the country in an effort to get picked as soon as possible in the baseball draft. The part of the game in which the military may have ideas to offer baseball comes not in the art of securing personnel, but in evaluating it for promotion.

Joshua Botteicher and Nickolas Hinton served as staff sergeants in the Air Force Security Forces, which function essentially as the military police of the Air Force. They were charged with evaluating troops under their command. One of the primary avenues of doing so is through the Enlisted Performance Report, or EPR, that the staff sergeant must file on each airman. The EPR is filed on a two-page, standardized form that includes a numerical assessment of a troop's performance on a simple one-to-five scale, similar to the standard baseball scouting report template that grades players on a scale of twenty to eighty. Corporations, too, commonly have standardized assessment forms that attempt to assign a numerical rating to each employee. What makes each industry and organization distinct is how that information is interpreted.

In the Air Force, "it's pretty much five or bust," Hinton said.[5] "Anything below a three is considered bad. Three to four is still considered bad. Five is what you want."

Hinton said he was given virtual autonomy to grade his troops as he saw fit, and while higher-ups had to sign off on the form, it was generally rubber-stamped. His description of the process depicts an operation similar to a baseball front office that places a great deal of trust in its scouts.

"They don't know every troop that goes by. They're in offices all

189

day," Hinton said of those to whom he reported. "I'm actually out on the road, and they're in the office, so they don't get the chance to know every troop."

Unlike scouts, who travel around following different players every night, staff sergeants are stationed with their troops, evaluating them as they work and in off hours as well. Botteicher is reluctant to put a number on just how long it takes to determine whether an airman will pan out or not, but he defines three months as a rough estimate.

"You get to that point, you kind of get comfortable," he said.[6] "You're in your rhythm. You go to work Monday through Friday at 7 o'clock. At 4 o'clock you get off. And for a lot of people, routine becomes boring. And when they get bored, they start to get lazy."

If they notice a troop going off-track, staff sergeants can, and are expected to, jump in and work with the airman to improve. That made Hinton and Botteicher part-scouts and part-coaches.

"Being a supervisor is more than just being a mentor; it's about teaching," Hinton said. "My job is to teach you to take my job."

That results in greater accountability than you find in baseball, Botteicher contends.

"If I had a troop that's no good, the first thing [supervisors] look at is me," he said, presenting a hypothetical scenario. "I have five troops. Four of them are great, one of them sucks. But they're still going to look at me and go, 'What's wrong with this one? No, we know the other four are great. What did you do wrong with this one?' That's how they look at it."

It's not easy working with recruits fresh out of high school, but just as there are college players in the baseball draft, not everyone who enters the military is eighteen or nineteen years old. Baseball prospects drafted out of college are usually farther along than their high school counterparts, and get promoted to the majors more quickly. But age doesn't make much difference in the military, Botteicher believes.

"Some people come in with a lot of experience. Some people join the Air Force when they're a little bit older. They think that helps out. And you find out that he's a twenty-eight-year-old child," he said.

Many times, promotion has more to do with contextual circumstances than performance, in baseball and in the military. An up-and-coming catcher at Double-A or Triple-A stands a much better chance of making the majors if the big club is thin behind the plate or suffers an injury. In the military, Hinton estimates that 90 percent of promotion comes down to timing.

"Let's say that you're better at the job than I am, but you're deployed overseas, and I'm stateside," he said. "So, if I want that job, and I put in for it, I may get it because you're overseas."

Politics are sometimes at play in promotions as well, whether it's a baseball club pushing its No. 1 draft pick up the minor league ladder and into the majors despite mediocre performance, or it's a troop who doesn't otherwise stand out from the pack but has developed the right relationships. In the military, that's particularly true for back-office jobs, Hinton said.

"We had a captain who really liked me because I worked with him on flight, and I knew I already had the job going into it, but he still had to open it up just to say, 'Hey, we interviewed these people. He's still the best candidate,'" he said.

But by and large, Botteicher thinks the Air Force is far more focused on merit than baseball is, concentrating on performance rather than reputation. In his view, the problem in baseball, and other sports, stems from long-term, guaranteed contracts.

"You've got to get your contracts better," Botteicher said. "What if one year leads to another bad year, and leads to another bad year, and on and on and on and on? In the Air Force, if we have that problem, boom, we've got to stop this right now. We've got to either make things better or get him out."

While a team may address the problems a player encounters during a down year, Hinton advises greater patience, and thinks it's important not to get caught up in results from a short period of time that don't match a player's full track record.

"I know that's the nature of the beast, but if we did that in the military, we'd be pretty shorthanded," he said.

Ultimately, military personnel are government employees, though their work and the way it's measured may not fit the profile of most federal, state, and local agencies. The scope of government service is so broad that it's hard to say any government job has much in common with the next, as Walter Caudle explained. Caudle has held consulting and managerial positions in multiple South Carolina state government agencies over the past two decades and specializes in human resource management, performance measurement, and training and organizational development.

"In terms of consistency of purpose, or whether or not things are truly measureable, it's a mixed bag," he said.[7] "Government employees run the gamut from laborers with minimal educations, barely high school educations, to PhDs, and everything in between."

Still, there are general standards and policies that apply to most government jobs that shape the way employees are selected and evaluated. With the exception of the military, most government agencies stage recruitment efforts only for top-level jobs, and that's even more so amid today's cutbacks, Caudle said. That doesn't mean the agencies aren't careful about whom they hire. Beyond the raw data of the information on an applicant's resume, there's observation in the interview process that often focuses on how the personality of a potential hire will gibe with the rest of the staff and the requirements of the job. The right personality is much more important in the working environment than commonly thought, as Caudle details.

"Nine times out of ten if you have a bad supervisor, or a bad employee, or a bad executive, it is because you have created a train wreck of processes and personalities, and/or you have someone who has horrible communication skills," he said.

It's more than just creating the right workplace chemistry.

"Let's say you've got a front-office function that interacts with the general public all day, every day," Caudle said. "Do you fill that position with the person who is so shy, quiet, and introverted, they can't even look up at the person at the counter when they come in? They may be the most technically proficient person, but if they can't interact with the customer and help get the customer where they need to go, that technical capability is worthless."

In spite of this, many agencies stop short of administering personality tests as part of the interview. That's because of legal liability the agency may incur if the test is used as a key determining factor in the hire, Caudle said.

"If you can't back up why you used that as an objective decision-making criteria, and it ever comes up, you've got trouble on your hands in terms of exposure for inappropriate hiring practices," he said.

Instead, hiring managers simply observe the candidates in the interview, and, as much as possible, try to get them to self-report — in other words, volunteer information about their personalities in response to questions. Many interviewers describe routine scenarios the candidates may encounter, and ask them what they would do if a co-worker needed help or a consumer presented a tricky request.

"A good manager will pick up on cues during an interview with the right questions," Caudle said. "Certain answers people give will tell you what you need to know in terms of, 'Can this person engage with outsiders, can this person engage with internal employees, can this person engage across different parts of an organization?'"

Liability concerns continue to play a significant role in how governments evaluate workers from the hiring process forward.

"If there's even the least hint of inequitable treatment, real or perceived, you could run afoul of what you're trying to accomplish," Caudle said. "Government agencies have scrapped some types of performance measurement models on the basis of one bad lawsuit."

That's one reason why most government employees are assessed using quantifiable benchmarks as opposed to subjective observation. If a government agency were a baseball front office, its system of evaluation would far more closely resemble that of the *Moneyball* A's than a traditional scout-reliant setup.

"Observation, in many cases, can't be measured. They may be able to measure it, but it can't be necessarily compared," Caudle said. "In most cases, government agencies are dealing with paper, or transactions, or processes that don't lend themselves to observation."

One of the goals of a performance evaluation system in government is to minimize the amount of interpretation involved, he added, identifying accountability for individual employees as the primary reason government personnel evaluation exists. The assessment lets the agency mete out discipline or take corrective measures if the employee does not meet the standards. Quantifying performance also allows governments to easily identify whom to trim when they must make staff cuts.

"If a governmental agency lays off employees, in most cases an employee's performance is calculated into an equation as to whether or not they are subject to separation if there is a reduction in force," Caudle said.

The same formulaic use of performance metrics is often used to determine how merit pay is awarded, though Caudle notes that such bonuses are handed out much less often than before. In baseball, save for decisions made by the most numbers-obsessed executives, there's far greater interpretation and discretion at play when players are drafted, awarded lucrative deals, and promoted. Teams aren't subject to the same liability as government agencies—and most businesses—are because, unlike most people, players work under contract. That's why we don't hear about highly touted prospects suing the teams that drafted them when they're released after failing to earn promotion past Double-A.

"Generally speaking, and I'm speaking in big, broad terms, a person under an employment contract doesn't have the same protections and/or rights that we talk about in these other situations," Caudle said.

Indeed, the uniform player contract for minor leaguers includes a skills clause that allows the team to part ways with the player if he's not performing as the club sees fit.[8] Such clauses don't necessarily preclude anyone from bringing a case, as might happen if a player intentionally violates the contract or if the team tries to back out of the deal, Caudle said. That sort of specific contractual language nonetheless creates significantly less grounds to do so.

While baseball is far from the only business to use contracts, the presence of those documents sets the sports industry apart from most of the corporate world, even as an increasing number of business school grads populate baseball front offices. The larger the business, the more likely it is that its system of human resource evaluation will be based upon measurable data, just like the government, Caudle explained. Caudle, who has owned and operated multiple professional service and hospitality firms outside his government work, understands that in small businesses, simple observation takes precedence over data in many cases.

"It is because of the lack of a dedicated personnel function. It is also the fact that in most cases there are not thoroughly written position descriptions," he said. "Everybody pretty much has to do some of everything. There's also informal merit pay or bonuses where a small business owner can say, 'I think you did a great job, here's a hundred bucks,' or, 'Here's a ham,' or whatever."

The same whims that can prompt a local shop owner to reward the employee of the month can lead to a pink slip for the same employee the next month, as Caudle points out. That could perhaps open the shop up to legal issues, though they'd probably be offset by the isolation of the incident. If a company fires a single employee in a year, it's less likely to be prosecuted for wrongful termination than a multinational conglomerate that sheds thousands of jobs at a time.

Ultimately, Caudle believes the best approach to measuring performance would balance some degree of professional judgment with a numbers-based evaluation. Whatever system is in place, the imperative is for everyone to know what the standard is. Alas, one arm of an organization doesn't always work in sync with the other. Sometimes, companies or government agencies will create elaborate measurement schemes that have little to do with the tasks employees perform on a daily basis, or aren't in line with what the organization's goals are, Caudle explained. He believes communication is central to avoiding this sort of problem. Those in executive positions must continuously review their work processes and listen to their employees and understand how they go about their tasks, and must set forth their directives with explanation that doesn't just lay out what to do, but why it needs to be done.

The implementation of new technology provides fertile ground for miscommunication. In the 1990s, Caudle was a manager in a South Carolina state agency that was transitioning to computers from a paper system that had relied on color-coded documents.

"When all this stuff starting going electronic, the IT people were all so happy," Caudle recalled. "They'd created these electronic screens that replicated all the same information. But the users were going crazy."

For decades, the staff had been able to identify standardized documents at a glance simply by observing their colors. The new computer system forced everyone in the office to spend extra time memorizing the names and numbers of the forms. The advantages that computer filing usually entails, like ease of sorting and the ability to quickly find a specific document, were curtailed during the initial implementation.

"There was a green form that was part of a key work process," Caudle explained. "We had to go in and tell the IT department, 'OK guys, guess what? You need to make the screen green.' And we're going, 'OK, look, this is why: People have been used to seeing this information for a hundred years on a green piece of paper. They're going crazy as it is migrating to electronics. Give them some transition and some comfort by giving them the green screen.'

"And the minute they colored those screens, we had a hundred employees say, 'Oh, thank God!'"

The same sort of disconnect can occur in baseball. A draftee who has been evaluated one way in high school or college, and thirty different ways by every team that scouted him, may not understand when his rookie league manager tells him he's being passed over for a promotion to Class A because the organization's advanced metrics show he doesn't hit to all fields against right-handers. All the player knows is he's got a strong arm and hit twenty home runs that season. He might start to overcompensate for deficiencies he doesn't understand, and stunt his growth as a prospect.

Those who are evaluated aren't the only ones who deal with change. Just as technology has allowed teams to store all kinds of video and data about players, people making hires in the business world increasingly rely upon social networks to connect with candidates. LinkedIn, which boasts more than two hundred million members,[9] has become an effective tool for Walsh, the corporate recruiter. It's largely replaced the need for him to obtain company rosters and gives him an invaluable avenue of obtaining information about potential hires. Knowing who works at a specific company or department is especially valuable information when he calls someone to network and seek out potential candidates.

"I'll throw a bunch of names at them, and I'll say, 'Hey, look, I've got this list of names, I've got a company roster, give me ten minutes of your time to kind of walk me through it," Walsh said. "I know who they are. I just don't want to call the person who's really not a fit."

Walsh estimates that for every ten names he brings up in conversations of this sort, two of them turn out to be strong candidates.

"If I can identify everybody in the stadium, and I can have three sections—happy, on the fence, and looking—then I know I won't waste my time on the happy people," he said.

Governments use social networks, too, but much of their recruiting is done at the top level, where the cursory glance at a profile doesn't fit the bill. For some of these high-profile positions, agencies form a search committee, though it's a tool that's used sparingly.

"Most state executive positions are either elected, appointed by the legislature, appointed by the governor, or appointed by a board that runs that agency," Caudle said. "And in those cases, they make their own decisions about how to hire or recruit."

Despite its limited use, the search committee is the closest analogy in government to the way a baseball front office considers whom it will draft. Search committees commonly take anywhere from thirty days to a year to find the right candidate, depending on the position to be filled and the circumstances involved.

"The likelihood of finding a quality, major university president in South Carolina is not as high as if you were in New York or California," Caudle said. "So that's why those types of searches generally end up going far afield, out of state, and take a longer period of time, while there is some interim person, usually the number two or three person already in place, doing the job if they haven't filled the job prior to the person leaving."

The more important and lucrative the position, the longer a search committee usually takes, Caudle said. The first step a search committee takes is to create a position description, just like the way nearly every other hiring entity in government and business begins the process.

"Even if it's an executive position, there are still some minimum standards that have to apply, if for no other reason than to justify the salary that has been approved for that position," Caudle said. "In [South Carolina] state government, there is an actual board that has to approve most agency head salaries."

Once it comes to consensus on what the job entails, a committee considers precisely what sort of candidate it's seeking. A small or medium-sized university is usually inclined to consider someone from a school of a similar size, unless the committee decides the college is in a growth mode and ready to make a splashy hire, Caudle said. A school may look to address an area of strength, like academics, or weakness, like fundraising. Sometimes, the committee may pass over an ambitious, well-qualified candidate if the school's goals are modest.

"Is the board looking for a caretaker or is the board looking for a catalyst?" Caudle asked. "If I come in all fancy and credentialed, and this, that and the other, and I'm talking about, 'Oh, well, I would love to come in and review the strategic plan, and I would like to make changes in X, Y and Z, and consider this, and talk about that,' and as a board all they want is a caretaker, congratulations, you just talked yourself right out of a second interview."

It's much like the question of whether a team should draft the best available talent or select players based on organizational need. Caudle's advice is that major hiring — or drafting — decisions should be made in line with a well-defined long-term plan.

"If you don't know what your organization is trying to do, or where it's trying to go, you can't make these kinds of informed decisions, which is how so many organizations within government get an appointed official as an executive who is not the right fit for the group," he said.

Baseball is worlds apart from government, just as it's vastly different from business and the military. Still, teams can learn from the methods each of these institutions uses to identify and develop talent within its ranks. There are plenty of people in front offices these days who apply their business experience to decision-making within the game. And although former military members are not nearly as much a part of baseball as they were in previous generations, particularly following World War II, their methodologies remain a self-evident influence in the game, from the Padres' camouflage jerseys to the Pirates' Navy SEAL training for instructional leaguers.[10] Largely absent in baseball are civilian government officials. The anti-bureaucracy climate of the past 30 years hasn't exactly popularized the work of a government manager as a model of efficiency. Yet surely there's room in the game for someone who can build and maintain an effective staff on a shrinking budget, particularly among small-market teams.

Epilogue

When we visited with Minnesota Twins farmhand Aaron Hicks in April of 2011, he was at the first real crossroads of his career. Early in his fourth professional season, the fourteenth overall pick of the 2008 draft was putting up pedestrian numbers at A-ball in Fort Myers. While the switch-hitting Hicks toiled in the minors, ten of the thirteen players drafted ahead of him were playing and, in some cases, excelling in the major leagues. At Fort Myers in 2011, Hicks hit just .242, though his seventy-eight walks in 528 plate appearances allowed him to finish the season with a respectable .354 on-base percentage. He also stole seventeen bases and hit thirty-one doubles. A lower-round draft pick trying to plug his way through the minors would have been elated by such a performance. But the expectations for Hicks were a lot higher. Jim Rantz, then the Twins minor league director, wasn't ready to panic, however. He said he was optimistic that the twenty-one-year-old would soon "figure it out," baseball parlance for a player learning enough about himself and the game to achieve a significant breakthrough in performance.

Still, the question lingered: Was Hicks still a candidate to become the five-tool star the Twins believed he would be, or was he on his way to becoming a first-round disappointment? In many ways, 2012 figured to be a critical year for him, at least in terms of his future in the Minnesota organization. After the completion of that season, the Twins would either have to place him on their forty-man roster or risk losing him in the Rule 5 draft.

Prior to having to make that difficult decision, the Twins gave Hicks every opportunity to shine. After his season in Fort Myers, he went to play in the Arizona Fall League. He credited that experience with helping him to validate Rantz's confidence in him. Playing with and against other top prospects in Arizona, Hicks realized it was time to get serious. He worked on improving his plate discipline and hitting to the opposite field.[1] And when he returned home to Long Beach, California, for a brief offseason, he spent considerable time on the golf course, but with a baseball-related purpose in mind.

"I play golf right-handed. I do everything right-handed," he said. "I think one of the main reasons I'm good at hitting a baseball right-handed is because of the eye-hand coordination I developed playing golf. I never felt the same confidence hitting left-handed. And neither did my coaches. In high school, they'd say, 'Hey, we've got the bases loaded. Can Aaron please hit right-handed, so we can win this game?' [Before the 2012 season], I fooled around with playing left-handed golf. I think it helped my left-handed baseball swing come along."

In August 2012, we checked in again on Hicks, who, by that time, was having his best season to date at Double-A New Britain. Thanks in part to his left-handed hitting prowess, he set personal highs in home runs, RBIs, stolen bases, and runs scored that year. In addition, he led the Eastern League in walks. At the end of the season, the Twins put Hicks on the 40-man roster and shipped him off to play winter ball in Venezuela.

Reflecting on his successful year at Double-A, Hicks discussed the challenges of facing and overcoming adversity in the minor leagues. "It doesn't matter how good you are, you're going to take your lumps at some point," he said. "If you can learn from that and get it behind you and over with, it's a lot easier to move forward. As my dad says, 'Eventually, it's just going to click, and everything's going to seem easier.'"

While Hicks was out of the country, his future with the Twins got even brighter. Over the course of a weeks bridging November and December, Minnesota traded starting outfielders Denard Span and Ben Revere to Washington and Philadelphia, respectively. Suddenly, Hicks was in a position to bypass Triple-A and earn the starting center field job with the Twins in 2013. He helped his cause in spring training by hitting .370 and belting three home runs in a game against the Phillies.

Aaron Hicks made the mental and physical adjustments necessary to improve his performance and keep his dream of playing in the major leagues alive. The departure of two everyday outfielders in Minnesota turned that dream into a reality. Then, he took a step back. As we reflect on the findings of our research, we should remain mindful of the role timing plays in separating the players who get their shot at the big time from the ones who can only sit around and wonder what might have been. During the 2013 regular season, Hicks got a crash course on the difference between spring training and the 162 games that count. As Minnesota's everyday center fielder, Hicks got off to a dreadful start, hitting just .113 in 71 April at-bats. Over the next three months, Hicks showed flashes of brilliance. In a May game against the White Sox, he belted two home runs and, in the field, soared high to keep an Adam Dunn drive from leaving the park. But Hicks' rookie season was marked by inconsistency. In early August, the Twins decided he required more seasoning and demoted him to Triple-A, where he stayed for the remainder of the 2013 season and hit just .222.

The scouts turned out in droves to catch a glimpse of the high school outfielder whom had every major league front office salivating. Not only could he run, hit, and field like a seasoned veteran, he was a straight-A student whom coaches and teammates described as "smart," "humble," and "wise beyond his years" before even getting around to talking about his ability on the baseball diamond. One teammate reminisced in a national sports magazine about having grown up with baseball's next can't-miss prospect: "He's the most level-headed guy I know, but when we were kids, he climbed trees all the time. And sometimes he fell out. We're talking twenty, thirty, sometimes forty feet down to the ground. But he never broke a bone. We started calling him 'The Terminator.' He's just indestructible."

Best of all to the teams that coveted him, the kid loved baseball. Despite receiving collegiate offers from every top baseball program in the country, he made it clear through his parents that he would sign a professional contract out of high school. Not only that, but he planned to do so without the assistance of an agent. His father, a successful hedge-fund manager, told reporters that his son wasn't going pro for the money. "He eats, breathes, and sleeps the game," his dad explained. "My son wants his baseball experience to stay as pure as possible. For him, that means conducting his own business, without the help of an agent."

Epilogue

To no one's surprise, the young man went number one overall on draft day. When he showed up at rookie ball, he was greeted by three dozen reporters, even though his manager had declared him off-limits to the media. "The kid's here to show what he can do on the ball field, but he won't be able to show anything on the ball field if he can't get to his locker and change into his uniform," the manager quipped.

Three weeks later, the attention hadn't dissipated a bit. In fact, it had increased. The young phenom went hitless in his first thirty-eight at-bats in the minors, leading some to wonder if he was the most over-hyped player in the history of the game. His manager finally gave him a day off to gather his thoughts. The kid spent that entire afternoon in the batting cage. That evening, he went to his apartment and watched a favorite movie. He vowed not to let himself get down. He knew he could play the game and that it was only a matter of time before he got his first hit, then his tenth hit, and so on. Despite starting 0 for 38, he finished the season with a batting average just below .300. And he never fell south of that mark again for the rest of his Hall-of-Fame career.

Just like George Plimpton's 168-mile-per-hour-throwing superman Sidd Finch, the player referenced above isn't real. If only he and others like him existed, major league teams would have long ago mastered the draft. As it stands, there are no guarantees in baseball, even at the top of the draft board. And as long as baseball front offices misgauge talent levels and players remain physically and mentally breakable, it will remain that way.

As we noted earlier, one-third of players drafted in the first round between 1990 and 2006 didn't make it past the minor leagues. Injury, poor performance, and a lack of resilience in the face of mental or phys-ical struggles were the three main reasons these top selections failed to reach the game's highest level. The individual stories of these players help provide a greater understanding of the game in general.

Our research shows teams became more successful during the first ten years of 2000s in turning top picks into major leaguers. This is some-what counterintuitive considering that decade saw a further proliferation of non-drafted Latin players who created greater competition for big league jobs. So why did teams have more success in the draft? Part of the answer certainly lies in technological advances that have made the task of gathering and sorting information on prospects much more manageable. In addition, showcases have allowed one-stop shopping that's made it easier for teams to keep tabs on top prospects, even as they may lead to group-think and teams missing out on hidden gems who aren't participating.

Group-think plays a large role in the first round. Top-prospect lists promulgated by publications including *Baseball America* more or less predetermine which players will get selected in the first round. Few if any teams want to risk scorn and potential embarrassment by picking a high school or college player much higher than anyone expected.

Our research shows that some organizations, including the San Diego Padres, endured years without drafting a player in *any* round who went on to have a serviceable major league career. Other teams, such as the St. Louis Cardinals, drafted and developed players so successfully that their minor league systems have long produced a steady flow of big league contributors. Meanwhile, the ups and downs experienced by the Minnesota Twins over the past twenty years appear directly connected to the team's success, or lack thereof, in the draft. A common thread in all three teams' draft fortunes speaks to a truism of the selection process as a whole: Much of the teams' varying levels of draft success between 1990 and 2006 came from players nabbed in the later rounds.

For all the advances in communications and information flow, the baseball draft is still largely centered on educated guesswork. The rise of superagents, like Scott Boras, have further complicated the process by dissuading teams from drafting players who might command too High-A price tag.

We believe an increased awareness of the frailty of the human body and mind has led to preventive measures that likely have allowed more young prospects to avoid or overcome the sort of physical and mental injuries that have diminished and ended the careers of others.

Whether a higher percentage of American-born draft picks would reach the majors if baseball instituted a full-fledged international draft remains an open question. But as the sport moves in that direction, we might find out the answer sooner rather than later.

The United States contains a vast minor league baseball infrastructure. Inexpensive game tickets, creative promotions, and cozy ballparks continue to lure millions to minor league fields every summer. But as our research shows, the minor league parks are also home to some of the most compelling narratives in baseball. Every player drafted into professional baseball carries the number of his pick with him for the rest of his career. And no player faces more pressure than the first-round pick. As former top draft choice David Yocum says about his career's ending prematurely in the minors due to injury, "It's not life or death, but at the time, it felt that way. Coming to terms with the fact that you're done is not an easy thing to do."[2]

Baseball is a game of perseverance. Scott Rice is proof of that. Rice, a first-round pick of the Orioles in 1999, made his major league debut in 2013. Pitching in middle relief for the Mets, Rice led the National League in appearances before undergoing season-ending hernia surgery with a few weeks remaining in the season.

Nothing about the baseball draft is easy. Whether it's a scout trying to convince his supervisor that their team should pick the high school third baseman over the college pitcher, the prospect standing in the batter's box against the country's top pitcher as dozens of scouts look on at a showcase, or the once-touted draftee hanging his head in a Class-A clubhouse after another 0 for 4 day, the draft is a heavy burden. If, as the saying goes, baseball is a game of failure, the draft is appropriately backbreaking.

Chapter Notes

Introduction

1. Jake Mauer, interview by Chuck Myron, Hammond Stadium, Fort Myers, Florida, April 25, 2011.

2. Aaron Hicks, interview by Chuck Myron, Hammond Stadium, Fort Myers, Florida, April 25, 2011.

3. Jim Rantz, telephone interview with Chuck Myron, May 23, 2011.

4. Matthew Stucko, "Ramapo Product Shooter Hunt Hoping New Fitness Regimen Puts Him Back on Path to Major Leagues," *Star-Ledger,* 15 Aug. 2010, http://www.nj.com/sports/njsports/index.ssf/2010/08/ramapo_product_shooter_hunt_ho.html (30 April 2011).

5. Aaron Gleeman, "Twins' First-Round Pick Alex Wimmers Shut Down After Six Straight Walks in First Start," NBCSports.com, 15 April 2011, http://hardballtalk.nbcsports.com/2011/04/15/twins-first-round-pick-alex-wimmers-shut-down-after-six-straight-walks-in-first-start/ (30 April 2011).

6. Joe Christensen, "Wimmers Now Faces Recovery," *Minneapolis Star Tribune,* 2 August 2012, http://www.startribune.com/sports/twins/164836046.html?refer=y (12 March 2013).

7. Chad Mottola, interview by Alan Maimon, Cashman Field, Las Vegas, Nevada, May 16, 2011.

8. David O'Brien, "Reds Call Worth Mottola's Wait," *South Florida Sun-Sentinel,* 2 June 1992, http://articles.sun-sentinel.com/1992-06-02/sports/9202120399_1_clay-daniel-sign-reds-scout (21 May 2011).

9. "Chad Mottola," Baseball-Reference.com, n.d., http://.baseball-reference.com/minors/player.cgi?id=mottol001cha (21 May 2011).

10. Gordon Edes, "He's Loved But Not Needed," *South Florida Sun-Sentinel,* 15 March 1996, http://articles.sun-sentinel.com/1996-03-15/sports/9603150099_1_reds-manager-chad-mottola-love (21 May 2011).

Chapter 1

1. Peter Morris, *A Game of Inches: The Stories Behind the Innovations That Shaped Baseball,* vol. 2: *The Game Behind the Scenes* (Lanham, MD: Ivan R. Dee, 2006), Chapter 13, page 6.

2. Ibid., 5–6.

3. Ibid., 6.

4. "National Agreement for the Government of Professional Base Ball Clubs," Doug Pappas's Business of Baseball Pages, n.d., http://roadsidephotos.sabr.org/baseball/1903NatAgree.htm (26 Oct. 2011).

5. Brian McKenna, "The Baseball Draft, Since 1892," Glimpses Into Baseball History, 26 Oct. 2010, http://baseballhistoryblog.com/tag/major-league-draft/ (19 Oct. 2011).

6. Ibid.

7. Ibid.

8. Ibid.

9. Ibid.

10. Robert Fredrick Burk, *Much More Than a Game* (Chapel Hill: University of North Carolina Press, 2001), 28.

11. Ibid., 29.

12. Pat Doyle, "Branch Rickey's Farm,"

Baseball Almanac, n.d., http://www.base ball-almanac.com/minor-league/minor 2005a.shtml (3 Nov. 2011).

13. Morris, 7–8.

14. Doyle.

15. McKenna.

16. Jim Hawkins, Dan Ewald and George Van Dusen, *The Detroit Tigers Encyclopedia* (Champaign, IL: Sports Publishing, 2002), 71.

17. Allan Simpson, "Bonus Concerns Created Draft; Yet Still Exist." *Baseball America*, 4 June 2005, http://www.base ballamerica.com/today/2005draft/ 050604bonus.html (3 Nov. 2011.)

18. Ibid.

19. Ibid.

20. Buzzie Bavasi and Jack Olsen, "The Real Secret of Trading," *Sports Illustrated*, 5 June 1967, 54 (SI Vault).

21. Ibid.

22. Simpson, "Bonus."

23. Jeff Blank, "Evolution of Draft," Jeff Blank Baseball Blog, n.d., http://www. jeffblankbaseball.com/?page_id=12 (19 Oct. 2011).

24. Simpson, "Bonus."

25. Robert Cull, *Rumors of Baseball's Demise: How the Balance of Competition Swung and the Critics Missed* (Jefferson, NC: McFarland, 2006), 81.

26. David George Surdam. *The Postwar Yankees: Baseball's Golden Age Revisited* (Lincoln, NE: University of Nebraska Press, 2008), 272.

27. Simpson, "Bonus."

28. Cull, 80–1.

29. "Minors OK Free Agent Draft in Surprise Move," *Daytona Beach Morning Journal*, 3 Dec. 1964, 14 (Google News Archive).

30. William Leggett, "Fresh Breezes from the Free-Agent Draft," *Sports Illustrated*, 1 May 1967, 26 (SI Vault).

31. Blank.

32. "Evolution of the Bonus Record," *Baseball America*, 4 June 2005, http://ww w.baseballamerica.com/today/2005draft/ 050604bonus1.html (3 Nov. 2011).

33. Rany Jazayerli, "Doctoring the Numbers: The Draft, Part 4," *Baseball Prospectus*, 2 June 2005, http://www.base ballprospectus.com/article.php?articleid =4090 (10 Nov. 2011).

34. Doug Pappas, "The J.D. Drew Saga," *Outside the Lines* 4, no. 2 (1998): 4.

35. Blank.

36. Cull, 81.

37. Ibid., 82.

38. Blank.

39. Cull, 82.

40. Ibid., 104.

41. Richard J. Peurzer, "The Kansas City Royals' Baseball Academy," *The National Pastime* 24 (2004): 5–6.

42. Ibid., 6.

43. William Leggett, "School's In: Watch Out for Baseball Players," *Sports Illustrated*, 23 Aug. 1971, 38. (SI Vault).

44. Peurzer, 7.

45. Ibid., 8.

46. Ibid., 12.

47. Ibid., 10.

48. Ibid., 10.

49. Simpson, Allan, "Draft Bonuses—Ten-Year Evolution," *Perfect Game USA*, 12 May 2011, http://www.perfectgame.org/ articles/View.aspx?article=5639 (8 Nov. 2011).

50. Simpson, "Bonus."

51. "Minors."

52. Blank.

53. "Major League Baseball Scouting Bureau Q&A," MLB.com, n.d., http:// mlb.mlb.com/mlb/official_info/about_ mlb/scouting_overview.jsp (7 Nov. 2011).

54. Cull, 104.

55. Ibid., 104.

56. Ibid., 86.

57. Ibid., 94.

58. Rausch, Gary, "Evolution of the Draft," MLB.com, 16 May 2002. http://ml b.mlb.com/news/article.jsp?ymd=20 020516&content_id=26646&vkey=news_ mlb&fext=.jsp&c_id=null (24 Oct. 2011).

59. "Draft May Bring Some Teams Instant Relief," *Rome News-Tribune*, 31 May 1987, 10B. (Google News Archive).

60. Ibid.

61. Paul D. Staudohar, Franklin Lowenthal, and Anthony K. Lima, "The Evolution of Baseball's Amateur Draft," *NINE: A Journal of Baseball History and Culture* 15.1 (2006): 37 (Project MUSE).

62. Steven Goldman, "The BP Broadside: The Most Disappointing Prospects of All Time, Part 4," *Baseball Prospectus*, 7

June 2011, http://www.baseballprospectus. com/article.php?articleid=14162 (8 Nov. 2011).

63. Rausch.

64. Simpson, "Bonus."

65. Blank.

66. "Evolution."

67. Jazayerli.

68. Ibid.

69. William Oscar Johnson and William Taaffe, "A Whole New Game," *Sports Illustrated*, 26 Dec. 1988, 34 (SI Vault).

70. Ibid.

71. "ESPN Contract Riles Broadcasters: Baseball Pact Viewed as Threat to Free Televised Sports," *Los Angeles Times*, 15 Sept. 1989 (*Los Angeles Times* Collections).

72. Blank.

73. Ibid.

74. Ibid.

75. Ibid.

76. Simpson, "Bonus."

77. Ibid.

78. Doug Pappas, "The J.D. Drew Saga." *Outside the Lines* 4, no. 2 (1998): 4.

79. Ibid.

80. Ibid.

81. Ibid.

82. Blank.

83. Simpson, "Bonus."

84. Rausch.

85. Ibid.

86. Blank.

87. "Coming This June: The MLB Draft on TV," ESPN.com, 7 May 2007, htt p://sports.espn.go.com/mlb/news/story ?id=2862901 (9 Nov. 2011).

88. Blank.

89. Ibid.

90. Ibid.

91. Ibid.

92. Ibid.

93. Simpson, "Bonus."

94. Ibid.

95. Jonathan Mayo, "Deadline for Top Draft Picks Looms," MLB.com, 15 August 2007, http://mlb.mlb.com/news/article.js p?ymd=20070813&content_id=2146282 &vkey=draft2007&fext=.jsp (10 Nov. 2011).

96. Ibid.

97. Simpson, "Bonus."

98. Jim Callis, "No Matter The Slots, Teams Spent Freely In 2011," *Baseball America*, 18 August 2011, http://www. baseballamerica.com/today/draft/news/ 2011/ 2612233.html (10 Nov. 2011).

99. Ibid.

100. Jim Breen, "Hard Slotting Is Bad for Baseball," FanGraphs, 9 Nov. 2011, http://www.fangraphs.com/blogs/index. php/hard-slotting-is-bad-for-baseball/ (9 Nov. 2011).

101. Callis, "No."

102. Ben Nicholson-Smith, "CBA Details: Luxury Tax, Draft, HGH, Replay," MLB Trade Rumors, 22 Nov. 2011, http:// www.mlbtraderumors.com/2011/11/cba-details-luxury-tax-draft-.html (23 Nov. 2011).

103. Ibid.

104. Jim Callis, "Draft Cap May Not Be So Harsh," *Baseball America*, 22 Nov. 2011, http://www.baseballamerica.com/blog/ draft/2011/11/draft-cap-may-not-be-so-harsh/ (23 Nov. 2011).

105. Ibid.

106. Ibid.

107. Ibid.

108. Ken Rosenthal, "MLB Deal a Dagger to Small-Market Teams," Fox Sports, 23 Nov. 2011, http://msn.foxsports.com/ mlb/story/MLB-deal-unfair-to-small-market-teams-112211 (23 Nov. 2011).

109. Nicholson-Smith.

110. Ibid.

111. Ibid.

112. Ibid.

Chapter 2

1. Gordon Edes, "Epstein Eager for Draft; Sox Have 7 Picks in First 5 Rounds," *Boston Globe*, 5 June 2008, C5, *Factiva*, Web (9 November 2011).

2. Tom Verducci, "Upton, Braun Help '05 Claim Top Spot in Ranking of Best Draft Classes," SI.com, n.d., http:// sportsillustrated.cnn.com/2011/writers/ tom_verducci/06/07/best.draft.classes /index.html (12 November 2011).

3. "Straight to the Major Leagues," *Baseball Almanac*, n.d., http://www. baseball-almanac.com/feats/feats9.shtml (13 November 2011).

4. Keith Law, "Wood Would Be Better for College," ESPN.com, 14 August 2006, http://sports.espn.go.com/espn/page2/story?page=law/060814 (13 November 2011).

5. Jerry Crasnick, "College Starters Who Rose Very Quickly," ESPN.com, 1 June 2011, http://m.espn.go.com/mlb/story?storyId=6612022&pg=2&wjb (12 November 2011).

6. "Amateur Baseball Draft History." The Baseball Cube, http://thebaseballcube.com/draft/byYear.asp?Y=2005, http://thebaseballcube.com/draft/byYear.asp?Y=1995 (15 November 2011).

7. Ibid.

8. Paul Nyman, "In the Beginning, God Created Heaven and Earth ..." *The Hardball Times*, 18 April 2008 (13 November 2011).

9. Genevra Pittman, "Are Lefty Pitchers More Injury-Prone?" Reuters, 25 June 2010, http://www.reuters.com/article/2010/06/25/us-lefty-pitchers-more-injury-prone-idUSTRE65O3XD20100625 (20 November 2011).

10. "2008 Baseball Payrolls, List," ESPN.com, n.d., http://sports.espn.go.com/espn/wire?section=mlb&id=3324146 (17 November 2011).

11. Ibid.

12. Matt Wein, "This Could be the End of Johnny V. as the Pirates Know Him," *Centre Daily Times*, 2 August 2007, 7 (Factiva, 28 November 2011).

13. Wayne Coffey, "Life Throws Phenom a Curve; Between the Seams," *New York Daily News*, 17 July 2006, C1 (Factiva, 1 December 2011).

14. Ibid.

Chapter 3

1. "Evolution of the Bonus Record," *Baseball America*, 4 June 2005, http://www.baseballamerica.com/today/2005draft/050604bonus1.html (2 May 2012).

2. Allan Simpson, "Signing Bonuses: No. 1 Overall Picks Year-by-Year," *Perfect Game*, 9 May 2011, http://www.perfectgame.org/articles/View.aspx?article=5609 (2 May 2012).

3. Ibid.

4. "Jaime Jones," Baseball-Reference.com, n.d., http://www.baseball-reference.com/minors/player.cgi?id=jones-015jam (2 May 2012).

5. "Mike Drumright," Baseball-Reference.com, n.d., http://www.baseball-reference.com/minors/player.cgi?id=drumri001mic (2 May 2012).

6. Tom Gage, "Pitcher finds new path; Struggles leave Drumright with different outlook, career," *Detroit News*, 2 August 2007, 5 (Factiva).

7. "About Us," Drumright Builders, n.d., http://www.drumrightbuilders.com/about/default.asp (2 May 2012). Updates and confirms the number of houses built per year.

8. Sean McAdam, "How long can things go right for Sox?" *South Coast Today*, 10 May 1998, http://www.southcoasttoday.com/apps/pbcs.dll/article?AID=/1998051 0/ NEWS/305109912 (3 May 2012).

9. Buster Olney, "A Met Prospect Walks Away From Baseball," *New York Times*, 30 May 1997, http://www.nytimes.com/1997/05/30/sports/a-met-prospect-walks-away-from-baseball.html?pagewanted=all&src=pm (30 April 2012).

10. Ibid.

11. Ibid.

12. Brent Schrotenboer, "After Bilking Athletes, Gillette Now a Pastor," SignOn San Diego.com, 15 February 2006, http://www.utsandiego.com/sports/20060215-9999-1s15gillette.html (3 May 2012).

13. Olney.

14. Alan Eskew, "KC's Fasano Belts Three Homers," CJOnline.com, 1 April 1999, http://cjonline.com/stories/040199/spo_kcfasano.shtml (3 May 2012).

15. "Without Lebron, Scorpions Score Road Win," *Yuma Sun*, 25 July 2006, http://www.yumasun.com/sports/game-22350-innings-lebron.html (3 May 2012).

16. "White Sox Select Long Beach State's Liefer," *Los Angeles Times*, 2 June 1995, http://articles.latimes.com/1995-06-02/sports/sp-8733_1_long-beach-state (4 May 2012).

17. Buster Olney, "Shepherd To Sign," *Baltimore Sun*, 17 August 1995, http://articles.baltimoresun.com/1995-08-17/

sports/1995229163_1_shepherd-orioles-alvie (7 May 2012).

18. Russ Charpentier, "Extra Innings: Miller Happy to Be Back," Cape Cod Online, 17 June 2009, http://www.capecod online.com/apps/pbcs.dll/article?AID=/ 20090617/SPORTS23/90618002/-1/N EWSMAP (18 May 2012).

19. Jim Salisbury, "Doster Gets Phils' 25th Spot; Miller Returned to Indians," Philly.com, 1 April 1999, http://articles.phi lly.com/1999-04-01/sports/25520833_1_ phillies-david-miller-ed-wade (23 May 2012).

20. Joseph Person, "'Never Too Late': Corey Jenkins Goes Back to School," Go Gamecocks.com, 21 March 2010, http:// www.thestate.com/2010/03/21/1209705/ corey-jenkins.html (30 April 2012).

21. Ibid.

22. John Harper, "The Shea Hey Kid Farmhand Morenz Could Be Next Great Yankee Center Fielder," *New York Daily News*, 27 August 1995, http://articles.nyda ilynews.com/1995-08-27/sports/179901 58_1_great-yankee-center-fielder-shea-morenz-oneonta-manager (4 May 2012).

23. Ibid.

24. Rafael Hermoso, "Padres Are Yank Pen Pals Send Relief for Ex-No. 1," *New York Daily News*, 24 August 1998, http:// articles.nydailynews.com/1998-08-24/ sports/18085667_1_yankees-mike-stan ton-ray-ricken, (4 May 2012).

25. "The Global Intelligence Files," WikiLeaks, 27 February 2012, http://wik ileaks.org/the-gifiles.html, (23 May 2012).

26. Eamon Javers, "Wikileaks Stratfor Memo Reminiscent of a Spy Novel," CNBC, 27 February 2012, http://www. cnbc.com/id/46535884, (4 May 2012).

27. Thomas Harding, "Redbird Shows Grit For Majors Hass's Work Ethic May Pay Over Long Run," *Commercial Appeal*, 17 June 1999, D1 (Factiva).

28. Ibid.

29. David Schoenfield, "The 100 Worst Draft Picks Ever," ESPN Page 2, 26 April 1996, http://sports.espn.go.com/espn/pag e2/story?page=schoenfield/060427 (8 May 2012).

30. Dave Sanford, "RC's Top 10 First Half Performances: #7," Royals Corner, 7 July 2006, royals.scout.com/2/545181.html (8 May 2012).

31. Amy K. Nelson, "Dream on a Shelf," ESPN Outside the Lines, n.d., http: //sports.espn.go.com/espn/eticket/story ?page=090423/harrington (16 May 2012).

32. Ibid.

33. John Maffei, "Harrington Headed Back into Draft," *Baseball America*, 28 May 2002, http://www.baseballamerica. com/today/news/harrington052802.html (16 May 2012).

34. Nelson.

35. John Manuel, "Harrington Fires Tanzer, Hires Boras," *Baseball America*, 26 September 2011, http://www.baseballamer ica.com/today/news/harrington0925.html (16 May 2012).

36. Nelson.

37. Maffei.

38. Pat Jordan, "The Holdout," *New York Times Magazine*, 18 July 2004, www. nytimes.com/2004/07/18/magazine/the-holdout.html?pagewanted=all&src=pm (16 May 2012).

39. Ibid.

40. Nelson.

41. Ibid.

42. J.J. Cooper, "Harrington Signs Deal with the Cubs," *Baseball America*, 10 October 2006, http://www.baseballamerica. com/today/minors/news/2006/262616. html (16 May 2012). Cooper's story holds that Harrington changed agents prior to the 2001 draft when he was taken by the Padres. Manuel makes it clear the switch occurred after the draft, and Nelson confirms Manuel's chronology.

43. Ibid.

44. Jordan.

45. Nelson.

46. Cooper.

47. Nelson.

48. Kirk Kenney, "Baseball Dream Won't Die Quietly," Sign On San Diego, 13 April 2005, http://www.signonsan diego.com/uniontrib/20050413/news_ 1s13dawgs.html (6 February 2012).

49. Ibid.

50. "Mark Phillips," Baseball-Refer ence.com, n.d., http://www.baseball-refer ence.com/minors/player.cgi?id=philli 002mar (10 May 2012).

51. Tyler Kepner, "BASEBALL; Padres' Prospect Is Key to Yanks' Trade," *New York Times*, 20 March 2003, http://www.nytimes.com/2003/03/20/sports/baseball-padres-prospect-is-key-to-yanks-trade.html (6 February 2012).

52. Tom Krasovic, "Former Top Padres Prospect at Bottom of Yanks' Ladder," Sign On San Diego, 27 June 2004, http://www.signonsandiego.com/uniontrib/20040627/news_1s27minors.html (6 February 2012).

53. Todd Traub, "Texas Notes: Torres Takes Long Road," MiLB.com, 26 July 2011, http://www.milb.com/news/article.jsp?ymd=20110725&content_id=22271924&vkey=news_l109&fext=.jsp&sid=l109 (6 February 2012).

54. Ibid.

55. Derrick Goold, "Goold: Grading Cards' Top Picks Since 2000," STLToday.com, 7 June 2011, http://www.stltoday.com/sports/baseball/professional/article_a97656f0–9120–11e0-b833–001a4bcf6878.html (10 May 2012).

56. Roch Kubatko, "Johnson Returns," *Baltimore Sun*, 24 August 2007, http://articles.baltimoresun.com/2007–08–24/sports/0708240275_1_shuey-orioles-olson (7 February 2012).

57. Danny Wild, "Chicago's Negron Suspended 50 games," MiLB.com, 8 January 2010, http://www.milb.com/news/article.jsp?ymd=20100108&content_id=7893332&vkey=news_milb&fext=.jsp (7 February 2012).

58. Hal McCoy, "Ask Hal: Ballpark Count for This Writer Is at 51," *Hamilton Journal-News*, n.d., http://www.journal-news.com/hamilton-sports/cincinnati-reds/ask-hal-ballpark-count-for-this-writer-is-at-51-624116.html?showComments=true&page=2&more_comments=false&viewAsSinglePage=true (11 May 2012).

59. Jim Callis, "Ask BA," *Baseball America*, 26 May 2008, http://www.baseballamerica.com/today/prospects/askba/2008/266153.html (11 May 2012).

60. Ibid.

61. McCoy.

62. Travis Young, "Twins Make Statement with Top Pick," *Baseball America*, 14 June 2007, http://www.baseballamerica.com/blog/draft/2007/06/twins-make-statement-with-top-pick/ (11 May 2012).

63. McCoy. Young contends the length of the contract was eight years while McCoy says it was for six.

64. Chris Kahrl, "Transaction Analysis, July 22–25, 2002," *Baseball Prospectus*, n.d., http://www.baseballprospectus.com/news/20020728trans.shtml (11 May 2012).

65. Brian Walton, "Whatever Happened To…Blake Williams," The Cardinal Nation, 12 September 2005, http://stlcardinals.scout.com/2/437629.html (8 February 2012).

66. Ibid.

67. Ibid.

68. Ibid.

69. Sickels, John. "2000 First Round Part Two." Minor League Ball, 20 May 2006, http://www.minorleagueball.com/2006/5/20/155954/967 (8 February 2012).

70. Ibid.

71. Ibid.

72. Brian McTaggart, "A-Rod hits 13th, 14th. Incredible," *Houston Chronicle*, 23 April 2007, http://blog.chron.com/gamedayastros/2007/04/a-rod-hits-13th-14th-incredible/ (8 February 2012).

73. Sickels.

74. Greg Johns, "Ex-Pro Baseball Player, 26, Joins UW football Team," *Seattle Post-Intelligencer*, 14 August 2008, http://www.seattlepi.com/sports/article/Ex-pro-baseball-player-26-joins-UW-football-team-1282303.php#page-1 (9 February 2012).

75. "Tripper Johnson," *University of Washington Football*, n.d., http://www.gohuskies.com/sports/m-footbl/mtt/johnson_tripper00.html (15 May 2012).

76. Lisa Winston, "Stalled Prospects Try to Make Up for Lost Time," *USA Today*, 24 April 2002, http://www.usatoday.com/sports/bbw/2002–04–24/minors.htm (9 February 2012).

77. Jason Guarente, "Familiar Name at Third for Barnstormers," Lancaster Online, 6 March 2009 http://lancasteronline.com/article/local/234675_Familiar-name-at-third-for-Barnstormers.html (9 February 2012).

78. Ibid.

Chapter 4

1. Buck Rapp; interview by Chuck Myron; Firemen's Field, Sebring, Florida; May 25, 2012.

2. Alex Mesa; interview by Chuck Myron; Firemen's Field, Sebring, Florida; May 25, 2012.

3. Tim McIlvaine; interview by Chuck Myron; Firemen's Field, Sebring, Florida; May 25, 2012.

4. Gib Bodet; interview by Chuck Myron; Firemen's Field, Sebring, Florida; May 25, 2012.

5. Addison Russell; interview by Chuck Myron; Firemen's Field, Sebring, Florida; May 25, 2012.

6. "Top 200 Prospects," *Baseball America*, 12 June 2012, 17.

7. Pat Borders; interview by Chuck Myron; Firemen's Field, Sebring, Florida; May 25, 2012.

8. Craig Faulkner; interview by Chuck Myron; Firemen's Field, Sebring, Florida; May 25, 2012.

9. Avery Romero; interview by Chuck Myron; Firemen's Field, Sebring, Florida; May 25, 2012.

10. Jim Callis, "What Happened at the Deadline," *Baseball America*, 13 July 2012, http://www.baseballamerica.com/blog/draft/2012/07/what-happened-at-the-deadline/ (17 July 2012).

11. Jim Callis, Twitter post, July 13, 2012, 4:08 p.m. https://twitter.com/jimcallisBA (17 July 2012).

12. Justin Barney, "Prep Baseball Stars Avery Romero, Hayden Hurst Cash In with Big Deals at Signing Deadline," *Florida Times-Union*, 13 July 2012, http://jacksonville.com/ sports/ high-schools/20 12–07–13/story/prep-baseball-stars-avery-romero-hayden-hurst-cash-big-deals (17 July 2012).

13. Hayden Hurst, email interview by Chuck Myron, August 31, 2012.

14. Luis Romero, email interview by Chuck Myron, July 17, 2012.

15. Barney.

16. Matt Kimbrel; interview by Chuck Myron; Firemen's Field, Sebring, Florida; May 25, 2012.

17. Brian Kraft; interview by Chuck Myron; Firemen's Field, Sebring, Florida; May 25, 2012.

18. Kevin Towers; interview by Alan Maimon; Salt River Fields at Talking Stick, Scottsdale, Arizona; March 19, 2012.

19. Jose Ortega; interview by Chuck Myron; Firemen's Field, Sebring, Florida; May 25, 2012.

20. Lewis Brinson; interview by Chuck Myron; Firemen's Field, Sebring, Florida; May 25, 2012.

21. Hayden Hurst; interview by Chuck Myron; Kenilworth Lodge, Sebring, Florida; May 25, 2012.

22. Pat Borzi, "Settlement Sheds Little Light on N.C.A.A. No-Agent Rule," *New York Times*, 23 July 2010, http://www.nytimes.com/2010/07/24/sports/baseball/24advisers.html (24 July 2012).

23. Ibid.

24. Ibid.

25. Aaron Fitt, "NCAA Tournament, 'No Agent' Rule Could Change," *Baseball America*, 10 January 2011, http://www.baseballamerica.com/today/college/news/2011/2611133.html (24 July 2012).

26. Aaron Fitt, "ABCA Notebook: Status Quo Prevails," *Baseball America*, 9 January 2012, http://www.baseballamerica.com/blog/college/2012/01/abca-notebook-status-quo-prevails/ (24 July 2012).

27. "FAQS," IMG Baseball Academy, n.d., http://www.imgacademies.com/baseball-academy/baseball-department/faqs/ (30 July 2012).

28. "Who We Are," Bucky Dent Baseball School, n.d., http://www.buckydentbaseball.com/?page_id=1181 (30 July 2012).

29. "2012–2013 IMG Academies School & Baseball Rate Card," IMG Baseball Academy, 2012, http://www.imgacademies.com/_assets/dynamic_media/media_bank/IMG-Academies/pdf-documents/Pricing/Rate_Cards/Baseball_2012_2013.pdf (30 July 2012).

30. "2012 Draft LIVE! Draft Pick Database," *Perfect Game*, n.d., http://www.perfectgame.org/Draft/Signings.aspx (30 July 2012).

31. Ibid.

32. "State & County Quick Facts," United States Census Bureau, 6 June 2012,

http://quickfacts.census.gov/qfd/states/
12/1264875.html (30 July 2012).

Chapter 5

1. Bill Shaikin, "Helping Baseball's Scouts in a Post-'Moneyball' World," *Los Angeles Times*, 13 January 2012, http://articles.latimes.com/2012/jan/13/sports/la-sp-shaikin-moneyball-20120114 (12 January 2013).
2. Quinn Roberts, "Scouts Dinner Thrills Star-Studded Audience," MLB.com, 13 January 2013, http://mlb.mlb.com/news/article.jsp?ymd=20130113&content_id= 40944056&vkey=news_mlb&c_id=mlb (13 January 2013).
3. Bob Nightengale, "Baseball Scouts Benefit from Beverly Hills Fundraiser," *USA Today*, 10 January 2013, http://www.usatoday.com/story/sports/mlb/2013/01/10/dennis-gilbert-scouts-foundation-dinner-bud-selig-harrison-ford-jim-palmer-beverly-hills/ 1823439/ (13 January 2013). Nightengale writes that nearly four million dollars has been raised, but Roberts' estimate is more modest, at "more than $1 million."
4. Jon Paul Morosi, "Baseball Eyes Jays' 2010 Draft Class," Fox Sports, 22 June 2012, www.google.com/url?sa=t&rct=j&q=baseballscouting draft&source=web&cd=13&cad =rja&ved=0CCkQFjACOAo&url=http://msn.foxsports.com/mlb/story/toronto-blue-jays-2010-draft-class-anti-moneyball-approach62312&ei=YjPyUO65FpHy9gTnnoCwDg&usg=AFQjCNGX9X5rAhvlGny3e3dNp9lbs0_O5g&bvm=bv.1357700187,d.eWU (12 January 2013).
5. Jim Bowden, "Differing GM Styles Slowing Trade Market," ESPN.com, 10 December 2012, http://insider.espn.go.com/blog/the-gms-office/post?id=5573&addata= 2009_insdr_mod_mlb_xxx_xxx&refresh=true&refresh=true (13 January 2013).
6. Morosi.
7. Ibid.
8. Ibid.
9. Jose Ortega; interview by Chuck Myron; Firemen's Field, Sebring, Florida; May 25, 2012.

10. Brian Kraft; interview by Chuck Myron; Firemen's Field, Sebring, Florida; May 25, 2012.
11. Gib Bodet; interview by Chuck Myron; Firemen's Field, Sebring, Florida; May 25, 2012.
12. Alex Mesa; interview by Chuck Myron; Firemen's Field, Sebring, Florida; May 25, 2012.

Chapter 6

1. Kevin Towers, interview by Alan Maimon, Salt River Fieldd at Talking Stick, Scottsdale, Arizona, March 19, 2012.
2. Tom Krasovic, "Moores' Deep Pockets Enable Padres to Spend Freely on Farm System," *San Diego Union-Tribune*, 6 June 1999 (Factiva, 21 January 2013).
3. Kevin Kernan, "Padres Sign Another of Their Top Draftees," *San Diego Union-Tribune*, 29 August 1993 (Factiva, 23 January 2013).
4. Ibid.
5. Nick Gates, "Delmonico Irked by Transfer Story," *Knoxville News-Sentinel*, 12 February 1996 (Factiva, 23 January 2013).
6. Ibid.
7. Amy K. Nelson, "OTL: Dream On A Shelf," ESPNwww, n.d., http://sports.espn. go.com/espn/eticket/story?page=0 90423/harrington (24 January 2013).
8. Ibid.
9. Ibid.
10. Ibid.
11. Bernie Wilson, "Padres Suspend Top Pick Matt Bush After Arrest," Associated Press, 21 June 2004 (Factiva, 5 February 2013).
12. Lee Jenkins, "Playing in Peoria, Former Top Pick Takes the Mound," *New York Times*, 22 June 2007 (Factiva, 5 February 2013).
13. Brent Schrotenboer, "Blue Jays Release Bush After Incident in Florida," *San Diego Union-Tribune*, 4 April 2009 (Factiva, 5 February 2013).
14. Ibid.
15. Marc Topkin, "Reliever Charged with DUI, Hit and Run," *Tampa Bay Times*, 23 March 2012 (Factiva, 5 February 2013).

16. Joe Smith, "Deal Upsets Victim's Family: Ex-Rays prospect Matt Bush gets 3.5 years, no probation for DUI hit-and-run," *Tampa Bay Times*, 19 December 2012 (Factiva, 6 February 2013).

17. Dennis Waszak, Jr., "First Pick Is High School SS," *Newark Star-Ledger*, via Associated Press, 8 June 2004 (Factiva, 5 February 2013).

Chapter 7

1. "Salt Lake Bees Walk Away with Lopsided Loss," *Deseret News*, 13 August 2008, http://www.deseretnews.com/article/700250523/Salt-Lake-Bees-walk-away-with-lopsided-loss.html (6 February 2013).

2. John Mozeliak, telephone interview by Chuck Myron, October 3, 2012.

3. Joe Lamie, "Day After Being Booed by Fans, Cardinals Trade Tyler Greene To Houston," FOX2now.com, 9 August 2012, http://fox2now.com/2012/08/09/day-after-being-booed-by-fans-cardinals-trade-tyler-greene-to-houston/ (11 February 2013).

4. Jeff Passan, "If Rasmus Wants Off Cards, Pujols Says Leave," Yahoo! Sports, 5 September 2010, http://sports.yahoo.com/mlb/news?slug=jp-rasmuspujols090510 (16 February 2013).

5. Keith Law, "Ranking the Farm Systems," ESPN.com, 4 February 2013, http://insider.espn.go.com/mlb/story/_/id/8902178/st-louis-cardinals-lead-keith-law-ranking-all-30-farm-systems-mlb (14 February 2013).

6. Keith Law, "Rangers' Farm System Still Loaded," ESPN.com, 27 January 2010, http://insider.espn.go.com/mlb/insider/columns/story?columnist=law_keith&id=4861174 (18 February 2013).

7. Rick Hummel, "Cardinals Lineup Is Stocked with Home-Grown Players," STLToday.com, 21 October 2012, http://www.stltoday.com/sports/baseball/professional/cardinals-lineup-is-stocked-with-home-grown-players/article_28d1f2ff-5f18-5af8-8356-df4026b1aeb8.html (28 February 2013).

8. Ibid.

9. Michael Wacha, interview by Chuck Myron, Roger Dean Stadium, Jupiter, Florida, August 17, 2012. Note: reference missing in text

Chapter 8

1. Dave Campbell, "Twins Dismiss GM Smith, Return Ryan As Interim," AP News Archive, 7 November 2011, http://www.apnewsarchive.com/2011/Twins-dismiss-GM-Smith—return-Ryan-as-interim/id-faf8156d70fa48dd8cf6230460ff4f1e (26 February 2013).

2. "2000 Major League Baseball Attendance & Miscellaneous," Baseball-Reference.com, n.d., http://www.baseball-reference.com/leagues/MLB/2000-misc.shtml (26 February 2013).

3. Dave Sheinin, "Draft Dodger: Scott Boras's Trailblazing History With the MLB Draft," *Washington Post*, 17 August 2009, http://www.washingtonpost.com/wp-dyn/content/article/2009/08/16/AR2009081602024.html (18 January 2013).

4. Ibid.

5. Mitch Stephens, "Starting Point: Snapshots of Major League's Semifinalist," MaxPreps.com, 16 October 2009, http://www.maxpreps.com/news/qHcRrrp7Ed6OEwAcxJTdpg/starting-point—snapshots-of-major-leagues-semifinalist.htm (27 February 2013).

6. Sheinin.

7. Doug Pappas, "The J.D. Drew Saga." *Outside the Lines* 4, no. 2 (1998): 3–4.

8. Jim Rantz, telephone interview with Chuck Myron, May 23, 2011.

9. Dennis Waszak Jr., "Twins: Tough Choice With Top Pick," AP News Archive, 4 June 2001, http://www.apnewsarchive.com/2001/Twins-Tough-Choice-With-Top-Pick/id-3f51351df0aa9eaa10e5c84c5c3c0ed4 (27 February 2013).

10. Ibid.

11. Tom Haudricourt, "Too High Price to Pay," *Milwaukee Journal Sentinel*, 5 June 2011, 6C (Google News Archive).

12. Ibid.

13. Bob Nightengale, "Catcher Joe Mauer Will Test Staying Power with Twins," *USA Today*, 17 February 2010,

http://usatoday30.usatoday.com/sports/baseball/al/twins/2010–02–16-mauer_N.htm (27 February 2013).

14. Brian Landman, "Top Quarterback Prospect Commits to Florida State," *St. Petersburg Times*, 2 February 2001, http://www.sptimes.com/News/020201/Sports/Top_quarterback_prosp.shtml (27 February 2013).

15. Haudricourt.

16. Allan Simpson, "Signing Bonuses: No. 1 Overall Picks Year-by-Year," *Perfect Game USA*, 9 May 2011, http://www.perfectgame.org/Articles/View.aspx?article=5609 (27 February 2013).

17. Allan Simpson, "Bonus Progression Record," *Perfect Game USA*, 9 May 2011, http://www.perfectgame.org/Articles/View.aspx?article=5607 (27 February 2013).

18. Ibid.

19. Jake Mauer; interview by Chuck Myron; Hammond Stadium, Fort Myers, Florida; April 25, 2011.

Chapter 9

1. Dave Anderson, "Phillies' Teenager Idolizes DiMaggio," *Miami News*, reprinted from *New York Times*, 24 July 1974, 13.

2. Ibid.

3. Ibid.

4. "14 Is Not the Player's Number — It's His Age," author unknown, *People* 2, no. 8, 19 August 1974, http://people.com/people/archive/article/0,,20064377,00.html (4 December 2012).

5. Dallas Green; interview by Alan Maimon; Conowingo, Maryland; September 16, 2012.

6. Allen Abel, "Major Leagues One Escape from Little Dominican Town That Produced Rico, Alfredo: It's Baseball or Life in Cane Fields," *(Toronto) Globe and Mail*, 21 July 1979, S8 (Factiva, 11 December 2012).

7. Dan Sewell, "Baseball's Latin-Flavored Trend to Grow," Associated Press, printed in *(Spartanburg, SC) Herald-Journal*, 10 May 1979, 11.

8. Ibid.

9. Stuart Anderson and L. Brian Andrew, "Coming to America: Immigrants, Baseball and the Contributions of Foreign-Born Players to America's Pastime," *National Foundation for American Policy*, October 2006, http://nfap.com/research activities/studies/baseballcoming1006.pdf (14 December 2012).

10. Rob Ruck, "Baseball's Recruitment Abuses," *Quarterly Americas*, Summer 2011, http://americasquarterly.org/node/2745.

11. Chris Kraul, "Venezuelan Baseball Dreams Survive Political Tensions," *Los Angeles Times*, 1 April 2011, http://articles.latimes.com/print/2011/apr/01/world/la-fg-venezuela-baseball-20110401 (2 January 2013).

12. Ruck.

13. Melissa Segura, "Drafted at 13, How One Player Changed International Signing Rules," SI.com, 2 July 2012, http://sportsillustrated.cnn.com/2012/writers/melissa_segura/ 07/02/jimy-kelly/index.html (5 January 2013).

14. Ruck.

15. Melissa Segura, "Prospect Testified that Nationals' Instructor Knew of His Fake Identity," SI.com, 21 September 2010, http://sportsillustrated.cnn.com/2010/baseball/mlb/ 09/20/nationals.baez/index.html (5 January 2013).

16. Ronald Blum, "Spending Drops 11 Percent in MLB Draft," Associated Press, 18 July 2012, http://bigstory.ap.org/article/spending-drops-11-pct-mlb-draft (2 January 2013).

17. Ibid.

18. Joanna Shepherd and George B. Shepherd, "U.S. Labor Market Regulation and the Export of Employment: Major League Baseball Replaces U.S. Players with Foreigners," *Emery Law and Economics Research Paper No. 7*, 2002, http://papers.ssrn.com/sol3/papers.cfm?abstract_id=370422 (16 December 2012).

19. Bob Nightengale, "African Americans in MLB: 8%, Lowest Since Integration Era," *USA Today*, 15 April 2012, http://content.usatoday.com/communities/dailypitch/post/2012/04/mlb-jackie-robinson-day-african-american-players/1 (16 December 2012).

20. Ibid.

21. "MLB Completes 2012 First-Year Player Draft," MLB.com, 6 June 2012, http://mlb.mlb.com/news/print.jsp?ymd =20120606&content_id=32872664&vkey =pr_mlb&c_id=mlb (17 December 2012).

22. "Spencer Fordin, "MLB sees diversity grow in Draft's first night," MLB.com, 7 June 2013, http://mlb.mlb.com/news/ article.jsp?ymd=20130607&content_ id=49891314&vkey=news_mlb&c_ id=mlb (28 September 2013).

23. Tim Keown, "Is Major League Baseball too Hispanic?" ESPN.com, 4 October 2011, http://espn.go.com/espn/ print?id=7058357&type=Story&image-sPrint=off (17 December 2012).

24. Shepherd and Shepherd.

25. "Can the Dominican Republic Avoid Puerto Rico's Fate?" author unknown, *The Economist*, 4 February 2012, http://economist.com/node/21546064/ (16 December 2012).

26. Ibid.

27. Evan Brunell, "Puerto Rico a Warning Sign for Worldwide Draft," CBS Sports.com, http://cbssports.com/mcc/bl ogs/entry/22297882/28713423 (16 December 2012).

28. Ibid.

29. Adry Torres, "MLB Draft: Correa Gives Hope to Puerto Rican Baseball," Fox News Latino, http://latino.foxnews.com/ latino/sports/2012/06/06/mlb-draft-correa-gives-hope-to-puerto-rican-baseball/ (17 December 2012).

30. Jeff Passan, "Alderson Addresses Dominican Corruption," Yahoo! Sports, 22 April 2010, http://sports.yahoo.com/ mlb/news?slug=jp-dominican04221 0&print=1 (18 December 2012).

31. *The Economist*.

32. Josh Leventhal, "Selig Calls International Draft 'Inevitable,'" *Baseball America*, 23 February 2012, http://base-ballamerica.com/today/majors/news/ 2012/2613020.html (17 December 2012).

33. Johanna Shepherd Bailey and George B. Shepherd, "Baseball's Accidental Racism: The Draft, African-American Players, and the Law," *Connecticut Law Review* 44, no.1 (November 2011).

34. Jim Callis. "Ask BA," BaseballAmerica.com, 19 September 2011, http://base-ballamerica.com/today/prospects/ask-ba/ 2011/2612377.html (19 December 2012). Note reference missing in text

Chapter 10

1. David Yocum, telephone interviews by Alan Maimon, December 12, 2012, December 18, 2012, and January 7, 2013.

2. "91st Round of the 1993 MLB June Amateur Draft," Baseball-Reference.com, n.d., http://baseball-reference.com/draft/ ?query_type=year_round&year_ID=1993 &draft_round=91&draft_type=junreg& (8 December 2012).

3. Rod Beaton, "These 14 Are Projected Top Picks," *USA Today*, 4 May 1995 (Factiva, 08C, 11 December 2012).

4. Alan Schmadtke, "FSU Baseball Team Beats 1st-Place Clemson Again," *Orlando Sentinel*, 23 April 1995 (Factiva, D4, 11 December 2012).

5. Alan Schmadtke, "Drew's Blast Lifts Seminoles," *Orlando Sentinel*, 3 June 1995 (Factiva, B1, 11 December 2012).

6. Tom Vint, "'Canes Tame Seminoles 4–2 at Rainy CWS," *Tampa Tribune*, via Associated Press, 5 June 1995 (Factiva, 11 December 2012).

7. Alan Schmadtke, "USC Ousts FSU, 16–11," *Orlando Sentinel*, 7 June 1995 (Factiva, D1, 11 December 2012).

8. Lawrence Rocca, "ON THE FARM: At Vero Beach, It's Always a Day Job," *Orange County Register*, 23 July 1995 (Factiva, 12 December 2012).

9. Rod Beaton, "Where Last Year's First-Rounders Are," *USA Today*, 4 June 1996 (Factiva, 13 December 2012).

Chapter 11

1. Adam Kilgore, "Stephen Strasburg's 2013 salary," *Washington Post*, 31 October 2012, http://washingtonpost.com /blogs/nationals-journal/wp/2012/10/31/ stephen-strasburgs-2013-salary (13 March 2013).

2. "2010 Washington Nationals," Baseball-Reference.com, n.d., http://baseball-

reference.com/teams/WSN/2010-sched ule-scores.shtml (4 January 2013).

3. Gene Cherry, "Rookie Strasburg Sidelined with Inflamed Shoulder," Reuters, 28 July 2010, http://reuters.com/ article/2010/07/28/us-baseball-nationals-strasburg-idUSTRE66R3KD20100728 (4 January 2013).

4. Nancy Kercheval, "Strasburg Heads Home to Recover After Successful Elbow Surgery," Bloomberg.com, 4 September 2010, http://.bloomberg.com/apps/news? pid= 2065100&sid=arspkEJDppTg (4 January 2013).

5. Adam Kilgore, "With Stephen Strasburg on an Innings Limit, the Nationals Will Not Manipulate His Schedule," *Washington Post*, 20 Feb. 2012, http:// washingtonpost.com/blogs/nationals-jour nal/post/with-stephen-strasburg-on-an-innings-limit-the-nationals-will-not-ma nipulate-his-schedule/2012/02/20/gI QAqvZUPR_blog.html (6 January 2013).

6. Adam Kilgore, "Stephen Strasburg Says Shutdown Is 'Something That I'm Not Happy About at All,'" *Washington Post*, 8 September, 2012, http://washingt onpost.com/blogs/nationals-journal/wp/ 2012/09/08/stephen-strasburg-says-shu tdown-is-something-that-im-not-happy-about-at-all/ (6 January 2013).

7. Paul White, "Nationals Clinch NL East and First Division Title," *USA Today*, 1 October 2012, http://usatoday.com/ story/sports/mlb/2012/10/01/nationals-clinch-nl-east/1607595/ (7 January 2013).

8. Jake Simpson, "Why the Nationals Are Right to Shut Down Stephen Stras burg," *The Atlantic*, August 2012, http://. theatlantic.com/entertainment/archive/ 2012/08/why-the-nationals-are-right-to-shut-down-stephen-strasburg/261451/ (14 February 2013).

9. Rick Hummel, "Cardinals Lineup Is Stocked with Home-Grown Players," STLToday.com, 21 October 21, http://. stltoday.com/sports/baseball/professional/ cardinals-lineup-is-stocked-with-home-grown-players/article_28d1f2ff–5f18– 5af8–8356-df4026b1aeb8.html (6 January 2013).

10. Dave Zirin, "Postmortem: The Now-Infamous and Indefensible Decision to Sit Stephen Strasburg," TheNation-www, 13 October 2012, http://.thenation. com/blog/ 170547/postmortem-now-infa-mous-and-indefensible-decision-sit-stephen-strasburg# (4 January 2013).

11. Nick Friedell, "Did Dusty Baker Learn Nothing from Mark Prior and Kerry Wood?" *Yahoo! Sports*, 8 May 2008, http:// sports.yahoo.com/mlb/blog/big_league_ stew/ post/Did-Dusty-Baker-learn-noth ing-from-Mark-Prior-an?urn=mlb,81407 (11 January 2013).

12. Dave van Dyck, "The Pitch on Pitch Counts," *Chicago Sun-Times*, 26 July 1998, *Factiva*, Web (11 January 2013).

13. Steve DeShazo, "Plenty of Stars in Year in Sports," *(Fredricksburg) Free-Lance Star*, 27 December 1997, 11, 13.

14. Tyler Kepner, "A Ballplayer's Beginnings: For Chris Stowe, Major League Dreams Are Being Played in a Minor Key," *Washington Post*, 5 August 1997, E1 (Factiva, 8 January 2013).

15. Ibid.

16. Ibid.

17. Steve DeShazo, "Expos, Stowe in Stalemate," *(Fredricksburg) Free-Lance Star*, 22 February 1999, B5.

18. Zachary Levine, "Skewed Left: Year of the Right-Handed Hitter," Baseball Prospectus, 27 November 2012, http://ba seballprospectus.com/article.php?articlei-d= 18995 (9 January 2013).

19. Ibid.

20. Rany Jazayerli, "A National Mistake: Why the Washington Nationals Were Wrong to Shut Down Stephen Strasburg," Grantland, 12 September 2012, http://gr antland.com/story/_/id/8369941/history-shows-washington-nationals-shut-steph en-strasburg-too-soon (4 January 2013).

21. Ibid.

22. Ibid.

23. Teddy Greenstein, "Hershiser's Project: Protect Young Arms," *Chicago Tribune*, 24 March 2006 (Factiva, 6 January 2013).

24. Ibid.

25. Ibid.

26. Alan Schwarz, "Pitch Counts: Calculated Risks," ESPN.com, 10 May 2004, http://sports.espn.go.com/mlb/columns/ story?columnist=schwarz_alan&id= 1790788 (6 January 2013).

27. Ibid.

28. James R. Andrews, M.D., and Glenn S. Fleisig, Ph.D., "Protecting Young Pitching Arms," *The Little League Pitch Count Regulation Guide for Parents, Coaches, and League Officials,* 2008, 2, http://littleleague.org/Assets/old_assets/media/pitch_count_publication_2008.pdf (6 January 2013).

29. Hayden Hurst; email interview by Chuck Myron; August 31, 2012.

30. Hays Carlyon, "Bolles Freshman Flirts with No-Hitter," *Florida Times-Union,* 1 May 2009 (Factiva, 11 January 2013).

31. Ibid.

32. "Bolles Pitcher Earns Spot with Team USA," *Florida Times-Union,* author unknown, 11 August 2009 (Factiva, 11 January 2013).

33. Justin Barney, "Prep Baseball Stars Avery Romero, Hayden Hurst Cash In with Big Deals at Signing Deadline," 13 July 2012, http://jacksonville.com/sports/high-schools/ 2012-07-13/story/prep-baseball-stars-avery-romero-hayden-hurst-cash-big-deals (11 January 2013).

Chapter 12

1. Doug Pappas, "The J.D. Drew Saga." *Outside the Lines* 4, no. 2 (1998): 3–4.

2. Bob Golon, *No Minor Accomplishment: The Revival of New Jersey Professional Baseball* (New Brunswick, NJ: Rutgers University Press, 2008), 28–9.

3. Dave Sheinin, "Draft Dodger: Scott Boras's Trailblazing History with the MLB Draft," *Washington Post,* 17 August 2009, http://www.washingtonpost.com/wp-dyn/content/article/2009/08/16/AR2009081602024.html (18 January 2013).

4. Ibid.

5. Ibid.

6. Ibid.

7. Ibid.

8. Pappas, 4; Allan Simpson, "Signing Bonuses: No. 1 Overall Picks Year-by-Year," *Perfect Game USA,* 9 May 2011, http://www.perfectgame.org/Articles/View.aspx? article=5609 (18 January 2013). Simpson cites Benson's bonus as two million dollars, while Pappas has it as $2.5 million.

9. Pappas, 4.

10. Ben Walker, "Randy Johnson Clone, College Record-Breaker Lead Draft List," AP News Archive, 2 June 1997, http://www.apnewsarchive.com/1997/Randy-Johnson-clone-college-record-breaker-lead-draft-list/id-7926f517bbf096d552eacbe6a78e9497 (25 January 2013).

11. Walker; Jim Salisbury, "A Wealth of Talent Best College Player Ever? It Might Be J.D. Drew," Philly.com, http://articles.philly.com/1997-05-30/sports/25565479_1_seminoles-coach-mike-martin-mark-barron-phils (21 January 2013).

12. Salisbury.

13. John F. Bonfatti, "Phillies Try to Sign J.D. Drew," AP News Archive, 25 May 1998, http://www.apnewsarchive.com/1998/Phillies-Try-To-Sign-J-D-Drew/id-ea441af54e6e86333c5a252ee5917ff5 (25 January 2013).

14. Ibid.

15. Salisbury.

16. Simpson.

17. Salisbury.

18. Ibid.

19. John F. Bonfatti, "Giles Thinks Phillies Won't Sign Drew Until Next Year," AP News Archive, 14 June 1997, http://www.apnewsarchive.com/1997/Giles-thinks-Phillies-won-t-sign-Drew-until-next-year/id-a270894964a77a73151f581266b92073 (25 January 2013).

20. Ibid.

21. Kevin Goldstein, "Future Shock: Boras vs. Baseball — A Primer," *Baseball Prospectus,* 30 August 2008, http://www.baseballprospectus.com/article.php?articleid= 8012 (25 January 2013).

22. Ibid.

23. I.J. Rosenberg, "J.D. Drew, Caught in the Middle (of Nowhere)," *Atlanta Journal-Constitution,* 6 August 1997, C6 (NewsBank).

24. "Agent For Phillies' Draft Choice Says Team Never Sent Him Contract Offer," AP News Archive, 24 June 1997, http://www.apnewsarchive.com/1997/Agent-for-Phillies-draft-choice-says-team-never-sent-him-contract-offer/id-4c2802e5ef43d58df9d3442bf9e75750 (25 January 2013).

25. Goldstein.

26. Mike Augustin, "Phillies Phenom a Saint after Contract Talks Stall," *Daily News (Bowling Green, Kentucky)*, 13 July 1997, 4-B. (Google News Archive).

27. Ibid.

28. Pappas, 4.

29. Jim Salisbury, "Arbitrator to Field Grievance Involving J.D. Drew," Philly.com, 30 January 1998, http://articles.philly.com/1998–01–30/sports/25747592_1_independent-arbitrator-amateur-draft-dana-eischen (23 January 2013).

30. Ibid.

31. Ibid.

32. John F. Bonfatti, "Phillies Criticize Drew Holdout," AP News Archive, 23 February 1998, http://www.apnewsarch ive.com/1998/Phillies-Criticize-Drew-s-H oldout/id-b31b069c66773cd52218824907 1f79c5 (24 January 2012), and "Drew Wants Free Agency," *Sports Illustrated*, 23 March 1998, 25 (SI Vault). The pithiest of comments came from catcher Mark Parent, who said, "I think a lot of guys resent him. Wouldn't you? I wouldn't cover his butt."

33. Ronald Blum, "Grievance by Players Might Affect Drafting of Amateurs," *Boca Raton News*, 21 March 1998, 4B (Google News Archive).

34. Ibid.

35. Ronald Blum, "MLB Fires Arbitrator from Ryan Braun Case," *Chicago Sun-Times*, 14 May 2012, http://www.suntimes.com/sports/baseball/12532868–419/mlb-fires-arbitrator-from-ryan-braun-case.html (24 January 2013).

36. Bonfatti, "Phillies Try."

37. Ibid.

38. John F. Bonfatti, "Montgomery Replaces Giles as Phillies' CEO," AP News Archive, 21 June 1997, http://www.apnews archive.com/1997/Montgomery-replaces-Giles-as-Phillies-CEO/id-815628b92ede a263b0b74d53d061bc11 (24 January 2013).

39. Jim Salisbury, "Lee Thomas Is Fired by the Phillies, The General Manager Since 1988 Had Only One Winning Year, the Magical Season of 1993," *Philly.com*, 10 December 1997, http://articles.philly.com/1997–12–10/news/25556098_1_major-leagues-lee-elia-ed-wade (24 January 2013).

40. Jim Salisbury, "Going, Going, Gone Phils and Drew Fail to Reach an Agreement," Philly.com, 26 May 1998, http://articles.philly.com/1998–05–26/sports/25741686_1_phils-original-offer-salary-structure (27 January 2013).

41. Ibid.

42. Jim Salisbury, "Phils Turn Attention to Other Prospects Now that J.D. Drew Is History, the Focus Is on the Trading Deadline and Next Draft," Philly.com, 27 May 1998, http://articles.philly.com/1998–05–27/sports/25741844_1_mike-arbuckle-boras-and-drew-pat-burrell (24 January 2013).

43. Salisbury, "Going."

44. Simpson.

45. Goldstein.

46. Ken Berger, "Phillies 7, Cardinals 5," AP News Archive, 10 August 1999, http://www.apnewsarchive.com/1999/Phillies-7-Cardinals-5/id-948df1f63e529e86cad15f02bb1b5b58 (25 January 2013).

47. A.J. Daulerio, "Philadelphia's Continuing Misguided Hatred oOf J.D. Drew," Deadspin, 19 June 2008, http://deadspin.com/5018042/philadelphias-continuing-misguided-hatred—of-jd-drew (25 January 2013).

48. Ibid.

49. Dave Sheinin, "Boras's Next Assault on Draft Might Come From Far East," *Washington Post*, 3 July 2009, http://www.washingtonpost.com/wp-dyn/content/article/2009/07/02/AR2009070201804.html (19 February 2013).

50. Ibid.

51. Ibid.

52. Jim Callis, "Ask BA," *Baseball America*, 18 June 2012, http://www.baseballamerica.com/today/prospects/ask-ba/2012/2613567.html (19 February 2013).

53. Sheinin, "Boras's."

54. Callis.

Chapter 13

1. Dave Tollett, telephone interview by Chuck Myron, April 18, 2012.

2. Yogi Berra, *The Yogi Book: I Really Didn't Say Everything I Said!* (New York: Workman, 1998), 69.

3. Tim McIlvaine; interview by Chuck Myron; Firemen's Field, Sebring, Florida; May 25, 2012.

4. Johnny Rodriguez, interview by Chuck Myron, Roger Dean Stadium, Jupiter, Florida, August 17, 2012.

5. Alex Mesa; interview by Chuck Myron; Firemen's Field, Sebring, Florida; May 25, 2012.

6. Alan S. Kornspan and Mary J. Mac-Cracken, "The Use of Psychology in Professional Baseball: The Pioneering Work of David F. Tracy," *NINE: A Journal of Baseball History and Culture* 11, no. 2 (2003): 36.

7. Christopher D. Green, "'America's First Sport Psychologist,'" American Psychological Association, April 2012, http://www.apa.org/monitor/2012/04/sport.aspx (13 December 2012).

8. Ibid.

9. Kornspan and MacCracken, 37.

10. Ibid., 39.

11. Bob Tewksbury, phone interview by Chuck Myron, March 2, 2012. Tewksbury references from other sources are specifically noted.

12. David Laurila, "Prospectus Q&A: Bob Tewksbury," *Baseball America*, 5 March 2007, http://www.baseballprospectus.com/article.php?articleid=5931 (11 December 2012).

13. Casey Tefertiller, "Front-Office Veteran Wins Hemond Award for Excellence in Player Development," *Baseball America*, 15 Dec. 2006, http://www.baseballamerica.com/ today/majors/awards/roland-hemond-award/2006/262951.html (28 November 2012).

14. T. Rees Shapiro, "Harvey Dorfman, Psychologist to Top Baseball Stars, Dies at 75," *Washington Post*, 3 March 2011, http://www.washingtonpost.com/wp-dyn/content/ article/2011/03/03/AR2011030304871.html (28 November 2012).

15. Ibid.

16. Ibid.

17. "Sports Psychology — Mental Game vs. Physical Game," CBS Healthwatch, June 2000, http://cbshealthwatch.medsca

pe.com/cx/viewarticle/217955, quoted in Kornspan and MacCracken, 40.

18. David Lennon, "Pelfrey Laments Death of Psychologist," *Newsday*, 1 March 2011, http://www.newsday.com/sports/ baseball/mets/pelfrey-laments-death-of-psychologist-1.2722598 (28 November 2012).

19. Ibid.

20. Harvey A. Dorfman and Karl Kuehl, *The Mental Game of Baseball: A Guide to Peak Performance* (South Bend, IN: Diamond Communications, 1995), 28.

21. Mark Sheldon, "Psychology in Baseball: Heroes Are Human," MLB.com, 10 August 2009, http://mlb.mlb.com/ news/article.jsp?ymd=20090809&content_id= 6334524&vkey=news_mlb&c_id=mlb&fext=.jsp (7 December 2012).

22. Danny Wild, "Stanley, Thompson Banned 50 games," MiLB.com, 27 March 2012, http://www.milb.com/news/article. jsp?ymd=20120327&content_id=27674424& fext=.jsp&vkey=news_milb (7 December 2012).

23. Cody Stanley; interview by Chuck Myron; Roger Dean Stadium, Jupiter, Florida; August 17, 2012.

24. Chuck Carree, "Setbacks Don't Define Wild Year for Stanley," *Star News Online*, 5 September 2012, http://www.starnewsonline.com/article/20120905/ COLUMNIST/ 120909871?p=1&tc=pg (13 December 2012).

25. Laurila.

26. Chris Ballard, "Moneyballsy," *Sports Illustrated*, 3 December 2012, 56.

27. "Rick Ankiel," Baseball-Reference.com, n.d., http://www.baseball-reference.com/minors/player.cgi?id=ankiel001ric (12 December 2012).

28. "Cardinals Insider: 10 Questions with Joe Strauss," STL Today.com, 1 November 2012, http://www.stltoday.com/ sports/baseball/professional/cardinals-insider-questions-with-joe-strauss/ article_ac23780c-239f-11e2-a22b-0019bb30f31a.html (12 December 2012).

29. Zach Links, "Astros Sign Rick Ankiel," MLB Trade Rumors, 17 January 2013, http://www.mlbtraderumors.com/ 2013/01/astros-sign-rick-ankiel.html (20 March 2013).

30. Sheldon; Jim Luttrell, "Putting the Pressure on a Diagnosis," *New York Times*, 6 June 2009, http://bats.blogs.nytimes.com/2009/06/06/putting-the-pressure-on-a-diagnosis (12 December 2012).

31. Luttrell.

32. Ibid.

33. Jonah Keri, *The Extra 2%* (New York: ESPN Books, 2011), 111.

34. Larry Stone, "The Art of Baseball: A Tradition of Superstition," *Seattle Times*, 26 September 2005, http://seattletimes.com/html/mariners/2002518797_artx25.html (13 December 2012).

35. Ibid.

Chapter 14

1. "Conversation With…Dean of Admission Janet Rapelye, Part I," http://www.princeton.edu/admission/multimedia/player/?id=5212 (26 July 2013).

2. Lawrence Mishel and Natalie Sabadish, "CEO Pay and the Top 1%: How Executive Compensation and Financial-Sector Pay Have Fueled Income Inequality," *Economic Policy Institute*, 2 May 2012, http://www.epi.org/publication/ib331-ceo-pay-top-1-percent (8 January 2013). The lower percentage is based on CEO compensation that includes salary, bonus, restricted stock grants, stock options granted, and long-term incentive payouts. The higher figure includes the amount of exercised stock options instead of those that have been granted.

3. Joe Walsh, telephone interview with Chuck Myron, October 1, 2012.

4. "Operation and Maintenance Overview Fiscal Year 2012 Budget Estimates," United States Department of Defense, February 2011, 166, http://comptroller.defense.gov/defbudget/fy2012/fy2012_OM_Overview.pdf (9 January 2013).

5. Nickolas Hinton, telephone interview by Chuck Myron, December 4, 2012.

6. Joshua Botteicher, telephone interview by Chuck Myron, December 5, 2012.

7. Walter Caudle, telephone interview by Chuck Myron, December 31, 2012.

8. Patrick Thornton, *Sports Law* (Sudbury, MA: Jones and Bartlett, 2011), 88.

9. "LinkedIn Reaches 200 Million Members Worldwide," LinkedIn Press Center, 9 January 2013, http://press.linkedin.com/News-Releases/165/LinkedIn-reaches-200-million-members-worldwide (11 January 2013).

10. Jeff Passan, "'Pirates' 'Hells Angels,' 'Navy SEALs' Minor League Training Methods Become MLB Joke," Yahoo! Sports, 21 September 2012, http://sports.yahoo.com/news/ pirates-hells-angels-navy-seals-minor-league-training-methods-become-mlb-joke.html (11 January 2013). Note reference missing in text

Epilogue

1. Aaron Hicks, interview by Alan Maimon, Trenton, New Jersey, August 28, 2012.

2. David Yocum, telephone interview by Alan Maimon, February 13, 2013.

Bibliography

Abel, Allen. "Major Leagues One Escape from Little Dominican Town That Produced Rico, Alfredo: It's Baseball or Life in Cane Fields." *(Toronto) Globe and Mail*, 21 July 1979, S8. (Factiva).

"About Us." *Drumright Builders*, n.d., http://www.drumrightbuilders.com/about/default.asp (2 May 2012).

"Agent For Phillies' Draft Choice Says Team Never Sent Him Contract Offer." AP News Archive, 24 June 1997, http://www.apnewsarchive.com/1997/Agent-for-Phillies-draft-choice-says-team-never-sent-him-contract-offer/id-4c2802e5ef43d58df9d3442bf9e75750 (25 January 2013).

"Amateur Baseball Draft History." thebaseballcube www. http://thebaseballcube.com/draft/byYear.asp?Y=2005, http://thebaseballcube.com/draft/byYear.asp?Y=1995 (15 November 2011).

Anderson, Dave. "Phillies' Teenager Idolizes DiMaggio." *Miami News*, reprinted from *New York Times*, 24 July 1974, 13.

Anderson, Stuart, and L. Brian Andrew. "Coming to America: Immigrants, Baseball and the Contributions of Foreign-Born Players to America's Pastime." *National Foundation for American Policy*, October 2006, http://nfap.com/researchactivities/studies/baseiballcoming1006.pdf (14 December 2012).

Andrews, James R., M.D., and Glenn S. Fleisig, Ph.D. "Protecting Young Pitching Arms," *The Little League Pitch Count Regulation Guide for Parents, Coaches, and League Officials.* 2008, 2, http:/littleleague.org/Assets/old_assets/media/pitch_count_publication_2008.pdf (6 January 2013).

Augustin, Mike. "Phillies Phenom a Saint After Contract Talks Stall." *Daily News (Bowling Green, Kentucky)*, 13 July 1997, 4-B. (Google News Archive).

Ballard, Chris, "Moneyballsy," *Sports Illustrated*, 3 December 2012, 50–9.

Barney, Justin. "Prep Baseball Stars Avery Romero, Hayden Hurst Cash In with Big Deals at Signing Deadline." *The Florida Times-Union*, 13 July 2012, http://jacksonville.com/sports/high-schools/2012-07-13/story/prep-baseball-stars-avery-romero-hayden-hurst-cash-big-deals (17 July 2012).

Bavasi, Buzzie, and Jack Olsen. "The Real Secret of Trading." *Sports Illustrated*, 5 June 1967, 47–54 (SI Vault).

Beaton, Rod. "These 14 Are Projected Top Picks." *USA Today*, 4 May 1995, 08C. (Factiva).

_____. "Where Last Year's First-Rounders Are." *USA Today*, 4 June 1996 (Factiva).

Berger, Ken. "Phillies 7, Cardinals 5." *AP News Archive*, 10 August 1999, http://www.apnewsarchive.com/1999/Phillies-7-Cardinals-5/id-948df1f63e529e86cad15f02bb1b5b58 (25 January 2013).

Berra, Yogi. *The Yogi Book: I Really Didn't Say Everything I Said!* New York: Workman, 1998.

Blank, Jeff. "Evolution of Draft." Jeff Blank Baseball Blog, n.d., http://www.jeffblankbaseball.com/?page_id=12 (19 Oct. 2011).

Blum, Ronald. "Grievance by Players Might Affect Drafting of Amateurs." *Boca Raton News*, via Associated Press, 21 March 1998, 4B (Google News Archive).

_____. "Spending Drops 11 Percent in MLB Draft." Associated Press, 18 July 2012, http://bigstory.ap.org/article/spending-drops-11-pct-mlb-draft (2 January 2013).

"Bolles Pitcher Earns Spot with Team USA." *Florida Times-Union.* 11 August 2009 (Factiva).

Bonfatti, John F. "Giles Thinks Phillies Won't Sign Drew Until Next Year." AP News Archive, 14 June 1997, http://www.apnewsarchive.com/1997/Giles-thinks-Phillies-won-t-sign-Drew-until-next-year/id-a270894964a77a73151f581266b92073 (25 January 2013).

_____. "MLB Fires Arbitrator from Ryan Braun Case." *Chicago Sun-Times*, via Associated Press, 14 May 2012, http://www.suntimes.com/sports/baseball/12532868-419/mlb-fires-arbitrator-from-ryan-braun-case.html (24 January 2013).

_____. "Montgomery Replaces Giles as Phillies' CEO." AP News Archive, 21 June 1997, http://www.apnewsarchive.com/1997/Montgomery-replaces-Giles-as-Phillies-CEO/id-815628b92edea263b0b74d53d061bc11 (24 January 2013).

_____. "Phillies Criticize Drew Holdout." AP News Archive, 23 February 1998, http://www.apnewsarchive.com/1998/Phillies-Criticize-Drew-s-Holdout/id-b31b069c66773cd522188249071f79c5 (24 January 2013).

_____. "Phillies Try to Sign J.D. Drew." AP News Archive, 25 May 1998, http://www.apnewsarchive.com/1998/Phillies-Try-To-Sign-J-D-Drew/id-ea441af54e6e86333c5a252ee5917ff5 (25 January 2013).

Borzi, Pat. "Settlement Sheds Little Light on N.C.A.A. No-Agent Rule." *New York Times*, 23 July 2010, http://www.nytimes.com/2010/07/24/sports/baseball/24advisers.html (24 July 2012).

Bowden, Jim. "Differing GM Styles Slowing Trade Market." ESPN.com, 10 December 2012, http://insider.espn.go.com/blog/the-gms-office/post?id=5573&addata=2009_insdr_mod_mlb_xxx_xxx&refresh=true&refresh=true (13 January 2013).

Breen, Jim. "Hard Slotting Is Bad for Baseball." *FanGraphs,* 9 November 2011, http://www.fangraphs.com/blogs/index.php/hard-slotting-is-bad-for-baseball/ (9 November 2011).

Brunell, Evan. "Puerto Rico a Warning Sign for Worldwide Draft." cbssports.com, http://cbssports.com/mcc/blogs/entry/22297882/28713423 (16 December 2012).

Burk, Robert Fredrick. *Much More Than a Game.* Chapel Hill: University of North Carolina Press, 2001.

Callis, Jim. "Ask BA." *Baseball America*, 26 May 2008, http://www.baseballamerica.com/today/prospects/ask-ba/2008/266153.html (11 May 2012).

_____. "Ask BA." *Baseball America,* 19 September 2011, http://baseballamerica.com/today/prospects/ask-ba/2011/2612377.html (19 December 2012).

_____. "Ask BA." *Baseball America,* 18 June 2012, http://www.baseballamerica.com/today/prospects/ask-ba/2012/2613567.html (19 February 2013).

_____. "Draft Cap May Not Be So Harsh." *Baseball America*, 22 Nov. 2011, http://www.baseballamerica.com/blog/draft/2011/11/draft-cap-may-not-be-so-harsh/ (23 Nov. 2011).

_____. "No Matter the Slots, Teams Spent Freely in 2011." *Baseball America,* 18 Aug. 2011, http://www.baseballamerica.com/today/draft/news/2011/2612233.html (10 Nov. 2011).

_____. Twitter post, July 13, 2012, 4:08 p.m. https://twitter.com/jimcallisBA (17 July 2012).

_____. "What Happened at the Deadline." *Baseball America,* 13 July 2012, http://www.baseballamerica.com/blog/draft/2012/07/what-happened-at-the-deadline/ (17 July 2012).

Campbell, Dave. "Twins Dismiss GM Smith, Return Ryan As Interim." AP News Archive, 7 November 2011, http://www.apnewsarchive.com/2011/Twins-dismiss-GM-Smith — return-Ryan-as-interim/id-faf8156d70fa48dd8cf6 230460ff4f1e (26 February 2013).

"Can the Dominican Republic Avoid Puerto Rico's Fate?" *The Economist*, 4 February 2012, http://economist.com/node/21546064/ (16 December 2012).

"Cardinals Insider: 10 Questions with Joe Strauss." Stltoday.com, 1 November 2012, http://www.stltoday.com/sports/baseball/professional/cardinals-insider-questions-with-joe-strauss/article_ac23780c-239f-11e2-a22b-0019bb30f31a.html (12 December 2012).

Carlyon, Hays. "Bolles freshman flirts with no-hitter." *Florida Times-Union*, 1 May 2009 (Factiva).

Carree, Chuck. "Setbacks Don't Define Wild Year for Stanley." *StarNews* Online, 5 September 2012, http://www.starnewsonline.com/article/20120905/COLUMNIST/120909871?p= 1&tc=pg (13 December 2012).

"Chad Mottola." Baseball-Reference.com. n.d., http://.baseball-reference.com/minors/player.cgi?id=mottol001cha (21 May 2011).

Charpentier, Russ. "Extra Innings: Miller Happy to be Back." CapeCodOnline.com, 17 June 2009, http://www.capecodonline.com/apps/pbcs.dll/article?AID=/20090617/SPORTS23/ 906180 02/-1/NEWSMAP (18 May 2012).

Cherry, Gene. "Rookie Strasburg Sidelined with Inflamed Shoulder." Reuters, 28 July 2010, http://reuters.com/article/2010/07/28/us-baseball-nationals-strasburg-idUSTRE66R3KD20100728 (4 January 2013).

Christensen, Joe. "Wimmers Now Faces Recovery." *Minneapolis Star Tribune*, 2 August 2012, http://www.startribune.com/sports/twins/164836046.html?refer=y (12 March 2013).

Coffey, Wayne. "Life Throws Phenom a Curve; Between the Seams." *New York Daily News*, 17 July 2006, C1 (Factiva).

"Coming this June: The MLB Draft on TV." ESPNwww, 7 May 2007, http://sports.espn.go.com/mlb/news/story?id=2862901 (9 November 2011).

"Conversation With...Dean of Admission Janet Rapelye, Part I," http://www.princeton.edu/admission/multimedia/player/?id=5212 (26 July 2013).Cooper, J.J. "Harrington Signs Deal with the Cubs." *Baseball America*, 10 October 2006, http://www.baseballamerica.com/today/minors/news/2006/262616.html (16 May 2012).

Crasnick, Jerry. "College Starters Who Rose Very Quickly," ESPN.com, 1 June 2011, http://m.espn.go.com/mlb/story?storyId=6612022&pg=2&wjb (12 November 2011).

Cull, Robert. *Rumors of Baseball's Demise: How the Balance of Competition Swung and the Critics Missed*. Jefferson, NC: McFarland, 2006.

Daulerio, A.J. "Philadelphia's Continuing Misguided Hatred of J.D. Drew." *Deadspin*, 19 June 2008, http://deadspin.com/5018042/philadelphias-continuing-misguided-hatred — of-jd-drew (25 January 2013).

DeShazo, Steve. "Expos, Stowe in Stalemate." *(Fredricksburg) Free-Lance Star*, 22 February 1999, B5.

_____. "Plenty of Stars in Year in Sports." *(Fredricksburg) Free-Lance Star*, 27 December 1997, 11, 13.

Dorfman, Harvey A., and Karl Kuehl. *The Mental Game of Baseball: A Guide to Peak Performance*. South Bend, IN: Diamond Communications, 1995.

Doyle, Pat. "Branch Rickey's Farm." *Baseball Almanac*, n.d, http://www.baseball-almanac.com/minor-league/minor2005a.shtml (3 November 2011).

"Draft May Bring Some Teams Instant Relief." *Rome News-Tribune*, 31 May 1987, 10B (Google News Archive).

"Drew Wants Free Agency." *Sports Illustrated*, 23 March 1998, 25 (SI Vault).

Edes, Gordon. "Epstein Eager for Draft; Sox Have 7 Picks in First 5 Rounds." *Boston Globe*, 5 June 2008, C5 (Factiva).

_____. "He's Loved but Not Needed." *South Florida Sun-Sentinel*, 15 March 1996, http://articles.sun-sentinel.com/1996-03-15/sports/9603150099_1_reds-manager-chad-mottola-love (21 May 2011).

Eskew, Alan. "KC's Fasano Belts Three

Homers." CJOnline.com, 1 April 1999, http://cjonline.com/stories/040199/spo_kcfasano.shtml (3 May 2012).

"ESPN Contract Riles Broadcasters: Baseball Pact Viewed as Threat to Free Televised Sports." *Los Angeles Times*, 15 September 1989 (*Los Angeles Times* Collections).

"Evolution of the Bonus Record." *Baseball America*, 4 June 2005, http://www.baseballamerica.com/today/2005draft/050604bonus1.html (3 Nov. 2011).

"FAQS." IMG Baseball Academy, n.d., http://www.imgacademies.com/baseball-academy/baseball-department/faqs/ (30 July 2012).

Fitt, Aaron. "ABCA Notebook: Status Quo Prevails." *Baseball America*, 9 January 2012, http://www.baseballamerica.com/blog/college/2012/01/abca-notebook-status-quo-prevails/ (24 July 2012).

_____. "NCAA Tournament, "'No Agent' Rule Could Change." *Baseball America*, 10 January 2011, http://www.baseballamerica.com/today/college/news/2011/2611133.html (24 July 2012).

Fordin, Spencer. "MLB Sees Diversity Grow in Draft's First Night." MLB.com, 7 June 2013, http://mlb.mlb.com/news/article.jsp?ymd=20130607&content_id=49891314&vkey=news_mlb&c_id=mlb (28 September 2013).

"14 Is Not the Player's Number — It's His Age." *People* 2, no. 8, 19 August 1974, http://people.com/people/archive/article/0,,20064377,00.html (4 December 2012).

Friedell, Nick. "Did Dusty Baker Learn Nothing from Mark Prior and Kerry Wood?" Yahoo! Sports, 8 May 2008, http://sports.yahoo.com/mlb/blog/big_league_stew/post/Did-Dusty-Baker-learn-nothing-from-Mark-Prior-an?urn=mlb,81407 (11 January 2013).

Gage, Tom. "Pitcher Finds New Path; Struggles Leave Drumright with Different Outlook, Career." *The Detroit News*, 2 August 2007, 5 (Factiva).

Gates, Nick. "Delmonico Irked by Transfer Story." *Knoxville News-Sentinel*, 12 February 1996 (Factiva).

Gleeman, Aaron. "Twins' First-Round Pick Alex Wimmers Shut Down After Six Straight Walks in First Start." NBCSports.com, 15 April 2011, http://hardballtalk.nbcsports.com/2011/04/15/twins-first-round-pick-alex-wimmers-shut-down-after-six-straight-walks-in-first-start/ (30 April 2011).

"The Global Intelligence Files." WikiLeaks, 27 February 2012, http://wikileaks.org/the-gifiles.html (23 May 2012).

Goldman, Steven. "The BP Broadside: The Most Disappointing Prospects of All Time, Part 4," *Baseball Prospectus*, 7 June 2011, http://www.baseballprospectus.com/article.php?articleid=14162 (8 November 2011).

Goldstein, Kevin. "Future Shock: Boras vs. Baseball — A Primer." *Baseball Prospectus*, 30 August 2008, http://www.baseballprospectus.com/article.php?articleid=8012 (25 January 2013).

Golon, Bob. *No Minor Accomplishment: The Revival of New Jersey Professional Baseball*. New Brunswick, NJ: Rutgers University Press, 2008.

Goold, Derrick. "Goold: Grading Cards' Top Picks Since 2000." STLTodaywww, 7 June 2011, http://www.stltoday.com/sports/baseball/professional/article_a97656f0-9120-11e0-b833-001a4bcf6878.html (10 May 2012).

Green, Christopher D. "'America's First Sport Psychologist.'" *American Psychological Association*, April 2012, http://www.apa.org/monitor/2012/04/sport.aspx (13 December 2012).

Greenstein, Teddy. "Hershiser's Project: Protect Young Arms." *Chicago Tribune*, 24 March 2006 (Factiva).

Guarente, Jason. "Familiar Name at Third for Barnstormers." Lancaster Online, 6 March 2009 http://lancasteronline.com/article/local/234675_Familiar-name-at-third-for-Barnstormers.html (9 February 2012).

Harding, Thomas. "Redbird Shows Grit for Majors Hass's Work Ethic May Pay Over Long Run." *Commercial Appeal*, 17 June 1999, D1 (Factiva).

Harper, John. "The Shea Hey Kid Farmhand Morenz Could Be Next Great Yankee Center Fielder." *New York Daily News*, 27 August 1995, http://articles.nydailynews.com/1995-08-27/sports/17990158_1_great-yankee-center-fielder-shea-morenz-oneonta-manager (4 May 2012).

Haudricourt, Tom. "Too High Price to Pay." *Milwaukee Journal Sentinel*, 5 June 2011, 6C (Google News Archive).

Hawkins, Jim, Dan Ewald, and George Van Dusen. *The Detroit Tigers Encyclopedia*. Champaign, IL: Sports, 2002.

Hermoso, Rafael. "Padres Are Yank Pen Pals Send Relief For Ex-No. 1." *New York Daily News*, 24 August 1998, http://articles.nydailynews.com/1998-08-24/sports/18085667_1_ yankees-mike-stanton-ray-ricken, (4 May 2012).

Hummel, Rick. "Cardinals Lineup Is Stocked with Home-Grown Players." STLToday.com, 21 October 2012, http://www.stltoday.com/sports/baseball/professional/cardinals-lineup-is-stocked-with-home-grown-players/article_28d1f2ff-5f18-5af8-8356-df4026b1aeb8.html (6 January 2013).

"Jaime Jones," *Baseball-Reference.com*, n. d., http://www.baseball-reference.com/minors/ player.cgi?id=jones-015jam (2 May 2012).

Javers, Eamon. "Wikileaks Stratfor Memo Reminiscent of a Spy Novel." CNBC, 27 February 2012, http://www.cnbc.com/id/46535884 (4 May 2012).

Jazayerli, Rany. "A National Mistake: Why the Washington Nationals Were Wrong to Shut Down Stephen Strasburg." Grantland, 12 September 2012, http://grantland.com/story/_/id/8369941/history-shows-washington-nationals-shut-stephen-strasburg-too-soon (4 January 2013).

_____. "Doctoring the Numbers: The Draft, Part 4." *Baseball Prospectus*, 2 June 2005, http://www.baseballprospectus.com/article.php?articleid=4090 (10 November 2011).

Jenkins, Lee. "Playing in Peoria, Former Top Pick Takes the Mound." *New York Times*, 22 June 2007 (Factiva).

Johns, Greg. "Ex-Pro Baseball Player, 26, Joins UW Football Team." *Seattle Post-Intelligencer*, 14 August 2008, http://www.seattlepi.com/sports/article/Ex-pro-baseball-player-26-joins-UW-football-team-1282303.php#page-1 (9 February 2012).

Johnson, William Oscar, and William Taaffe. "A Whole New Game." *Sports Illustrated*, 26 Dec. 1988, 34–42. (SI Vault).

Jordan, Pat. "The Holdout." *New York Times Magazine*, 18 July 2004, http://www.nytimes.com/ 2004/07/18/magazine/the-holdout.html?pagewanted=all&src=pm (16 May 2012).

Kahrl, Chris. "Transaction Analysis, July 22–25, 2002." *Baseball Prospectus*, n.d., http://www.baseballprospectus.com/news/20020728trans.shtml (11 May 2012).

Kenney, Kirk. "Baseball Dream Won't Die Quietly." SignOn San Diego.com, 13 April 2005, http://www.signonsandiego.com/uniontrib/20050413/news_1s13dawgs.html (6 February 2012).

Keown, Tim. "Is Major League Baseball too Hispanic?" ESPN.com, 4 October 2011, http://espn.go.com/espn/print?id=7058357&type=Story&imagesPrint=off (17 December 2012).

Kepner, Tyler. "A Ballplayer's Beginnings: For Chris Stowe, Major League Dreams Are Being Played in a Minor Key." *Washington Post*, 5 August 1997, E1 (Factiva).

_____. "BASEBALL; Padres' Prospect Is Key to Yanks' Trade." *New York Times*, 20 March 2003, http://www.nytimes.com/2003/03/20/sports/baseball-padres-prospect-is-key-to-yanks-trade.html (6 February 2012).

Kercheval, Nancy. "Strasburg Heads Home to Recover After Successful Elbow Surgery." Bloomberg.com, 4 September 2010, http://www.bloomberg.com/apps/news?pid=2065100&sid=arspkEJDppTg (4 January 2013).

Keri, Jonah. *The Extra 2%*. New York: ESPN, 2011.

Kernan, Kevin. "Padres Sign Another of Their Top Draftees." *San Diego Union-Tribune*, 29 August 1993 (Factiva).

Kilgore, Adam. "Stephen Strasburg Says Shutdown Is 'Something that I'm Not Happy About at All.'" *Washington Post*, 8 September 2012, http://washington post.com/blogs/nationals-journal/wp/2012/09/08/stephen-strasburg-says-shutdown-is-something-that-im-not-happy-about-at-all/ (6 January 2013).

_____. "Stephen Strasburg's 2013 salary." *Washington Post*, 31 October 2012, http://washingtonpost.com/blogs/nationals-journal/wp/2012/10/31/stephen-strasburgs-2013-salary (13 March 2013).

_____. "With Stephen Strasburg on an Innings Limit, the Nationals Will Not Manipulate His Schedule." *Washington Post*, 20 February 2012, http://washingtonpost.com/blogs/ nationals-journal/post/with-stephen-strasburg-on-an-innings-limit-the-nationals-will-not-manipulate-his-schedule/2012/02/20/gIQAqvZUPR_blog.html (6 January 2013).

Kornspan, Alan S., and Mary J. Mac-Cracken. "The Use of Psychology in Professional Baseball: The Pioneering Work of David F. Tracy." *NINE: A Journal of Baseball History and Culture* 11, no. 2 (2003): 36–43.

Krasovic, Tom. "Former Top Padres Prospect at Bottom of Yanks' Ladder." SignOn San Diego.com, 27 June 2004, http://www.signonsandiego.com/uniontrib/20040627/news_ 1s27minors.html (6 February 2012).

_____. "Moores' Deep Pockets Enable Padres to Spend Freely on Farm System." *San Diego Union-Tribune*, 6 June 1999 (Factiva).

Kraul, Chris. "Venezuelan Baseball Dreams Survive Political Tensions." *Los Angeles Times*, 1 April 2011, http://articles.latimes.com/print/2011/apr/01/world/la-fg-venezuela-baseball-20110401 (2 January 2013).

Kubatko, Roch. "Johnson Returns." *The Baltimore Sun*, 24 August 2007, http://articles.baltimoresun.com/2007-08-24/sports/0708240275_1_shuey-orioles-olson (7 February 2012).

Lamie, Joe. "Day After Being Booed by Fans, Cardinals Trade Tyler Greene to Houston." FOX2now.com, 9 August 2012, http://fox2now.com/2012/08/09/day-after-being-booed-by-fans-cardinals-trade-tyler-greene-to-houston/ (11 February 2013).

Landman, Brian. "Top Quarterback Prospect Commits to Florida State." *St. Petersburg Times*, 2 February 2001, http://www.sptimes.com/News/020201/Sports/Top_quarterback_ prosp.shtml (27 February 2013).

Laurila, David. "Prospectus Q&A: Bob Tewksbury." *Baseball America*, 5 March 2007, http://www.baseballprospectus.com/article.php?articleid=5931 (11 December 2012).

Law, Keith. "Rangers' Farm System Still Loaded." ESPN.com, 27 January 2010, http://insider.espn.go.com/mlb/insider/columns/story?columnist=law_keith&id=4861174 (18 February 2013).

_____. "Ranking the Farm Systems." ESPN.com, 4 February 2013, http://insider.espn.go.com/mlb/story/_/id/8902178/st-louis-cardinals-lead-keith-law-ranking-all-30-farm-systems-mlb (14 February 2013).

_____. "Wood Would Be Better for College." ESPN.com, 14 August 2006, http://sports.espn.go.com/espn/page2/story?page=law/060814 (13 November 2011).

Leggett, William. "Fresh Breezes from the Free-Agent Draft." *Sports Illustrated*, 1 May 1967, 26. (SI Vault).

_____. "School's In: Watch Out for Baseball Players." *Sports Illustrated*, 23 August 1971, 38–9. (SI Vault).

Lennon, David. "Pelfrey Laments Death of Psychologist." *Newsday*, 1 March 2011, http://www.newsday.com/sports/baseball/mets/pelfrey-laments-death-of-psychologist-1.2722598 (28 November 2012).

Leventhal, Josh. "Selig Calls International Draft 'Inevitable.'" *Baseball America*, 23 February 2012, http://baseballamerica.com/today/majors/news/2012/2613020.html (17 December 2012).

Levine, Zachary. "Skewed Left: Year of the Right-Handed Hitter." *Baseball*

Prospectus, 27 November 2012, http://b aseballprospectus.com/article.php? articleid=18995 (9 January 2013).

"LinkedIn reaches 200 Million Members Worldwide." LinkedIn Press Center, 9 January 2013, http://press.linkedin.com /News-Releases/165/LinkedIn-reaches-200-million-members-worldwide (11 January 2013).

Links, Zach. "Astros Sign Rick Ankiel." MLB Trade Rumors, 17 January 2013, http://www.mlbtraderumors.com/2013/ 01/astros-sign-rick-ankiel.html (20 March 2013).

Luttrell, Jim. "Putting the Pressure on a Diagnosis." *New York Times*, 6 June 2009, http://bats.blogs.nytimes.com/ 2009/06/06/putting-the-pressure-on-a-diagnosis (12 December 2012).

Maffei, John. "Harrington Headed Back into Draft." *Baseball America*, 28 May 2002, http://www.baseballamerica. com/today/news/harrington052802. html (16 May 2012).

"Major League Baseball Scouting Bureau Q&A." MLB.com, n.d., http://mlb.mlb. com/mlb/ official_info/about_mlb/sc outing_overview.jsp (7 November 2011).

Manuel, John. "Harrington Fires Tanzer, Hires Boras." *Baseball America*, 26 September 2011, http://www.baseballamer ica.com/today/news/harrington0925. html (16 May 2012).

"Mark Phillips." *Baseball-Reference.com*, n.d., http://www.baseball-reference.co m/minors/ player.cgi?id=philli002mar (10 May 2012).

Mayo, Jonathan. "Deadline for Top Draft Picks Looms." MLB.com, 15 August 2007, http://mlb.mlb.com/news/article. jsp?ymd=20070813&content_id= 2146282&vkey=draft2007&fext=.jsp (10 Nov. 2011).

McAdam, Sean. "How Long Can Things Go Right for Sox?" South Coast Today, 10 May 1998, http://www.southcoastto day.com/apps/pbcs.dll/article?AID=/ 19980510/NEWS/305109912 (3 May 2012).

McCoy, Hal. "Ask Hal: Ballpark Count for This Writer Is at 51." *Hamilton Journal-News*, n.d., http://www.journal-news. com/hamilton-sports/cincinnati-reds/ ask-hal-ballpark-count-for-this-writer-is-at-51–624116.html?showCommen ts=true&page=2&more_comments= false&viewAsSinglePage=true (11 May 2012).

McKenna, Brian. "The Baseball Draft, Since 1892." *Glimpses Into Baseball History*, 26 October 2010, http://baseball-historyblog.com/tag/major-league-draft/ (19 October 2011).

McTaggart, Brian. "A-Rod hits 13th, 14th. Incredible." *Houston Chronicle*, 23 April 2007, http://blog.chron.com/ gamedayastros/2007/04/a-rod-hits-13th-14th-incredible/ (8 February 2012).

"Mike Drumright," Baseball-Reference, n.d., http://www.baseball-reference. com/minors/ player.cgi?id=d rumri001mic (2 May 2012).

"Minors OK Free Agent Draft in Surprise Move." *Daytona Beach Morning Journal*, 3 December 1964, 14 (Google News Archive).

Mishel, Lawrence, and Natalie Sabadish. "CEO Pay and the Top 1%: How Executive Compensation and Financial-Sector Pay Have Fueled Income Inequality." *Economic Policy Institute*, 2 May 2012, http://www.epi.org/publica tion/ib331-ceo-pay-top-1-percent (8 January 2013).

"MLB Completes 2012 First-Year Player Draft." MLB.com. 6 June 2012, http:// mlb.mlb.com/news/print.jsp?ymd=20 120606&content_id=32872664&vkey= pr_mlb&c_id=mlb (17 December 2012).

Morosi, Jon Paul. "Baseball Eyes Jays' 2010 Draft Class." Fox Sports, 22 June 2012, www.google.com/url?sa=t&rct=j &q=baseball scouting draft&source= web&cd=13&cad=rja&ved=0CCkQF-jACOAo&url=http://msn.foxsports. com/mlb/story/toronto-blue-jays-2010-draft-class-anti-moneyball-approach-062312&ei=YjPyUO65FpHy9gTnnoCw Dg&usg=AFQjCNGX9X5rAhvlGny3e3 d N p 9 1 b s 0 _ O 5 g & b v m = b v . 1357700187,d.eWU (12 January 2013).

Morris, Peter. *A Game of Inches: The Stories Behind the Innovations That Shaped Baseball.* Vol. 2, *The Game Behind the Scenes.* Lanham, MD: Ivan R. Dee, 2006.

"National Agreement for the Government of Professional Base Ball Clubs." *Doug Pappas's Business of Baseball Pages,* n.d., http://roadsidephotos.sabr.org/basebal l/1903NatAgree.htm (26 October 2011).

Nelson, Amy K. "OTL: Dream On A Shelf." ESPNwww, n.d., http://sports. espn.go.com/espn/eticket/story?pag e=090423/harrington (16 May 2012).

Nicholson-Smith, Ben. "CBA Details: Luxury Tax, Draft, HGH, Replay." MLB Trade Rumors, 22 Nov. 2011, http://www.mlbtraderumors.com/2011/ 11/cba-details-luxury-tax-draft-.html (23 Nov. 2011).

Nightengale, Bob. "African Americans in MLB: 8%, Lowest Since Integration Era." *USA Today,* 15 April 2012, http:// content.usatoday.com/communities/ dailypitch/post/2012/04/mlb-jackie-robinson-day-african-american-players/1 (16 December 2012).

_____. "Baseball Scouts Benefit from Beverly Hills Fundraiser." *USA Today,* 10 January 2013, http://www.usatoday. com/story/sports/mlb/2013/01/10/ dennis-gilbert-scouts-foundation-dinner-bud-selig-harrison-ford-jim-palmer-beverly-hills/1823439/ (13 January 2013).

_____. "Catcher Joe Mauer Will Test Staying Power with Twins." *USA Today,* 17 February 2010, http://usatoday30. usatoday.com/sports/baseball/al/twins/ 2010-02-16-mauer_N.htm (27 February 2013).

"91st Round of the 1993 MLB June Amateur Draft." Baseball-Reference n.d., http://baseball-reference.com/ draft/?query_type=year_round&year_ ID=1993&draft_ round=91&draft_ty pe=junreg& (8 December 2012).

Nyman, Paul. "In the Beginning, God Created Heaven and Earth ..." *Hardball Times,* 18 April 2008 (13 November 2011).

O'Brien, David. "Reds Call Worth Mottola's Wait." *South Florida Sun-Sentinel,* 2 June 1992, http://articles.sun-sentinel.com/1992-06-02/sports/ 9202120399_1_clay-daniel-sign-reds-scout (15 June 2011).

Olney, Buster. "A Met Prospect Walks Away from Baseball." *New York Times,* 30 May 1997, http://www.nytimes.com/ 1997/05/30/sports/a-met-prospect-walks-away-from-baseball.html?pa gewanted=all&src=pm (30 April 2012).

_____. "Shepherd to Sign." *Baltimore Sun,* 17 August 1995, http://articles. baltimoresun.com/ 1995-08-17/sports/ 1995229163_1_shepherd-orioles-alvie (7 May 2012).

"Operation and Maintenance Overview Fiscal Year 2012 Budget Estimates." *United States Department of Defense,* February 2011, 166, http://comptroller. defense.gov/defbudget/ fy2012/fy2012 _OM_Overview.pdf (9 January 2013).

Pappas, Doug. "The J.D. Drew Saga." *Outside the Lines* 4, no. 2 (1998): 3–4.

Passan, Jeff. "Alderson Addresses Dominican Corruption." Yahoo! Sports, 22 April 2010, http://sports.yahoo.com/ mlb/news?slug=jp-dominican0422 10&print=1 (18 December 2012).

_____. "If Rasmus Wants Off Cards, Pujols Says Leave." Yahoo! Sports, 5 September 2010, http://sports.yahoo. com/mlb/news?slug=jp-rasmuspujo ls090510 (16 February 2013).

_____. "Pirates' 'Hells Angels,' 'Navy SEALs' minor league training methods become MLB joke." Yahoo! Sports, 21 September 2012, http://sports.yahoo. com/news/pirates-hells-angels-navy-seals-minor-league-training-methods-become-mlb-joke-.html (11 January 2013).

Person, Joseph. "'Never Too Late': Corey Jenkins Goes Back to School." GoGame cocks.com, 21 March 2010, http://www. thestate.com/2010/03/21/1209705/ corey-jenkins.html (30 April 2012).

Peurzer, Richard J. "The Kansas City Royals' Baseball Academy." *The National Pastime* 24 (2004): 3–12.

Pittman, Geneva. "Are Lefty Pitchers More Injury-Prone?" Reuters, 25 June

2010, http://www.reuters.com/article/ 2010/06/25/us-lefty-pitchers-more-injury-prone-idUSTRE65O3XD2 0100625 (20 November 2011).

Rausch, Gary. "Evolution of the Draft." MLB.com, 16 May 2002. http://mlb. mlb.com/news/ article.jsp?ymd=20020 516&content_id=26646&vkey=news_m lb&fext=.jsp&c_id=null (24 Oct. 2011).

"Rick Ankiel." Baseball-Reference.com, n.d., http://www.baseball-reference. com/minors/ player.cgi?id=ankiel001ric (12 December 2012).

Roberts, Quinn. "Scouts Dinner Thrills Star-Studded Audience." MLB.com, 13 January 2013, http://mlb.mlb.com/ news/article.jsp?ymd=20130113&content_id=40944056&vkey=news_mlb&c_id=mlb (13 January 2013).

Rocca, Lawrence. "ON THE FARM: At Vero Beach, It's Always a Day Job." *Orange County Register*, 23 July 1995 (Factiva).

Rosenberg, I.J. "J.D. Drew, Caught in the Middle (of Nowhere)." *Atlanta Journal-Constitution*, 6 August 1997, C6 (NewsBank).

Rosenthal, Ken. "MLB Deal a Dagger to Small-Market Teams." Fox Sports, 23 November 2011, http://msn.foxsports. com/mlb/story/MLB-deal-unfair-to-small-market-teams-112211 (23 Nov. 2011).

Ruck, Rob. "Baseball's Recruitment Abuses." *Quarterly Americas*, Summer 2011, http://americasquarterly.org/node /2745 (16 December 2012).

Salisbury, Jim. "Arbitrator to Field Grievance Involving J.D. Drew." Philly.com, 30 January 1998, http://articles.philly. com/1998–01–30/sports/25747592_1_ independent-arbitrator-amateur-draft-dana-eischen (23 January 2013).

_____. "Doster Gets Phils' 25th Spot; Miller Returned to Indians." Philly. com, 1 April 1999, http://articles.philly. com/1999–04–01/sports/25520833_1_ phillies-david-miller-ed-wade (23 May 2012).

_____. "Going, Going, Gone Phils and Drew Fail to Reach an Agreement." Philly.com, 26 May 1998, http://articles.

philly.com/1998–05–26/sports/ 25741686_1_phils-original-offer-salary-structure (27 January 2013).

_____. "Lee Thomas Is Fired by the Phillies, the General Manager Since 1988 Had Only One Winning Year, the Magical Season Of 1993." Philly.com, 10 December 1997, http://articles.philly. com/1997–12–10/news/25556098_1_ major-leagues-lee-elia-ed-wade (24 January 2013).

_____. "Phils Turn Attention to Other Prospects Now That J.D. Drew Is History, the Focus Is on the Trading Deadline and Next Draft." Philly.com, 27 May 1998, http://articles.philly.com/ 1998–05–27/sports/25741844_1_mike-arbuckle-boras-and-drew-pat-burrell (24 January 2013).

_____. "A Wealth of Talent Best College Player Ever? It Might Be J.D. Drew." Philly.com, http://articles.philly.com/19 97–05–30/sports/25565479_1_seminole s-coach-mike-martin-mark-barron-phils (21 January 2013).

"Salt Lake Bees Walk Away with Lopsided Loss." *Deseret News*, 13 August 2008, http://www.deseretnews.com/article/ 700250523/Salt-Lake-Bees-walk-away-with-lopsided-loss.html (6 February 2013).

Sanford, Dave. "RC's Top 10 First Half Performances: #7." Royals Corner, 7 July 2006, royals.scout.com/2/545181. html (8 May 2012).

Schmadtke, Alan. "Drew's Blast Lifts Seminoles." *Orlando Sentinel*, 3 June 1995, B1 (Factiva).

_____. "FSU Baseball Team Beats 1st-Place Clemson Again." *Orlando Sentinel*, 23 April 1995, D4 (Factiva).

_____. "USC Ousts FSU, 16–1." *Orlando Sentinel*, 7 June 1995, D1 (Factiva).

Schoenfield, David. "The 100 Worst Draft Picks Ever." ESPN Page 2, 26 April 1996, http://sports.espn.go.com/espn/ page2/story?page=schoenfield/060427 (8 May 2012).

Schrotenboer, Brent. "After Bilking Athletes, Gillette Now a Pastor." SignOn San Diego.com, 15 February 2006, http://www.utsandiego.com/sports/

20060215–9999–1s15gillette.html (3 May 2012).

_____. "Blue Jays Release Bush After Incident in Florida." *San Diego Union-Tribune*, 4 April 2009 (Factiva).

Schwarz, Alan. "Pitch Counts: Calculated Risks." ESPN.com, 10 May 2004, http://sports.espn.go. com/mlb/columns/story?columnist=schwarz_alan&id=1790788 (6 January 2013).

Segura, Melissa. "Drafted at 13, How One Player Changed International Signing Rules." SI.com, 2 July 2012, http://sportsillustrated.cnn.com/2012/writers/melissa_segura/07/02/jimy-kelly/index.html (5 January 2013).

_____. "Prospect Testified that Nationals' Instructor Knew of his Fake Identity." SI.com, 21 September 2010, http://sportsillustrated.cnn.com/2010/baseball/mlb/09/20/nationals.baez/ index.html (5 January 2013).

Sewell, Dan. "Baseball's Latin-Flavored Trend to Grow." *(Spartanburg, SC) Herald-Journal*, via Associated Press, 10 May 1979, 11 (Google News Archive).

Shaikin, Bill. "Helping baseball's Scouts in a Post-'Moneyball' World." *Los Angeles Times*, 13 January 2012, http://articles.latimes.com/2012/jan/13/sports/la-sp-shaikin-moneyball-20120114 (12 January 2013).

Shapiro, T. Rees. "Harvey Dorfman, Psychologist to Top Baseball Stars, Dies at 75." *Washington Post*, 3 March 2011, http://www.washingtonpost.com/wp-dyn/content/article/2011/03/03/AR2011030304871.html (28 November 2012).

Sheinin, Dave. "Boras's Next Assault on Draft Might Come From Far East." *Washington Post*, 3 July 2009, http://www.washingtonpost.com/wp-dyn/content/article/2009/07/02/AR2009070201804.html (19 February 2013).

_____. "Draft Dodger: Scott Boras's Trailblazing History with the MLB Draft." *Washington Post*, 17 August 2009, http://www.washingtonpost.com/wp-dyn/content/article/2009/08/16/AR2009081602024.html (18 January 2013).

Sheldon, Mark. "Psychology in Baseball: Heroes Are Human," MLB.com, 10 August 2009, http://mlb.mlb.com/news/article.jsp?ymd=20090809&content_id=6334524&vkey=news_mlb&c_id=mlb&fext=.jsp (7 December 2012).

Shepherd, Joanna, and George B. Shepherd. "U.S. Labor Market Regulation and the Export of Employment: Major League Baseball Replaces U.S. Players with Foreigners." *Emery Law and Economics Research Paper No. 7*, 2002, http://papers.ssrn.com/sol3/papers.cfm?abstract_id=370422 (16 December 2012).

Shepherd-Bailey, Johanna, and George B. Shepherd. "Baseball's Accidental Racism: The Draft, African-American Players, and the Law." *Connecticut Law Review*, no.1 (November 2011).

Sickels, John. "2000 First Round Part Two." Minor League Ball, 20 May 2006, http://www. minorleagueball.com/2006/5/20/155954/967 (8 February 2012).

Simpson, Allan. "Bonus Concerns Created Draft; Yet Still Exist." *Baseball America*, 4 June 2005, http://www.baseballamerica.com/today/2005draft/050604bonus.html (3 November 2011).

_____. "Bonus Progression Record." *Perfect Game USA*, 9 May 2011, http://www.perfectgame.org/Articles/View.aspx?article=5607 (27 February 2013).

_____. "Draft Bonuses—Ten-Year Evolution." *Perfect Game USA*, 12 May 2011, http://www.perfectgame.org/articles/View.aspx?article=5639 (8 Nov. 2011).

_____. "Signing Bonuses: No. 1 Overall Picks Year-by-Year." *Perfect Game USA*, 9 May 2011, http://www.perfectgame.org/articles/View.aspx?article=5609 (2 May 2012).

Simpson, Jake. "Why the Nationals Are Right to Shut Down Stephen Strasburg." *The Atlantic*, August 2012, http://.theatlantic.com/entertainment/archive/2012/08/why-the-nationals-are-right-to-shut-down-stephen-strasburg/261451/ (14 February 2013).

Smith, Joe. "Deal Upsets Victim's Family: Ex-Rays Prospect Matt Bush Gets 3.5 years, No Probation for DUI Hit-and-

Run." *Tampa Bay Times*, 19 December 2012 (Factiva).

"Sports Psychology — Mental Game vs. Physical Game." CBS Healthwatch, June 2000, http://cbshealthwatch.medscape.com/cx/viewarticle/217955, quoted in Kornspan and MacCracken, 40.

"State & County Quick Facts." United States Census Bureau, 6 June 2012, http://quickfacts.census.gov/qfd/states/12/1264875.html (30 July 2012).

Staudohar, Paul D., Franklin Lowenthal, and Anthony K. Lima. "The Evolution of Baseball's Amateur Draft." *NINE: A Journal of Baseball History and Culture* 15.1 (2006): 27–44. (Project MUSE).

Stephens, Mitch. "Starting Point: Snapshots of Major League's Semifinalist." MaxPreps.com, 16 October 2009, http://www.maxpreps.com/news/qHcRrrp7Ed6OEwAcxJTdpg/starting-point—snapshots-of-major-leagues-semifinalist.htm (27 February 2013).

Stone, Larry. "The Art of Baseball: A Tradition of Superstition." *Seattle Times*, 26 September 2005, http://seattletimes.com/html/mariners/2002518797_artx25.html (13 December 2012).

"Straight to the Major Leagues." *Baseball Almanac*, n.d., http://www.baseball-almanac.com/ feats/feats9.shtml (13 November 2011).

Stucko, Matthew. "Ramapo Product Shooter Hunt Hoping New Fitness Regimen Puts Him Back on Path to Major Leagues." *The Star-Ledger*, 15 August 2010, http://www.nj.com/sports/njsports/index.ssf/2010/08/ramapo_product_shooter_hunt_ho.html (30 April 2011).

Surdam, David George. *The Postwar Yankees: Baseball's Golden Age Revisited.* Lincoln: University of Nebraska Press, 2008.

Tefertiller, Casey. "Front-Office Veteran Wins Hemond Award for Excellence in Player Development." *Baseball America*, 15 December 2006, http://www.baseballamerica.com/ today/majors/awards/roland-hemond-award/2006/262951.html (28 November 2012).

Thornton, Patrick. *Sports Law.* Sudbury, MA: Jones and Bartlett, 2011.

"Top 200 Prospects." *Baseball America*, 12 June 2012, 17.

Topkin, Marc. "Reliever Charged with DUI, Hit and Run." *Tampa Bay Times*, 23 March 2012 (Factiva).

Torres, Adry. "MLB Draft: Correa Gives Hope to Puerto Rican Baseball." Fox News Latino, http://latino.foxnews.com/latino/sports/2012/06/06/mlb-draft-correa-gives-hope-to-puerto-rican-baseball/ (17 December 2012).

Traub, Todd. "Texas Notes: Torres Takes Long Road." MiLB.com, 26 July 2011, http://www.milb.com/news/article.jsp?ymd=20110725&content_id=22271924&vkey=news_l109&fext=.jsp&sid=l109 (6 February 2012).

"Tripper Johnson." *University of Washington Football*, n.d., http://www.gohuskies.com/sports/m-footbl/mtt/johnson-_tripper00.html (15 May 2012).

"2000 Major League Baseball Attendance and Miscellaneous." Baseball-Reference www, n.d., http://www.baseball-reference.com/leagues/MLB/2000-misc.shtml (26 February 2013).

"2008 Baseball Payrolls, List." ESPNwww, n.d. http://sports.espn.go.com/espn/wire?section=mlb&id=3324146 (17 November 2011).

"2010 Washington Nationals." Baseball-Reference n.d., http://baseball-reference.com/teams/WSN/2010-schedule-scores.shtml (4 January 2013).

"2012 Draft LIVE! Draft Pick Database." *Perfect Game*, n.d., http://www.perfectgame.org/Draft/Signings.aspx (30 July 2012).

"2012–2013 IMG Academies School & Baseball Rate Card." *IMG Baseball Academy*, 2012, http://www.imgacademies.com/_assets/dynamic_media/media_bank/IMG-Academies/ pdf-documents/Pricing/Rate_Cards/Baseball_2012_2013.pdf (30 July 2012).

Van Dyck, Dave. "The Pitch on Pitch Counts." *Chicago Sun-Times*, 26 July 1998 (Factiva).

Verducci, Tom. "Upton, Braun Help '05

Claim Top Spot in Ranking of Best Draft Classes." SI.com, n.d., http://sportsillustrated.cnn.com/2011/writers/tom_verducci/06/06/best.draft.classes/index.html (12 November 2011).

Vint, Tom. "'Canes Tame Seminoles 4–2 at Rainy CWS." *Tampa Tribune,* via Associated Press, 5 June 1995 (Factiva).

Walker, Ben. "Randy Johnson Clone, College Record-Breaker Lead Draft List." AP News Archive, 2 June 1997, http://www.apnewsarchive.com/1997/Randy-Johnson-clone-college-record-breaker-lead-draft-list/id-7926f517bbf096d552eacbe6a78e9497 (25 January 2013).

Walton, Brian. "Whatever Happened To ... Blake Williams." The Cardinal Nation.com, 12 September 2005, http://stlcardinals.scout.com/2/437629.html (8 February 2012).

Waszak, Dennis, Jr. "First Pick Is High School SS." *Newark Star-Ledger,* via Associated Press, 8 June 2004 (Factiva).

_____. "Twins: Tough Choice with Top Pick." AP News Archive, 4 June 2001, http://www.apnewsarchive.com/2001/Twins-Tough-Choice-With-Top-Pick/id-3f51351df0aa9eaa10e5c84c5c3c0ed4 (27 February 2013).

Wein, Matt. "This Could be the End of Johnny V. as the Pirates Know Him." *Centre Daily Times,* 2 August 2007, 7 (Factiva).

White, Paul. "Nationals Clinch NL East and First Division Title." *USA Today,* 1 October 2012, http://usatoday.com/story/sports/mlb/2012/10/01/nationals-clinch-nl-east/1607595/ (7 January 2013).

"White Sox Select Long Beach State's Liefer." *Los Angeles Times,* 2 June 1995, http://articles.latimes.com/1995–06–02/sports/sp-8733_1_long-beach-state (4 May 2012).

"Who We Are." Bucky Dent Baseball School, n.d., http://www.buckydentbaseball.com/?page_id=1181 (30 July 2012).

Wild, Danny. "Chicago's Negron Suspended 50 Games." MiLB.com, 8 January 2010, http://www.milb.com/news/article.jsp?ymd=20100108&content_id=7893332&vkey=news_milb&fext=.jsp (7 February 2012).

_____. "Stanley, Thompson Banned 50 Games." MiLB.com, 27 March 2012, http://www.milb.com/news/article.jsp?ymd=20120327&content_id=27674424&fext=.jsp&vkey=news_milb (7 December 2012).

Wilson, Bernie. "Padres Suspend Top Pick Matt Bush After Arrest." Associated Press, 21 June 2004 (Factiva).

Winston, Lisa. "Stalled Prospects Try to Make Up for Lost Time." *USA Today,* 24 April 2002, http://www.usatoday.com/sports/bbw/2002–04–24/minors.htm (9 February 2012).

"Without Lebron, Scorpions Score Road Win." *Yuma Sun,* 25 July 2006, http://www.yumasun.com/sports/game-22350-innings-lebron.html (3 May 2012).

Young, Travis. "Twins Make Statement With Top Pick." *Baseball America,* 14 June 2007, http://www.baseballamerica.com/blog/draft/2007/06/twins-make-statement-with-top-pick/ (11 May 2012).

Zirin, Dave. "Postmortem: The Now-Infamous and Indefensible Decision to Sit Stephen Strasburg." *The Nation,* 13 October 2012, *http://.thenation.com/blog/170547/ postmortem-now-infamous-and-indefensible-decision-sit-stephen-strasburg#* (4 January 2013).

Index

Index

Index

Index

Index

Index

Index

Index